1700

Organization and Leadership in the Local Church

Kenneth K. Kilinski
and
Jerry C. Wofford

ORGANIZATION AND LEADERSHIP in the LOCAL CHURCH

Kenneth K. Kilinski and Jerry C. Wofford

Academie Books
Grand Rapids, Michigan
Zondervan Publishing House

Copyright © 1973 by The Zondervan Corporation
Grand Rapids, Michigan

ACADEMIE BOOKS are printed by Zondervan
Publishing House, 1415 Lake Drive, S.E.,
Grand Rapids, Michigan 49506

Library of Congress Catalog Card Number 72-95532

ISBN 0-310-26810-9

Printed in the United States of America

89 90 91 92 93 94 95 / AH / 22 21 20 19 18 17 16

Dedicated with love and appreciation to

Donna

and

Vera

Contents

Figures 9
Miscellaneous Tables 11
Introduction 13
Acknowledgments 17

PART ONE: The Equipping of the Saints:
          The Challenge of Guidance Toward Spiritual Maturation
1   The Three-dimensional Man 21
2   Fostering Spiritual Maturation 33
3   Recognizing and Developing Spiritual Gifts 46
4   Selecting and Training Church Personnel 55

PART TWO: The Work of Service:
          The Challenge of Leadership
5   Choosing Your Leadership Style 69
6   Motivating People for Action 79
7   The Dynamics of Small-Group Behavior 88
8   Interpersonal Conflict 98
9   Reasoning Together Through Communication 110
10   Overcoming Resistance to Change 121

PART THREE: The Building Up of the Body of Christ:
          The Challenge of Building the Church Organization
11   The Church Organism and Community 133
12   Objectives of the Church 137
13   Building the Organization Structure 142
14   Authority and the Power to Influence 152
15   Building a Team-centered Organization 159
16   Formal Organization Structuring 165
17   The Vocational Staff 171
18   Work Goals and Evaluation 179
19   Long-range Planning 186
20   Annual Planning of Church Goals 192
21   Budgeting and Accounting Procedure 197
22   Decision and Indecision 213
23   The Church Facilities 222
Conclusion 228
Appendix A 231
Appendix B 239
Appendix C 241
Bibliography 247
Index 251

Figures

1. The Interplay of Life's Forces   28

2. Motivational Forces and the Inner Law   31

3. Maturation in Christ   35

4. Leader Dimensions   75

5. Performance Effectiveness Equation   79

6. Motivation Cycle   80

7. Four Communications Styles   117

8. The Linking System of Church Organization   146

9. The Linking System of Church
       Organization for a Small Church   148

10. The Authority-centered Sunday School   162

11. The Team-centered Approach   163

12. Vocational Staff   174

13. Departmentalization Chart   191

Miscellaneous Tables

Membership Profile   57-61

Survey of Leadership Opinions   70-73

Typical Leadership Behaviors   74

Characteristics of Ineffective
    and Effective Organizations   143, 144

Ingredients of a Team-centered Organization   160

Job Descriptions   168-170, 239, 240

Basic Accounting Records   201-212

Activities, Interest, and Proficiency Questionnaire   231-238

Personal Growth Inventories   241-246

Introduction

Can the church survive in the midst of the changes of the twentieth century? Is the local church relevant to human needs in today's society? Or is the church merely the limb of a dying culture? Does the church today have authority as the body of Christ? These cries of doubt are being voiced within and outside of the Christian community. Perhaps the greatest challenge to the church comes from the under-thirty generation — a generation that abhors hypocrisy, has no roots in tradition, and is unwilling to march in step for duty alone. These are not just idle queries of a restless and brash youth; they are concerns that weigh heavily upon pastors, theologians, and laymen throughout all segments of Christendom. Churches and denominations are losing membership and support at a time of unparalleled population growth. The loss is felt most strongly among the young people.

Responses to the call for change are coming from every side — liberal and conservative, layman and clergy, local churches and national Christian organizations. Some call for the elimination of the local church, some call for radical change, others call for retrenchment; but each is calling for a response to the winds of social change that are threatening to rip the church community from its foundation. The time has come for the local church to reexamine its purposes, principles, and practices and to confront the demands of our generation with renewed confidence and energy.

This book is based upon three assumptions about the changes that are occurring in our society and offers what the authors consider to be the most effective attack for the church in fulfilling its commission in the decades ahead. First, we assume that we are in the midst of an international cultural change which will bring us to a place that is different from where we have been and from where we are. We assume that the change in society is fundamental and not a passing fancy. It is rooted in deep philosophical and psychological foundations. Permissiveness in the home and the humanistic-existential philosophies have erased the force of the traditional values for order, stratification, rationality, and absolutes — no longer are traditional moral standards adhered to without challenge; no longer are "self-evident truths" seen as self-evident; no longer is consistency and logic held to be more valid than feeling and experience. The rights of ownership, authority, and position are dying. In their place is emerging a concept of human dignity that exalts mankind but ignores the man. Value for human equality is removing the individual rights for property and power and replacing them with a democratic rule of equals and a mutual sharing of the bounty of the nation. We see on the horizon a personal ethic that is based upon individual experience and feeling rather than universal standards. We are assuming that these trends in society will be fully embraced by a large segment of the population and that elements of the underlying philosophy will become accepted (perhaps unconsciously) by almost everyone.

Second, we assume that certain principles of church dogma have Scriptural foundations, have been maintained by churches of every century, and are essential to the survival and effectiveness of the church. In *The Church at the End of the 20th Century,* Francis Schaeffer discusses eight fundamental absolutes or forms of church polity:

1. The local congregations are to exist and are to be made up of Christians (Acts 16:4, 5).
2. These congregations are to meet together in a special way on the first day of the week (1 Corinthians 16:2 and Acts 20:7).
3. There are to be church elders who have responsibility for the local churches (Acts 14:23).
4. There should be deacons responsible for the community of the church in the area of material things (Acts 6:1-6).
5. The church is to take discipline seriously (1 Corinthians 5:1-5).
6. There are specific qualifications for elders and deacons (1 Timothy 3:1-13 and Titus 1:5-9).
7. There is a place for form on a wider basis than the local church (Acts 15:1 describes a church council).
8. Two sacraments — baptism and the Lord's Supper — are to be practiced.[1]

Other fundamental absolutes seem to be of equal significance for the church and we consider them to be central to the church of any age:

1. The basic enduring purposes of the church are to evangelize (Acts 1:8), to foster spiritual maturation (1 Cor. 6:19, 20), to build fellowship and love (Heb. 10:24, 25), and to minister to the needs of the body (Eph. 4:11, 12).
2. All church affairs are to be handled decently and in order (1 Cor. 14:40). Irrespective of the extent that uninhibited, existential experiences may be encouraged in the church we must not lose sight of the requirement to do all things in an orderly fashion.
3. The church is to be organized in a unified, systematic, and functional manner (Eph. 4:16). As a physical body is beautifully structured with many parts working in harmony and efficiency, so ought the church to be set into an orderly design so that each person can contribute according to his talents and gifts to the total working of the church body.
4. The basic methods of communicating the message of God through preaching, teaching, and example are *not* to be ignored (1 Cor. 1:18-21; Matt. 28:19; and Phil. 3:17).

Our third assumption is that there are certain freedoms of the church which are not restrained by the Scripture and within which the church can operate to fulfill its basic purposes. We further assume that we can examine the nature of our society and culture and develop certain con-

---

[1]Francis Schaeffer, *The Church at the End of the 20th Century,* (Downers Grove, Ill.: Inter-Varsity Press, 1970), pp. 61-67.

structs and practices that can be broadly applied to augment the effectiveness of the church in our day. As Francis Schaeffer has aptly asserted, "Anything the New Testament does not command in regard to church form is a freedom to be exercised under the leadership of the Holy Spirit for that particular time and place."[2] Where the Scripture is silent the church will speak. Often we feel, for example, that the church is remaining silent on such matters as the time and number of Sunday services — that we are simply following tradition. However, whether we have made a conscious decision or have blindly followed custom, we are speaking loudly on the time and the number of services by our practice.

We contend that the demands of our generation call for change but not for disintegration. When a person adopts a new diet or changes from a sedentary job to a strenuous one, his body must adapt. Certain parts of the body must be built up, others will naturally weaken, several parts may operate differently; yet no one would advise the person to cut off an arm, to walk on his hands, or to become a horse. So it is with the church: as it confronts new challenges and needs it must function in a new way, it must develop new abilities and allow others to weaken by disuse; but it must not lose essential parts, fall into disarray, or try to change its Scriptural form.

The intent of this book is to look at the local church in the midst of the forces generated by our age and to analyze the primary functions of the church in light of the challenges before us. We shall set forth the principles, practices, and concepts which seem to be realistic and effective for the church of today and of the decades ahead. In the belief that the most effective approach for a local church is adaptation rather than revolution, we shall lay a foundation for progressive change within the concept of a congregation that holds tenaciously to the Scriptural forms but has the will and the capacity for fulfilling its basic purposes through the exercise of its freedoms. Although a revolutionary new church concept is more exciting in its idealized concept, the ideals often prove unrealistic when subjected to the scrutiny of actual practice. Progressive changes are often tempered by the fires that give them life.

This book is divided into three major parts which parallel the inspired text of Ephesians 4:11, 12. In Part I we will consider "the equipping of the saints" or the challenge of guiding Christians toward spiritual maturity. To accomplish this, we will look at the nature of the person in his human and spiritual makeup. We will be concerned with the way in which the spiritual life grows into dominance and the ways in which one's spiritual stature may be enhanced. We will also examine both the role of fellowship with others in Christian love as a basis for spiritual growth and the destructive forces involved in interpersonal conflict. Another aspect of the "equipping of the saints" is the recognition and

---

[2]*Ibid.*, p. 59-67.

15

development of spiritual gifts in view of the selection and development of church personnel.

In Part II we will attack the problem of "the work of service." In this section we will consider the role and functions of the church leader in equipping others to do the work of the ministry. In the light of this, we shall look at the characteristics of an effective leader and the styles of behavior which he exhibits. We will also look at the activities of the leader as he serves the church body in motivating the members to attain their common goal, helping them to make the church one that attracts others and assures a smooth flow of communication.

In Part III we will consider the "building up of the body of Christ" through administration and organization. We will deal with the problems of orderly and systematic organization in planning. This will involve the challenge of establishing goals and objectives. To carry these out, we will identify the authority relationships and the responsibilities and jobs that are essential for meeting the unified objectives. This will be followed by the establishment of performance standards and a "coaching" style of approach to aid in performance effectiveness. The second part of this challenge is that of decision making and planning. The problems of short-term as well as long-range planning will be considered.

Through a discussion of these vital challenges, we hope to provide guidelines that will be helpful in handling problems confronted by church leadership and to illustrate the use of these approaches in the local church.

Acknowledgments

The reader will soon notice that this book is not the result of untried classroom theory, but rather the practice of theory tried in the classroom of experience. In this case, the classroom has been the congregation of the Pantego Bible Church located in Arlington, Texas. It is to this body of believers that we are deeply indebted for being willing to present problems, raise questions, and be a living laboratory in which numerous experiments have been tried — many resulting in positive conclusions, and many having been failures.

We are also grateful for the contribution of Mr. James Rushing III in providing the expertise for establishing an accounting system in chapter twenty-one. Mr. Rushing is Church Treasurer at Pantego Bible Church and draws upon his background as a Certified Public Accountant to give direction in handling the Lord's money.

A special "thank you" to those who assisted in the production of the manuscript by typing and proofreading — Mrs. Ruth Gay, Mrs. Faye Hinds, Mrs. Lorry Lutz, Mrs. Elizabeth Carter — as well as to Mr. Gerard Terpstra of Zondervan Publishing House for his editorial help.

PART ONE

The Equipping of the Saints:

The Challenge of Guidance Toward Spiritual Maturation

1

The Three-dimensional Man

Sam is a hard-working, moderately successful businessman and entrepreneur of around fifty years of age. He often works long hours during his company's busy season. Early in life, family poverty forced him to work at many jobs — jobs ranging from carrying papers at 4:30 in the morning to serving as a gardener around the neighborhood. By doing far beyond the normal amount of work, he was able to complete the requirements for a degree in the local college. His strong drive toward the achievement of his personal goals seems obvious; in fact, he has the ulcers to prove it. At the same time, however, he manifests a strong need for the acceptance and love of others, especially those in his church. His warmth, ready smile, and open expressiveness of feeling, combined with his frank and direct approach to problems endears him to many. This need for acceptance and love stems from his early years, a time in which love was denied him by an overworked mother and a father who had left home. Although his mother was loving, he learned that he must first shower her with love to get her to leave the housework for which she had so little time and to give him the attention that he wanted.

The question is "Would this man be an effective lay leader of the church?" You might respond with an emphatic yes. You argue, "He is a man with developed qualities of responsibility and warmth. Since he has followed a pattern of hard work and achievement throughout life, surely he would apply these attitudes to a church office and do a fine job here as well. By possessing the love and warmth that would inspire those whom he would lead, he would be a fine church leader."

On the other hand, you might conclude, "This is a man who is driven by the desire to accomplish personal, secular success. It is unfortunate, but this man has developed a selfish attitude to gain those things for himself that he was denied in childhood. He would take the job readily," you predict, "but when he accepted it with all the accompanying status, respect, and recognition, he would have met his goals and would not give up time from his company to donate to the church. A man like this would use the church to fulfill his own desires; he would not be used of God."

Which position is correct? Either could be right. We cannot predict the effectiveness of Sam for church leadership, for we have seen only two dimensions of the three-dimensional man. Let us explain.

In Romans 7:14-25 Paul describes the nature of the Christian as follows:

> For we know that the Law is spiritual; but I am of flesh, sold into bondage to sin. For that which I am doing, I do not understand; for I am not practicing what I would like to do, but I am doing the very thing I hate. But if I do the very thing I do not wish to do, I agree with the Law, confessing that it is good. So now, no longer am I the one doing it, but sin which indwells me. For I know that nothing good dwells in me, that is, in my flesh; for the wishing is present in me, but the doing of the good is not. For the good that I wish, I do not do; but I practice the very evil that I do not wish. But if I am doing the very thing I do not wish, I am no longer the one doing it, but sin which dwells in me. I find then the principle that evil is present in me, the one who wishes to do good. For I joyfully concur with the law of God in the inner man, but I see a different law in the members of my body, waging war against the law of my mind, and making me a prisoner of the law of sin which is in my members. Wretched man that I am! Who will set me free from the body of this death? Thanks be to God through Jesus Christ our Lord.

Paul describes the psychology of the Christian personality in terms of three dimensions: the motivational dimension (natural man, Rom. 7:18), the "inner law" dimension (Law of God, Rom. 7:22), and the self (the "I" which controls one's will and actions, Rom. 7:19, 20).

THE FIRST DIMENSION: MOTIVATIONAL NATURE

Somewhere in the world at this instant a child is being born, a unique infant unlike any other in all of history. The thousands of genes which program his physiological future have never before been united in just this combination. Yet in another sense he is like all other men. His body is designed with the necessary equipment to allow him to survive in a potentially hostile world. Much of this equipment was acquired by Adam before his fall; indeed some of it made his fall possible. But most of it is essential to the survival of man in the post-Edenic environment. A primary factor in the physical system, the motivational process, Paul points out as a major determinant of his own behavior. The newborn infant has an almost complete set of physiological needs which will determine the direction of his behavior during the first few months of life. His need for food activates his behavior associated with nursing. His need to avoid pain stands guard to help him alert his mother to his slightest discomfort. But the little fellow is destined for far greater complexity of behavior motivation. Soon his highly advanced capacity to learn will begin to mold his personality. From his basic need to avoid pain, he will learn to avoid all threatening situations: the hot stove, the sharp knife, the angry big brother, and the myriad of things that he discovers as potentially destructive. This broader need we refer to as his need for security. At the same time he will be learning to love the warmth and care of his parents and to fear their wrath. If he is bathed in their consistent love, he will grow to need to share the love of others in a firm and positive way. If he is less fortunate and finds the love mingled with disgust and rejection, he may grow to search for love like the hungry wolf that expects to be chased away the moment the hen house is in sight, always seeking but never fully able to find. Either way, he will learn to need to love, to belong, and to interact with others.

As the infant grows old enough to reach beyond his crib, he begins to move into the curious world around him. No longer dependent upon others for his every need, he must fend for himself. He will learn to outwit his siblings for the attention of his parents, to care for his toys, to clean his room, to dress himself, and to perform in school. In terms of broad categories of needs, we can say that he will develop needs for esteem, achievement, recognition, and power. His needs may become stronger or weaker than those of the children 'around him, but he will find that these needs have a critical influence on his life.

So we have the first dimension: the motivational or natural man — the universal Adamic man whose very body and world necessitates a self-oriented life. If the person could grow to adulthood with this basic motivational dimension unbridled, he would be more savage and more violent than any killer lion. His cunning and his undisciplined skill in developing and using destructive weapons would leave the world ravaged in his wake.

THE SECOND DIMENSION: THE INNER LAW

The bridling influence comes with the "inner law." During the early developmental years, the child will be acquiring the standards and values that God has implanted in his society through His Word, His imprint in nature, and civic laws. He will quickly learn from the words and actions of his parents that many of his favorite activities are "no-no's." He must not hit baby sister; he must not take away the neighbor boy's train; he must not grab food from the host's table; he must be truthful and admit his wrongs; he must eat properly, dress neatly, and try to make life livable for his parents.

He will develop a set of standards or laws of conduct that are essential to his functioning in society. If something goes wrong and his inner law of conscience becomes underdeveloped, he is to be pitied as much as the child that is born without the sense of pain. Just as one who has no nerve endings to sense pain and thus cannot avoid severe burns or cuts, so the person with a weak conscience is incapable of reacting with a normal sense of guilt when he hurts another person or sins against God. He does not even think twice of actions that would leave another person racked in guilt and remorse. He often regards himself as superior to others in being uninhibited by their standards, yet he is actually a misfit, disowned by his own family and unable to maintain friends. The sociopath, as psychologists have called him, usually is exposed to the standards of society and of his parents but rejects these values.

THE THIRD DIMENSION: THE SELF

We are created in the image of God and consequently we are persons — we have a will, ability for discernment, creativity, and communication skills. The self is that aspect of the individual that determines his actions. The self is the central element of the person and includes the self-will, the decision functions, the creative capacity, and the capacity for communication. Although the self was created in the image of God, it is not currently operating in the original perfect state; it is fallen. In its present state the self is incapable of relating to God; an infinite gap stands between God and the self. The self has the desire for good but not the facility to perform that good. It strives hopelessly to bridge the gap and to obtain the joy, the peace, the kindness, and the fulfillment for which it was created; but having chosen to exercise his self-will against God's will, man lost the capability to achieve these goals. The self is in an incessant struggle and lacks the facility to find peace. We seek fulfillment in many achievements, adventures, and conquests but find our latter condition to be still less satisfying. Our only hope is in Christ.

As motivational forces begin to build the energy for action by the individual, the inner law of conscience is continuing its vigil to bring the action into its standard of good or right. The self must decide between the impulses of the motivational forces for an immediate gratification of needs that ignores moral qualities and the conscience whose total concern is for the values of right or wrong. If the needs are felt too strongly or if the conscience is too weak, the self becomes dominated by basic motives. If the conscience is too moralistic and rigid, the self becomes the slave of every petty whim of unrealistic standards. In every person the self is fighting an endless battle to resolve the conflict between the motivational forces and the conscience. Under its own power the self cannot stop the battle; it can only referee. The only hope of inner peace is the Holy Spirit.

The Spirit is an influence upon the man and not a component of his basic nature; He indwells the person and may control the self of the Christian. The Spirit comes into the life of every believer at the point in time that he receives Christ, for a person is, in fact, renewed by the Spirit (Titus 3:5, 6). At this time the leadership of the Spirit becomes accessible (1 Cor. 3:16). The believer has the potential to become controlled by the Spirit as he yields his life (Rom. 12:1, 2). This growth occurs as we increase in our faith (Heb. 11:6), as we study His revelation of Himself (1 Peter 2:2), as we consistently enter into prayerful communication with God through His Son (1 Thess. 5:17), and as we yield ourselves to the leadership of the Spirit (Rom. 8:9). The effects of the influence of the Spirit are numerous. "The fruit of the Spirit is love, joy, peace, patience, kindness, goodness, faithfulness, gentleness, self control" (Gal. 5:22).

The Spirit has a profound impact on the personal life of the yielded Christian, affording him love, joy, and peace. His influence on the relationship of the Christian to others is also far-reaching in significance, for the Spirit provides patience, kindness, gentleness, and moderation. Perhaps more important are the effects of the Spirit in our relationship to God as His control brings faithfulness and goodness.

Influence of the Spirit on the Personal Life

The Spirit of God causes us to *love* others in a special way, this love extending beyond our family and friends to include even our enemies. In contrast, the love that is associated with the motivation dimension is based upon the person's expectation that his needs will be met through his relationship with the person loved and therefore it cannot extend to his enemies.

The *joy* provided by the Spirit also surpasses human experience or understanding. Everyone knows the delight of accomplishing a long-sought goal, seeing a work of art, or sharing an evening with friends. This form of joy is based upon the motivational factors. Our human make-up provides for the pleasant feelings associated with the fulfillment of our values, wants, and needs. But the Spirit affords a joy that supersedes human emotions and satisfactions. It is a comfort in the face of distress, a hope in the face of failure, an enduring joy that circumstances cannot destroy.

The *peace* of the Spirit intervenes to quell and even to extinguish the war that rages within the natural human life, establishing a peace that provides a rest, a tranquillity, a freedom from worry, and a restraint to anxiety.

Influence of the Spirit on Our Relationship to Others

In our relationship to others the Spirit gives patience, kindness, and gentleness. Our *patience* in the Spirit is not an uneasy, watch-checking, foot-stomping, deep-sighing endurance. It is a patience based on a respect for the other person, a love for him, and a willingness to sacrifice time and, indeed, even our own lives. Spirit-filled *kindness* and *gentleness* toward others are also unique. These qualities do not represent our attempt to manipulate someone else into helping us. They are not characterized by a saccharine sweetness that covers hostility, but they are given as a means of showing our love and concern for another person, coupled with our desire to help him bear his burdens.

Moderation is established as we find our selfish wants and needs under the control of the Spirit within us. No longer harboring an outpouring of anger and resentment produced by the fear that our personal needs and wants will not be satisfied, we do not need to use all of our energy to control our fears and anxieties. We do not overreact to the frustrations of our environment, but find them to be within the reach of our easy control.

Influence of the Spirit on Our Relationship to God

The Spirit-controlled attitude toward God is portrayed in our faith and our goodness. Our *faith,* developed as we experience God's protection, care, and power in dealing with our lives, will give us assurance and confidence in meeting every hardship under His protection. *Goodness* develops as we come to desire to please God and to yield our every activity to His will.

It is apparent that the Spirit can have an unparalleled influence on our thoughts and actions if we are truly yielded to His leadership.

THE WAR AND PEACE OF THE CHRISTIAN LIFE

The motivational forces within the person are numerous and powerful. In striving for their fulfillment, the self is energized in a manner that creates a physiological and psychological distress. If our needs for food, water, oxygen, and the like are not satisfied, we cannot survive. Our bodies are designed to signal with severe discontent as these needs grow more pressing. Through the process of development of such psychological needs as security, affiliation, achievement, and esteem, these feelings of discontent are transferred in their full intensity. We often react with as much anxiety to the fear of being embarrassed as we would to prolonged hunger.

As our inner law of conscience develops, it comes into opposition to the satisfaction of the motivational dimension. The child would like to satisfy his hunger by eating rapidly with his most trusted grasping devices — his hands; however, the law of the table says, "No. Eat slowly with your fork; chew each bite well; be graceful; don't reach; eat from your own plate; take only your fair share." The motivational force of hunger and the desire for independence war with the laws of good manners. With the coming of adolescence, a new basic need develops whose satisfaction is almost totally denied, i.e., sex. The sex drive grows to become a strong force in behavior. Yet, the laws of society, parents, and, for the scripturally trained, the Bible, deny direct expression of the sex drive between people until the marriage relationship is established. Some parents instill so strong a fear into the adolescent to assure compliance to the inner law of conscience that he is racked with anxiety even in the proper expression of sex in marriage. The war between the sex drive and the conscience is well-attested in the life of every person who reaches adulthood.

In a more subtle way, psychological needs such as the need to belong and the need for esteem and achievement also become restrained in their fulfillment by the inner law. We are taught to achieve in school, at home, and on the playing fields. But our parents usually throw in a few restraints: "Don't cheat." "Don't lie to get ahead." "Don't steal for your grubstake." "Don't walk over others to get to the top." "Don't boast of your victories; be modest." On and on the list goes. For every need there are associated restraints upon its fulfillment.

Our lives are in the constant turmoil of a psychic war. It is a war that we cannot win, and we cannot end. As Paul described it, "For I joyfully concur with the law of God in the inner man, but I see a different law in the members of my body, waging war against the law of my mind" (Rom. 7:22, 23). In the final analysis, we are unknowingly striving for the fulfillment found only in God, as St. Augustine asserted, "For thou hast created us for thyself, and our heart cannot be quieted till it may find repose in thee."

Each person must face the decision. Will he maintain the battle and retain autonomy of the self to rule his life alone or will he invite the Spirit into his life and find fulfillment?

The person who receives Christ into his life obtains a potential for revolutionary change. The Spirit begins immediately to take a position of influence in the life, but the influence is only at the initial stage. As life is yielded increasingly to the Spirit, one's potential becomes realized. The Spirit begins to provide peace that ends the hopeless war within the life, and the joy and love that give substance and meaning to our existence. The longing of the human life is eternally satisfied in the presence of the Spirit. Both the Christian and the non-Christian have the war, but only the Christian can have the peace.

DANGER: A LIFE OUT OF CONTROL

If you are a church leader, it is your challenge to understand and to deal with people with every conceivable combination of forces from the three dimensions. As the arrows of Figure 1 indicate, the forces may be varied in strength (different lengths of arrows) as well as in types of needs and standards (different kinds of arrows). All of these forces act upon the self.

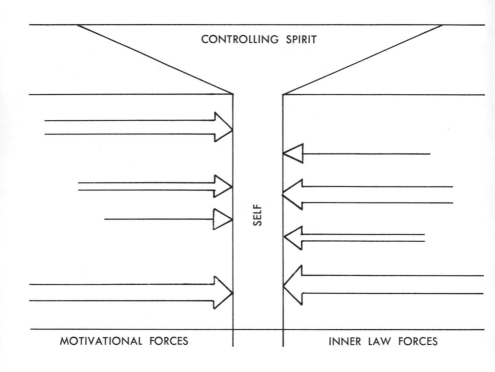

FIGURE 1 — The Interplay of Life's Forces

The person easiest to understand and deal with is the person whose motivational and inner law forces are in the normal range of strength. Problems intensify within the life when one of these dimensions is too strong or too weak.

A Life With Motivational Forces That Are Too Weak

Let's take the case of Harley. Reared in a secure home environment in which he was pampered and overprotected, he was late in his development in everything from toilet training to riding a bike. Because little was expected of him, he was never encouraged to enter sports or to make good grades. He would wander along to school with no concern about being late. If he became intrigued by a cat playing by the road and was an hour late, his parents understood. Happy Harley is now an adult, but he is still unreliable, lazy, and irresponsible. A Christian now, he has tried using his teaching talent in Sunday school, but he failed to prepare and couldn't be counted on to make it to his class. Harley is a fellow who has very weak motivational forces for achievement, esteem, recognition, and power. His behavior is good, but there is not a lot of it. As he matures spiritually, he will become motivated to work for the Lord, but persons of less maturity may do much more in areas of service. It is doubtful that Harley will ever be one of the Lord's dynamos.

A Life With Motivational Forces That Are Too Strong

William is a striking example of the highly motivated person. He has made a spectacular career in the company of which he is now president. William comes from a broken home, from which his father deserted when he was a boy and ceased to provide the partial support that he had been contributing while living in the home. Forced to leave school early, William went to work to help support his younger siblings. He did this conscientiously, even while attending high school, working nights and weekends. His mother, although domineering, seemed sweet and well-meaning, but he has felt like an outcast ever since his unhappy childhood days, always ashamed of his home.

One of William's traits is his persistent drive to improve his education and knowledge. Although he did not obtain a college degree, he is quite well-informed, largely through self-education. He is very well read and has taken carefully selected undergraduate and graduate courses. He sets himself increasingly difficult objectives in order to become skillful and better-trained. Being very sensitive to criticism, he reacts strongly to any personal failures of which he is aware. Praise and recognition from others exhilarate him and make him optimistic for a while, although he is troubled by the tendency to blame himself for everything that goes wrong.

Always eager to improve things, especially his company's profits, he remains intense, earnest, and conscientious, insisting upon introducing changes despite powerful and determined opposition, and never willing to compromise. The problem that William will have as he begins to grow in his spiritual life is placing his personal drives and ambitions under the control of the Spirit. He must learn to focus his attention on the will of God rather than on his own goals for success. As he does so, his high drive level will provide energy for an active, useful Christian life. His insecurities will also need to be yielded to the assurances of God that when one is in His will, he can do all things.

A Life With a Conscience That Is Too Strong

A neat, attractive, and fastidious person, Carol is one whose inner law of conscience is unrealistically severe. As a child she was expected to act like a grownup. Everyone knew she was bright and her parents seemed to think she should be perfect. Yet she never felt accepted or deeply loved by her parents because, no matter how hard she tried, they were never really pleased for long. They occasionally praised her, but always seemed to find something to criticize. Her father was a very austere and aloof businessman who had little time for her. Within Carol raged the war of life in all its crossfires and explosions. Yet, judging her by her stiff, formal manner, one would think that she had been in cold storage for the summer with her furs. Much of her time is spent in daily rituals; indeed, each day has been reduced to a restricted routine of prescribed activities and schedules. Every act is gauged in the light of a crushing standard. Her motivational forces are strong, but they are opposed by an overpowering conscience. Like Harley, Carol is unable to find a suitable area of continuous service. She faces a teaching or work assignment with great trepidation, and even though she usually performs well, she comes away in a state of severe anxiety and near exhaustion. For Carol to grow in the Spirit will mean putting her cares and anxieties one by one into the protection and comfort that is promised to those who will yield to Him in faith. Until she has overcome her problem in this way, her church leaders must shield her by not asking her to take difficult areas of responsibility.

A Life With a Conscience That Is Too Weak

Dr. Frank D—, a dentist who was highly intelligent and clever, lacked the influence of a normal inner law. He was interviewed while awaiting electrocution for murder. In high school he had pilfered and later in dental college he had rifled lockers and stolen models of teeth made by other students, and he had been chronically untruthful. Upon graduation from dental school, he went to South Africa, set up a practice, and stole all the gold, silver, and platinum he could lay his hands on. In addition, he was sexually promiscuous.

While in South Africa, he decided to commit certain murders. He had not yet met his chosen victims, but he knew them as reputable, wealthy people in his hometown. He subsequently sailed for New York where he enrolled in college courses in bacteriology and toxicology in preparation for the murders. He simultaneously had self-flattering notices appear in his hometown newspapers, setting the stage for his arrival.

Soon after establishing a dental practice in his hometown, he received an invitation to a social affair given by the family that he planned to murder. In a short time, he married the daughter of the family. He explained what happened next:

"The old lady [his mother-in-law] was a cinch, but what a time I

30

had with the old man. I gave the old lady some arsenic and she passed out quietly. I wet the old man's shoes and dampened the seat of the automobile and left the car windows open. That night he had a sore throat and I treated it by painting it with diphtheria germs, but I'll be darned if they would take. He skinned his shinbone on a box I had placed in his path, and I rubbed in tetanus, but no good! Next I fed him typhoid bacilli, pneumococci, and every germ I could think of, but it was no use. So I decided to give him arsenic. That worked.

"I almost did not complete the last of my planned murders. My wife is such a good pianist and I love beautiful music."

Frank was a person who lacked the basic fiber of the inner law. He did not have the sense of guilt that is necessary to guide the normal person into a truly satisfying life. He represents the extreme degree of weakness of the conscience. A person like Frank is very unlikely to come to the point of receiving Christ as Savior. He has rebelled against the principles of Christ and does not accept the fact that he is a sinner. Sociopaths who have received Christ are those who have been placed in a traumatic situation in which life seems hopeless and they come to see that they were wrong. They suddenly realize that they are sinners and turn to Christ. Such conversions often appear spectacular because the entering of the Spirit effects a radical personality change. They have accepted the inner law of the Spirit which begins to govern their lives. The conscience may still be weak in a number of problem areas, but if they continue to yield to the Spirit, it strengthens rapidly.

The strength of the motivational forces and the inner law may range from extremely strong through the normal levels to extremely weak, as shown in Figure 2.

FIGURE 2 — Motivational Forces and the Inner Law

It should be emphasized that Harley, William, Carol, and Frank are at the extremes of the scale. Most people would be closer to the center, having a weak conscience in a few areas, but not totally without principles. Similarly, many people are highly motivated or have a few unrealistic standards, but few people are as strongly driven as William or as inhibited by their conscience as Carol. Christians who have the fewest problems in working with others and in avoiding interpersonal conflicts are those who approach the center point on both dimensions.

However, the overriding determinant is the degree both to which the self is yielded to the Spirit, and to which its decisions are based upon His leading.

THE CHURCH LEADER LOOKS AT THE THREE-DIMENSIONAL MAN

What does the three-dimensional nature of man have to say concerning the church leader? What type of person should be selected to take positions of responsibility in the church? How may we work most effectively with people of various motivational and inner law strengths?

As the Holy Spirit takes control of the self through the process of Christian maturation, the dimensions begin to move toward the center. The extreme motivation begins to mellow and the extreme tyranny of the conscience begins to move toward a realistic consciousness of actual sins against God. The unmotivated begins to find purpose and to develop interests and concern. If a person remains under the grip of one of the extremes, then he has not yet matured in the Spirit. He must be helped spiritually, but not placed in a position of responsibility.

As a leader evaluates people for church service, he has the tendency to jump to the conclusion that a life that is balanced in terms of the human dimensions is one that is prepared for service. A Christian who has grown up in a well-balanced family in which love was shown to the children may be personally likeable, friendly, self-confident, and responsible, but a spiritual infant. If he has not yielded to the Spirit, he is quite unprepared to lead the way for others.

Persons who were at the extremes in their human dimensions and who have come under the power of the Spirit are often the strongest church workers. The person who is basically strong in the motivational dimension may perform with delightful energy and dedication when he is led of the Spirit to work on a property or finance committee, a building committee, a youth program, or in some other area of service. Each of us has observed numerous persons who, like Carol, were overly bound by an unrealistic conscience in specific areas of their lives but became effective Sunday School teachers or workers with children. Their promptness and careful attention to detail can be very valuable traits if they are under the control of the Spirit. It is apparent that the consideration in placing a person in a position of responsibility is the level of his spiritual maturity and not his personal appeal. The concepts of the three-dimensional nature of man will serve as an essential foundation for understanding as we consider the functions of the leadership of the church throughout the remainder of the book.

2

Fostering Spiritual Maturation

The church must provide a proper climate for spiritual growth — an environment that stimulates and nurtures the newborn babe as he develops toward maturity. Fellow Christians must encourage, instruct, and share with one another so that each is aided in his progress in the Christian life. The purpose of this chapter is to explore the methods by which a church may provide fertile soil for the support of rapid growth. As a basis for consideration of these methods, let us look at the evidences and principles that should guide our analysis of these methods.

EVIDENCES OF SPIRITUAL MATURITY

We can always recognize the Madison Avenue type of executive. Irrespective of the current fashion in dress, he always stands out as neat and well-groomed, wearing a carefully pressed suit which invariably includes a vest. His recently trimmed hair has no doubt been put in that permanent array by the corner stylist. With a manner bold and firm and speech just a bit too proper, he depicts the man that has adapted to the image of his profession and status. Similarly, a mature Christian is one whose speech and actions reveal his character. Because he has conformed to the image of God within and bears the imprint of the characteristics of the God who controls his life, he possesses qualities

33

that characterize him as a person of great faith, learned in the Word, and yielded to the will of God moment by moment. As we become acquainted with him, his Christian qualities shine through and emanate as an invisible glow over his life.

How would you describe the most spiritually mature person you ever met? On first acquaintance you might notice that he has inner peace, lacking the anxieties, fears, and worries that have become the symbol of our generation. You soon recognize the manifestation of his love in its unspoken presence, extending to non-Christians as well as to Christians. His love for non-Christians is tempered with a touch of sympathy, concern, and mercy as he sees them striving for fulfillment like Don Quixote jostling with the windmill — empty of satisfaction or hope. As you interact with him, you discover a consistent standard of goodness and justice that pervades every avenue of his life. His kindness and acceptance do not hide the strong values which permeate his behavior and thought, for he consistently applies biblical standards to his own life, and maintains patience and gentleness toward others. His discussions are based upon truth and candor, conveying a wisdom and judgment that cannot be attributed merely to his formal education. Finding his fulfillment in God, he becomes a person of moderation — he has no need to overeat, to overspend, to flaunt his knowledge or experience, to go to excesses in dress, to exhibit his property or his piety. In being bold to speak the Gospel of Christ and to share with others the reason for the hope that he has, he applies the Scripture as a foundation for the creative solution of the problems at hand, not bound by tradition but employing the principles of the Word as a framework for solving problems in the contemporary environment. In daily living, he exhibits the fruit of the Spirit — love, joy, peace, longsuffering, gentleness, goodness, faith, meekness, temperance (Gal. 5:22, 23).

PRINCIPLES OF SPIRITUAL GROWTH

How does one reach Christian maturity? Theodore Epp illustrates the path to spiritual maturity as a triangle with Christ as its center. It rests on the Word of God and ascends by way of faith and obedience (Figure 3).[1]

Paul expressed his yearning for deeper fellowship with Christ by saying, ". . . [that I] may be found in Him, not having a righteousness of my own derived from the law, but that which through faith in Christ, the righteousness which comes from God on the basis of faith" (Phil. 3:9). Christ must be the center of our life, infiltrating every aspect of our being, because He lives in us (Gal. 2:20).

---

[1]Theodore Epp, *Principles of Spiritual Growth,* (Lincoln, Neb.: Back-to-the-Bible Publishers, 1967), pp. 10-15.

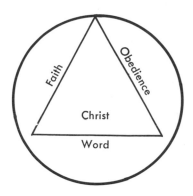

FIGURE 3 — Maturation in Christ

The Word

The foundation of growth is the knowledge of His Word. We appropriate the revelation of God for ourselves as we study the Word. "Like newborn babes, long for the pure milk of the word, that by it you may grow" (1 Pet. 2:2). The Word is God's communication to man. In His image we were created as communicating beings. It is not surprising that as a communicating Being He would communicate to us or that His communication would be perfect. To think otherwise would be an absurdity. Thus "all Scripture is inspired by God and profitable for teaching, for reproof, for correction, for training in righteousness" (2 Tim. 3:16). If we are to know and follow the direction of any person, we must hear and know that person's communication to us. To abide in Christ, we must receive His communication and know it. "Thy word have I treasured in my heart that I may not sin against Thee" (Ps. 119:11). In prayer as we wait in silence, listening to God's will for the moment, He will often communicate to us by way of His Word which we have made a permanent channel for His communication by study and memorization. "He who has My commandments, and keeps them, he it is who loves Me; and he who loves Me shall be loved by My Father, and I will love him and will disclose Myself to him" (John 14:21). We must first have His commandments that are found only in His Word. Then as we keep them and love Him, He will love us and will reveal Himself even more deeply to us.

Faith

Faith requires a knowledge of the Word. "Faith comes from hearing, and hearing by the word of Christ" (Rom. 10:17). Abraham provides an outstanding example of faith, for "with respect to the promise of

God, he did not waver in unbelief, but grew strong in faith, giving glory to God, and being fully assured that what He had promised, He was able also to perform. Therefore also IT WAS RECKONED TO HIM AS RIGHTEOUSNESS" (Rom. 4:20-22). Abraham was prepared to subordinate his will to that of God even to the·sacrifice of his only son at his own hand, but he could do this only because of his complete confidence in God.

Just as faith is based upon knowledge of the Word, so obedience requires faith. We cannot allow ourselves to be controlled by one in whom we lack faith.

Obedience

We sin because our self-will conflicts with the standards of God. Our only hope for avoiding sin is the power of Christ in our lives leading us to yield to His will. As we see this truth, we begin to recognize that our attempts at self-fulfillment through our work, our educational pursuits, our daily spending, and even our family are sin if they are not yielded to Him. They are sin in the same way that stealing, drunkenness, murder, or hate are sin, according to the full intent of God's Law — the Law given that we may recognize our separation from the will of God and return to Him through Christ for our fulfillment. "Even so consider yourselves to be dead to sin, but alive to God in Christ Jesus. Therefore do not let sin reign in your mortal body that you should obey its lusts, and do not go on presenting the members of your body to sin as instruments of unrighteousness; but present yourselves to God as those alive from the dead, and your members as instruments of righteousness to God" (Rom. 6:11-13). We grow spiritually as we submit each area and each moment of our lives to God.

This submission begins with self-evaluation. "But let a man examine himself . . ." (1 Cor. 11-28). We should examine ourselves to see which aspects of our lives are not conformed to the image of Christ. This evaluation is not intended as a basis for self-condemnation or remorse, but as a basis for submission and growth. Submission is the essence of confession. We know that if we confess our sins they are forgiven, and God restores fellowship with us. "If we confess our sins, He is faithful and righteous to forgive us our sins and to cleanse us from all unrighteousness" (1 John 1:9).

We must present ourselves to Him. "I urge you therefore, brethren, by the mercies of God, to present your bodies a living and holy sacrifice, acceptable to God, which is your spiritual service of worship" (Rom. 12:1). Not only must we commit ourselves to Him in an act of self-sacrifice, but we also must continue to allow His Being to be our fulfillment. "But I say, walk by the Spirit, and you will not carry out the desire of the flesh" (Gal. 5:16).

As with physical growth, spiritual development occurs one step at a time. Some of these are giant steps; others are infinitesimal, yet each step follows the pattern of knowledge, faith, and obedience.

Five key elements are necessary for one to make strides of progress in spiritual maturation. (1) First, we must identify an area of our life which we are attempting to fulfill outside of Christ. This may be a significant area of our lives or only a question of what we shall do for the next moment. (2) We then apply the Word of God to the issue by searching the Scripture or by simply reflecting on the relevant areas of the Bible with which we have familiarity. (3) Next comes self-examination; we must look within ourselves to identify the needs, fears, anxieties, resentments, worries, etc., that are preventing our yielding to the will of God. If we experience such emotions, then we are dealing with an area of our life in which our self-will is struggling for the gratification of our needs. Since we are frustrated in our attempts at handling the area, we strive all the harder to handle the problem on our own. If you are completely honest with yourself, you will find that you rather enjoy your worries and your depressions because they indicate to you that you are in the battle, fighting valiantly the struggles of life. Anxieties may then be used to control the lives of others — to gain their sympathy and compliance. Our human nature does not want to give these over to God. (4) If we are to grow, we must yield to God in an attitude of total surrender of self-will. We need not spend time in more than a brief confession of our past failure to yield, but concentrate primarily on what His will is for the next moment. (5) Finally, we receive His answer and act on faith. We must have faith that He answers at the instant of our prayer; if this faith exists, then we will begin to act accordingly. If you have yielded your resentment of a neighbor to God and ask for love, then you should immediately perform an act of love toward the neighbor. If you have asked for wisdom, then begin immediately to put it to practice. If you have yielded your home to God, then decide immediately what will be your first act of worship or service through the home and follow up quickly.

Let us illustrate with a step of growth in the life of Ray. Most people would say that Ray is an introvert, or at least quite reserved. His growth in Christ has been slow, and periods of regression in the Christian walk have retarded his progress. Occasionally, he has witnessed to members of his family or others who shared their lives with him. In college he even mustered the courage to go with a friend on an evangelistic visit into the streets of the local slum area. Nevertheless, he has been afraid to share his faith at work for fear of being considered a radical, telling himself, "The Christian faith is a highly personal and private experience. . . . My *life* is my witness before unbelievers."

He sponsored a Christian luncheon for people at work in which a regular speaker was engaged who chose as his topic for the series, "Sharing Your Faith at Work." After two weeks of discussion on wit-

37

nessing, the group was reduced from ten participants to three. Ray felt the challenge to witness at work was too strong a diet and wanted to ask the speaker to change the subject matter (note [1] above: attempting to fulfill — outside of Christ — the area of witnessing), but he knew that in the final analysis, witnessing was the responsibility that the group needed to face because it was a key command given in the Scripture ([2] applying the Word of God). Ray was experiencing deep conflict. Could he witness to others at work as the speaker urged? He was not the type to confront others with their need for Christ. The battle within his mind continued for hours as he pondered and prayed about the direction in which he should move. In thinking through the conflict, he realized that his failure to witness to unbelivers was based on the fear of being viewed as a radical or fanatic, and thereby losing respect. Was he "ashamed of the gospel of Christ?" His reluctant but honest answer was yes ([3] self-examination).

Suddenly, he realized that he had been praying amiss by pitting his own will against the speaker's desires for him. He must yield the area of witnessing in total surrender to God's will. This he did in a single sentence spoken to God; immediately he felt joy and peace as though a great burden had been lifted from his shoulders ([4] yielding to God). As he met fellow workers, he had a feeling of expectancy that God might open the door for his witness. Coupled with this expectancy was a fresh feeling of love. Apparently the area of witnessing had been a great barrier for Ray in his spiritual growth, for he found a new perspective on his entire life as he examined every area of life that came to mind and then yielded it to God. His new-found joy of living made witnessing to unbelievers a natural part of daily conversation. He simply explained the reason for the hope and joy in his life and invited others to receive that life for themselves ([5] receiving the answer and acting on faith). Next, let us consider the approaches by which church leaders can encourage spiritual maturation through fellowship and instruction.

FELLOWSHIP AS A PATH TO SPIRITUAL GROWTH

In the final analysis, progress in spiritual growth is the strictly personal experience of yielding our will through Christ. However, the fellowship of others is an important stimulant to this growth because a person rarely grows if he isolates himself from the fellowship of others. As we gather with others in Christ's name, we have the assurance that we can experience His presence among us. "For where two or three have gathered together in My name, there I am in their midst" (Matt. 18:20). Beyond this, we know that we hold a responsibility to one another. "Let us consider how to stimulate one another to love and good deeds, not forsaking our own assembling together, as is the habit of some, but encouraging one another; and all the more, as you see the day drawing near" (Heb. 10:24, 25). This is one of the most frequently quoted verses in many churches; usually the quotation starts in the middle of the verse (and of the thought) and is used as a means of warning members of failure to assemble. The verse does not encourage assembly simply to gather together, but rather we are to gather in His name and for a purpose — to help others to grow by encouraging, challenging, and exhorting them to love and to good works. The verse does not suggest that one person is to continually exhort the rest but that we are to "consider how to stimulate one another." Thus a mutual sharing is commanded in these verses. If churches are finding fewer and fewer people who consistently assemble together, perhaps it is because of our failure to do so for the right purpose or because our method does not encourage us to "stimulate one another to love and good deeds."

In recent years voices have been heard across the country, pleading for a return to an assembly of the body for mutual sharing in the pattern of the early church. Several have shifted their emphasis away from the lecture approach toward fellowship; some are doing so within the structure of the church as it is formally constituted, while others are making a radical departure from the traditional concept of the church.

Fellowship that will serve as a stimulant for spiritual growth has certain distinctives that differentiate it from simple affiliation with others. (1) Edifying fellowship is based on an encouragement toward good works. The church which enjoys the edifying fellowship is one in which members encourage one another to seek the goodness of God in their daily activities. They lovingly identify for each other those activities which seem to be based upon self-will and point out the way of fulfillment by surrendering them to God. (2) Edifying fellowship is based on Christian love. Love of others and love of God are inseparable. As we find a new depth of love for God, we find our love for others magnified. But it is equally true that as we experience Christian love for others, we find a deeper love for God. It is impossible for a blind man to appreciate the beauty of a rose garden. Likewise, if a person has not experienced Christian love for another person it is impossible for him to understand the love of God or to love Him fully: "If some one says, 'I love God,' and hates his brother, he is a liar: for the one who does not love his brother whom he has seen, cannot love God whom he has not seen. And this commandment we have from Him, that the one who loves God should love his brother also" (1 John 4:20, 21). (3) Edifying fellowship is based on a knowledge of one another. Each of us has a true self and each has a mask that covers some portion of the true person. A meaningful love relationship is directed toward the person; no one can love a mask. Christian fellowship must encourage an openness that strips away the mask and allows the true person to emerge. The true person is always lovely even though he is in a fallen state;

because he is created by and in the image of God, he is far more lovable than any mask created by fallen man to cover his fears and feelings of inadequacy. In the edifying fellowship we must honestly expose our true person: our values, virtues, strengths, weaknesses, burdens, blessings, fears, guilt, anxieties, resentments, loves, faith, and distrust. Seeing others love us just as we are, we can readily see how God with His perfect love can also love us. His Word takes on new meaning, our faith grows, and we cherish the opportunity to serve Him.

How do we appropriate the edifying fellowship to the life of the church? The number of approaches are perhaps limited only by the restraints of our creativity. An edifying fellowship has been found within the meetings of large congregations as well as in small groups and in two-person encounters.

Congregational Fellowship

A highly successful climate for an edifying fellowship has been developed in the Peninsula Bible Church under the leadership of Mr. Ray Stedman by the conduct of what he calls "body life" services. His evening service is devoted to a time of fellowship for the total church family. Applying the concepts of the unified body of Christ emphasized in Ephesians 4, he encourages church members to share their burdens and blessings with one another and to pray for one another. After a person has stood in the congregation to share his feelings, needs, and concerns, others may relate their similar experiences, burdens, or needs; they may refer to a scriptural teaching that casts light on the problem, or they may relate their insights concerning it. Out of their openness and honesty grows a close bond of love. Mr. Stedman has helped many churches to place a "body life" service at the heart of their church life.

Other churches have found the following to be meaningful: a Thanksgiving service in which blessings of the previous year are shared, a time of prayer request followed by prayer, a testimony time during a service. Though they have the value of involving the members in the lives of one another, these various types of worship usually lack the openness, depth, and regularity that are essential to an edifying fellowship.

Small Group Fellowship

Lawrence Richards advocates a change in church functioning toward the fellowship and involvement patterns of the early church. He envisions a church with three structural groupings — the family unit, the growth cell group, and the congregation. The total family unit is held together for study and fellowship "classes." Families meet together in growth cells for study of the Word with all members of the cell assuming the responsibility to study, pray, plan, minister, and share in the group. Small congregations of about 250 adults with their children meet once weekly for a three-hour block of time. This meeting involves a sermon followed by panels, discussions in small groups, and other means of interaction. This fellowship- and interaction-oriented church framework provides a basis for the responsibility, communication, study, and fellowship essential to spiritual growth. While he does involve the total congregation in one phase of church life, Richards places primary emphasis upon the small group. Sunday school classes are made up of the growth cell of five families or ten single adults. In these classes the families share their thoughts and experiences regarding biblical passages. Richards' concept does not assure an edifying fellowship but it does provide the opportunity for it. The experience of the edifying fellowship could be brought into his church concept at the growth cell level without modification of the structure.[2]

Another small group approach to the edifying fellowship is the "yokefellow group" developed under the guidance and encouragement of Cecil Osborne. Yokefellow groups allow a sharing and a fellowship that is similar to "body life," but encourage a deeper and more intense relationship of Christian love. These groups of six to twelve people meet in homes on a weekly or bi-weekly basis to encourage one another in their daily discipline of prayer and Bible study as well as to share their burdens. Topics are discussed that encourage the group members to examine themselves — their fears, anxieties, guilts, lack of faith, resentments — and to place themselves before the others without their psychological masks for cover-up. As the real person emerges, the Christian's love for this true person grows and he comes to accept and understand more fully the unmerited love and grace of God.[3]

Perhaps the essence of the yokefellow group is best conveyed by way of an illustration. The group which we shall describe is made up of seven people: two married couples, two women who attend without their husbands, and the male leader. The group has been meeting bi-weekly for almost a year. At the time of the first meeting, the group members knew one another only as acquaintances or not at all. During the first three sessions respectively the discussion topics concerned barriers to the Christian's relationship to God, such as anxieties, resentments, guilt, and fear; barriers to self-acceptance; and barriers to relationship to others. During these three meetings the members of the group felt that they were being extremely open in relating their burdens and needs, and, in terms of normal contacts, they *were*; but they were aware that there were still many thoughts that they could not express — experiences about which they felt guilt, resentments toward their spouses and friends that they would hardly admit to themselves, fear of rejection that ran

---

[2]Lawrence Richards, *A New Face for the Church,* (Grand Rapids: Zondervan Publishing House, 1970), p. 152.

[3]Cecil G. Osborne, *The Art of Understanding Yourself,* (Grand Rapids: Zondervan Publishing House, 1970), pp. 24-36.

deep into the history of each member. With each successive meeting they were able to become more open and to reveal honestly more of their true nature. Instead of finding that others were shocked or rejecting, they found love and acceptance in the true meaning of Christian love. The members of the group became close friends. One couple who had felt inadequate in making friends before found new confidence in being accepted and soon had surrounded themselves with a broad range of Christian friends.

As their experiences with Christ were shared in their devotional and Bible study times, they were able to "stimulate one another to love and good deeds." Their devotional and study times became more consistent and lengthened. They shared their victories and new insights into the Christian life and found that this stimulated the growth of others and spread to have a profound effect upon their churches and even upon the community.

The yokefellow groups are similar to many other sharing groups which operate within various church organizations. "Integrity therapy" is an approach developed by John Drakeford for involving groups of Christians in the therapy and growth experience emerging out of the confession of sins. In the integrity therapy groups the members are encouraged to assume responsibility for their actions, to confess their sins to one another, and to pray for one another. The warmth of acceptance of others and growth in the Spirit also follow as a result of this open confession and prayer.

Perhaps the most practical and effective form for Christian group life is that described by Lyman Coleman as "growth by groups." This type of fellowship does not require a trained leader and has a proper emphasis upon Bible study, prayer, and action, as well as open sharing. In addition, it provides for an expanding influence by adding new people and by division as the group becomes large.[4]

Although these groups may be called by many names — cell, yoke-fellow, integrity therapy, growth groups, and the like — their fundamental value is in fulfilling the scriptural exhortation to assemble for the purpose of promoting love and good works in the lives of their members. These good works may be centered upon confession of sins, Bible study, sharing of experiences, conversational prayer, encouragement of daily devotion, or some combination of these. The values of this type of fellowship for spiritual growth are in evidence both in the instruction of the Word and in the experience of those who have been involved in the groups.

Two-Person Fellowship

Perhaps the most familiar of the edifying fellowship experiences is

---

[4]Lyman Coleman, *Growth by Groups: Prologue,* (Huntingdon Valley, Penn.: Christian Outreach, 1967).

that found in counseling someone who has a personal problem. Sometimes a troubled person hopes for an easy solution, while other times he simply wishes to place his burden on the broad shoulders of the counselor. In any case, the criteria for effective counseling is the same as that for the edifying fellowship — the counselor must convey a fundamental acceptance and love that cannot be shocked or threatened out of existence, the counselee must become open and show a trust in the counselor, and the counselor must encourage the counselee to find peace in Christ. Perhaps the greatest difficulty in pastoral counseling is that the time available for it does not allow for the fellowship that could go beyond the immediate problem situation and continue to help the person to grow toward spiritual maturation. Perhaps people who are gifted with the ability to understand, accept, love, listen, and encourage others should be enlisted in a program of counseling for the church that would allow a long-range fellowship to grow. Such an arrangement can be developed between certain members of a local church. When a member carrying a particular burden is found, fellow Christians who have the gift of helping others may be called upon to provide the needed relationship of love and understanding.

INSTRUCTION AS A PATH TO SPIRITUAL GROWTH

Understanding God's revelation through the Word remains the foundation for spiritual growth. As we increase our fellowship, we must not allow it to replace the study and teaching of the Word. Some of today's churches have moved away from the study of the Word toward either a purely fellowship or social service orientation. Social service *is* an important activity for the Christian; by example and word Christ taught us to help others. Yet the acts of goodness must follow yieldedness to God. Doing good deeds as a result of human motivation is simply another futile attempt at satisfying our needs by the exercise of our own will. These acts, as well as other attempts at fulfillment outside of submission to and following God, will give a shallow satisfaction. Our problem today in the instruction of the Word is one of communicating the scriptural message in a manner that provides a foundation for growth and action. In past centuries people learned much from listening to speakers whom they enjoyed as a break from the routines of life. Today the Christian message competes with a vast array of communication media. Consequently, we have become increasingly less responsive to oratory as a means of communication. We now want to have action and visual cues as well as auditory ones. In addition, people today are less responsive to the spoken word. Television advertising has conditioned them to distrust what others tell them. In our work, we are no longer expected to jump when the boss yells. A more humanistic leadership form which assumes that a person should be led rather than driven to perform has become popular. We do not listen to a person in authority with the same unchallenging loyalty that prevailed a century ago.

Instruction of the Word must be reevaluated with the same openness to innovation that is necessary for a reevaluation of fellowship. Again, let us consider the methods of instruction with total congregations, small groups, and two-person meetings.

Small Group Instruction

In order for instruction and study of the Word to be effective, it must be (1) regular, (2) relevant to the life of the learner, and (3) made a part of the behavior and thought of the learner. Much teaching in the church has traditionally been done in small groups of twenty or fewer people. Such groups encourage discussion and involvement in thinking through the area of study. In small groups the participants usually feel more free to express their opinions and to describe how the ideas apply to their own lives. For this reason Sunday schools should be structured to have small classes and home Bible studies should be organized to be available to all who are interested. In fact, all small group study may be shifted to the home as a way of increasing fellowship while encouraging the relevancy of the instruction. Prayer groups also provide a basis for instruction. Members of these groups often wish to discuss the biblical basis of problems with which they are dealing. As prayers are answered, members of the group come to better understand God's work in their lives and in the world.

Congregational Instruction

Providing instruction to a total congregation in a way that is relevant while optimizing its application to the lives of the people is a difficult assignment. To make the instruction relevant one must be able to discern the concerns and thoughts of those who are listening. Some type of feedback system is required, such as frequent visiting with church members. The best feedback is gained when this visiting is over lunch or for several hours in the evening. This allows the conversation to go beyond the superficial level and into the real concerns of life. Feedback can also be gained within the congregational meeting. Lawrence Richards advocates one congregational meeting each Sunday of three-hours' duration in which the pastor presents a message that is vital "to the present life and growth of the people."[5] Following the sermon, the congregation is given time to react by exploring in small groups the implications of the Word studied in the sermon for the life of those involved. A question-and-answer session following the sermon also allows feedback as well as helping the congregation to clarify the implication of the message to them.

---

[5]Richards, *A New Face,* p. 34.

A time of sharing the experiences that members have had with the message will further help to illustrate its application for the present life situations of other people. Methods of bringing the message into focus, such as role playing, study, and discussion of someone's actual experience that has been written or that can be presented orally, will emphasize the application of the Word. Decision sessions are often preferable to discussion sessions following a sermon. In the decision session the participants are asked first to discuss various methods of applying the sermon content, and then to decide how they will apply it to their own lives. Brainstorming, buzz groups, debate, open-ended study, research, and report are among the many instructional methods which emphasize feedback and application. Any of these methods should prove useful following a sermon, to help bring the message to vitality in the life of the member.

Two-Person Instruction

An important pattern of the New Testament is that of the two-man teams serving and studying together. The two-person instruction approach has hardly been explored in most churches. The closest thing that is practiced in the church today is the family worship time. Some churches have used prayer partners, Scripture memorization teams, and visitation teams. Some have used "faith training" as a means of teaching faithfulness. In the "faith training" program young Christians are taken to a distant city with no money or food and are instructed in how to trust God to meet their needs as they serve Him and seek His will. For several days they must find their way on faith. The incidences of God's revealing His protection of them are often dramatic and always convincing.

The fostering of spiritual maturation by the church is of unexcelled significance to the fulfillment of its great commission from God. The principles of growth in Christ based upon study of the Word, faith, and obedience have no time constraints. Yet the methods by which they can best be fostered in a local church are open to innovation by the leadership of each church. Although some methods have general applicability, the most effective approaches will vary from church to church and from time to time. It is our hope that these concepts and examples will stimulate your imagination and creativity in the development of methods to increase the knowledge and understanding of the Word among your people, to build their faith, and to bring them into an obedience to God.

3

Recognizing and Developing Spiritual Gifts

According to Ephesians 4:12, the work of the ministry is not the responsibility of the paid professional; it is the job of the saints — every believer. The church continues to suffer from the fifteenth-century syndrome which inactivated the laymen and virtually deified the clergy. Today when a job needs to be done, it is not uncommon to hear the words "Let's hire someone to do it." As a result, if a sermon is to be preached, we hire a professional preacher; if a window is to be replaced, we engage a glazier; if a nursery is to be cared for, we pay a sitter, etc., ad infinitum. As someone has graphically put it, the local church is like a football game: twenty-two men are down on the field, desperately needing rest, while there are ten thousand cheering spectators who desperately need exercise.

The answer to the problem of getting the fans out of the stands and onto the playing field is to secure, not more cheerleaders, but more coaches — coaches who recognize the vast potential going to waste. The undiscovered secret which gets the fans out of the stands and into the work of the ministry centers around the subject of "spiritual gifts."

The Meaning of Spiritual Gifts

The concept of spiritual gifts is seen in the setting of the "body life." Romans 12 presents the context for Christian service: individual submission to God and a recognition of the need for and the responsibility to other members of the Body of Christ, which is the church. The church, in Scripture, is seen through the perspective of seven figures of speech, one of which is the human body, a picture which shows the intricate unity and function of the church with Jesus Christ as the controlling Head. In the human body there are many different parts, such as the hand, the foot, the ear, and the eye, yet each is part of the whole and has a very important function. If one part of the body does not operate correctly, the whole body suffers because of it. Thus a broken arm limits the body and curtails its effectiveness as well.

It is in this context that the apostle Paul writes, "So we, who are many, are one body in Christ, and individually members one of another. And . . . we have gifts that differ according to the grace given to us . . ." (Rom. 12:5, 6). Each member, then, is important and each member must function if the body is to be healthy. Therefore, God has given to every member in the body of Christ a gift to carry out his responsibility.

The idea of spiritual gifts is revealed in various words used in the New Testament. The primary word is *charisma* which means "a gift of grace." This word is used in Romans 12:6 and in 1 Corinthians 12:4, 9, 28, 30, and 31. The other word which identifies the subject is *pneumatikon;* when used with the article, it indicates "the things of the spirit," or "spiritual gifts." This word is used in the opening verses of 1 Corinthians 12 to introduce the subject of spiritual gifts which Paul discusses in chapters 12, 13, and 14.

From the context of the passages in which the words are used, and the meaning of the words themselves, the following definition for the term "spiritual gifts" is submitted. *Spiritual gifts are divine enablements given to every Christian through which he is able to serve the body of Christ, the results of which are due to the power of divine grace operating by the Holy Spirit.*

The Purpose of Spiritual Gifts

Because the work of the ministry is a spiritual work, God provides a spiritual enablement so that His church may carry it out. It is little wonder then that the work of the ministry fails in the local church when there is a failure to understand the spiritual nature of the work. Churches are prone to entrust the work of the ministry to people who exhibit natural ability to do the task but who fail miserably because they have no spiritual enablement.

In Ephesians 4:7 the apostle Paul identifies the concept of spiritual

47

gifts and in verse 12 he reveals the purpose of these gifts. Thus he says, "But to each one of us grace was given according to the measure of Christ's gift . . . for the equipping of the saints for the work of service, to the building up of the body of Christ." Therefore, there is a threefold purpose of spiritual gifts: The first is the perfecting or the "mending" of the saints. The word "equipping" or "perfecting" comes from a late and rare word *katartismon,* which conveys the idea of completely furnishing a house. This same sense is used in 2 Timothy 3:16, 17 where we see the purpose of Scripture in verse 12: "that the man of God may be adequate, equipped for every good work." The good works that the believer accomplishes are not the result of his self-effort, but of the fulfilled purpose of spiritual gifts manifested in his life.

Secondly, the purpose of spiritual gifts is not only to make the individual complete, but, to make him complete in order that he may do a good work, that is, the work of service. By sharing the true concept of spiritual gifts which God has given to every believer to do His work, we can get the spectators out of the stands and down onto the playing field.

The third reason is the ultimate goal of all these great gifts, and that is the edifying of the body of Christ, or as the Scripture more accurately states it, "the building up" of the body in Christ. Thus we can see that the strength of the church today is dependent on an understanding and implementation of the spiritual gifts in the lives of the believers.

THE IDENTIFICATION OF GIFTS

There being no question as to the meaning and the importance of spiritual gifts as seen in their purpose, the next question that proceeds logically is "What are the spiritual gifts that are to be used to equip the saints for the work of service so that the body of Christ may be strong?"

In an examination of the Scriptures dealing with spiritual gifts, we find that there are sixteen spiritual gifts identified in the New Testament. One can find these in Romans 12, 1 Corinthians 12, and Ephesians 4. Of the sixteen gifts, certain ones were designed primarily for the incubation stage of the church. An example of such a gift is that of "apostle." That this is a spiritual gift is clearly seen from its inclusion with the gifts in 1 Corinthians 12:28-31 and Ephesians 4:7-12. The gift of the office of apostle and prophet was used in laying the foundation of the church (Eph. 2:2). Its temporary character is seen in one of the requirements of an apostle: he must be one who was an eyewitness to the resurrection of Jesus (Acts 1:22). This characteristic along with the apostle's having been chosen directly by the Lord Himself (Matt. 10:1, 2; Rom. 1:1) and his endowment with miraculous powers, which were a divine credential of the office (Matt. 10:1; Heb. 2:4), has led Protestant theology to accept the fact of the cessation of the apostolic gift at the end of the first century.

Since the principle of a temporary gift is evident in Scripture, it leads one to question the possibility of other spiritual gifts that may be of a temporary nature. The earmark of this identification is seen in spiritual gifts which reveal an unusual display of the miraculous, i.e., healing, foretelling the future, or intervention in the realm of nature. A number of gifts bearing this mark were used exclusively by the apostles for the purpose of authenticating their verbal message from the Lord. However, with the completion of the written Word and the ministry of the Spirit of God in His convicting power, the need for unusual miraculous phenomena has ceased.

One is quick to acknowledge, however, that not all evangelical protestants hold to a theological position of "temporary gifts." Those of a charismatic position would take issue with the cessation of healings, speaking in tongues, and other unusual displays of miracles which could be identified as "sign" gifts (1 Cor. 12:22). According to Hebrews 2:3, 4, these sign gifts were obviously used to confirm the message of the Lord to those who heard the apostles preach: "How shall we escape if we neglect so great a salvation? After it was at the first spoken through the Lord, it was confirmed to us by those who heard, God also bearing witness with them, both by signs and wonders and by various miracles and by gifts of the Holy Spirit according to His own will."

Since the intent of this discussion is to relate the importance of spiritual gifts to the Body of Christ in the areas of organization and leadership, we will concentrate on the "serving" gifts rather than the "sign" gifts which confirm the message. A fuller discussion on the theology of spiritual gifts may be found in Walvoord's *The Holy Spirit,*[1] and Hodges' "The Purpose of Tongues."[2]

The serving gifts, which relate to *katartismon,* the "perfecting of the saints," furnishing them for the work of service for the purpose of building up the Body of Christ, constitute nine of the sixteen gifts mentioned in Scripture. They are the following: the gift of teaching, the work of pastor-teacher, evangelism, exhortation, administration, helps, cheerful mercy, giving, and faith. We shall consider them individually in their relationship to the building up of the Body.

The Gift of Teaching

The gift of teaching is mentioned in all three passages dealing with spiritual gifts: Romans 12:7, 1 Corinthians 12:28, and Ephesians 4:11. The gift of teaching is the divine enablement whereby a believer is able to communicate the Word of God by explaining and applying the truth of the Scriptures. The gift of teaching is not reserved only for seminary

---

[1]John F. Walvoord, *The Holy Spirit,* (Wheaton, Illinois: Van Kampen Press, 1954), pp. 163-188.

[2]Zane C. Hodges, "The Purpose of Tongues," *Bibliotheca Sacra,* 1963, Vol. 120, No. 479, pp. 226-233.

graduates but is available by divine bestowal to every believer in the body. Every Christian has an equal source for instruction — the Word of God and the teaching ministry of the Holy Spirit; however, not every believer possesses the ability to teach or to cause learning to take place unless he is endowed with the "gift" of teaching.

The gift of teaching is not limited to age categories, either for the one doing the teaching or the ones being taught. In other words, a teen-ager can possess the gift of teaching as well as a seasoned, mature Christian. Likewise, a person who has the gift of teaching will be able to communicate the truth to children as well as to adults. There is not a gift specifically for teaching adults or for teaching children, but simply the gift of teaching.

The Gift of Pastor-Teacher

This gift is mentioned only in Ephesians 4:11. The primary emphasis is on the pastoral aspect. The word "pastor" comes from the Greek *poimenas,* "shepherd." It carries with it the idea of "one caring for the sheep." There is more to shepherding than just feeding the flock; there must be protection, concern, discipline, personal attention, self-sacrifice, and a sense of responsibility on the part of the owner of the flock. The gift of pastor provides an understanding and a sensitivity with regard to the needs of people. The gift of pastor is not limited to the vocational minister. Many people in the body of Christ have the gift of shepherd-ing and should be exercising this gift.

A man may have the gift of teaching without the gift of pastor, but he cannot have the gift of pastor without having the gift of teaching. The Ephesians 4:11 structure links pastors and teachers with the con-tinuative conjunction "kai," which creates a unity of thought and intent. Thus the pastor will be able to feed his flock through the teaching of the Word. The teaching situation does not necessarily occur in a formal pupit or classroom situation, but may be on a person-to-person basis. A Sunday school teacher may have the gift of pastor-teacher and have an effective ministry even though there may be only five members in his class. On the other hand, a man may have the gift of teaching and perform the superficial duties of the pastor of a large congregation, yet without the gift of pastor he will not be able to meet the needs of his congregation.

The Gift of Evangelism

This gift is also mentioned in Ephesians 4:11. The gift of evangelism is the divine enablement within a believer to proclaim the Gospel, the Good News, and to witness the result of men being born again into the family of God. Just as learning is the result of the gift of teaching, so salvation is the result of the gift of evangelism.

The gift of evangelism is easily seen in the ministry of Billy Graham.

50

He preaches a simple message, showing man's need, God's provision, and man's responsibility to receive God's free gift of salvation. And then, miraculously, without coercion, hundreds respond to receive Christ as their personal Savior. This is a demonstration of the gift of evangelism.

However, we must not confuse mass evangelism and personal evangelism as being different gifts. The gift is the same. One may be led of God to witness on a personal basis with the joy of seeing individuals respond positively to the claims of Christ. He, too, has the gift of evangelism.

In 2 Timothy 4:5, Paul exhorts Timothy to do the "work" of an evangelist. Since Timothy had been sent to Ephesus to exercise his gift of pastor-teacher, it is possible that he did not have the gift of evangelism, but still had the responsibility of preaching the Gospel. This leads one to conclude that not everyone who witnesses will see great results, nor is he to be discouraged or guilt-ridden if he does not. It's just possible that the witness does not have the gift of evangelism. God did not sovereignly bestow it.

The Gift of Exhortation

The term "exhortation" comes from *parakaleō*, "to call for; to summon; to entreat" (Rom. 12:8). This word is also translated "to admonish, encourage, and exhort." It is a word of motivation for action. The gift of exhortation is accompanied by the divine enablement whereby people respond practically to the teaching of the Word. It is the gift of exhortation which provides the ability for a man to disciple another in the things of the Lord, to stimulate the faith of others.

The Gift of Administration

The work of the ministry, whether in a local church or on the mission field, demands a certain amount of administration. The biblical principle of orderliness commits the church to this. "Let all things be done properly and in an orderly manner" (1 Cor. 14:40) is to be the guideline.

Administration is not simply organization. Nor is administration manipulation. Administration is the ability to "rule" within the body of Christ. First Corinthians 12:28 designates the same gift as "governments" *(kubernaō)* "to guide and pilot." The word in Romans 12:8 is *proistemi,* "to preside, rule, govern, to set over." In either case it has the idea of guiding and directing a segment of the body of Christ. In the local church this gift should be possessed and exercised by those appointed as elders and deacons.

The Gift of Helps

The gift of helps is described by two designations. In Romans 12:7 it is the word *diakonia,* "service, ministry," and in 1 Corinthians 12:28, it is the word *antilampsis,* "a laying hold of, an exchange." In both instances it has the idea of one helping carry the burden of another. The gift of helps can be seen in the unassuming person who sees to it that the flowers for the sanctuary are brought and arranged, or that a family in need has their needs met, or that the person in the hospital has a visitor with whom to pass the lonesome hours.

God gives some believers a special sensitivity to the need of others and the ability to do something about those needs without saying, "Is there anything I can do to help?"

The Gift of Cheerful Mercy

Closely akin to the gift of helps is the gift of mercy. It differs from helps in that this gift focuses on the individuals within the body who need help rather than on the activities to be performed.

The gift is mentioned only in Romans 12:8 and has a dual thrust. It comes from *eleos,* meaning "compassion, mercy, and pity," and a qualifying adjective describes how the gift is to be demonstrated: *hilaroteti,* "with hilarity or cheerfulness."

A believer having the gift of mercy is sensitive to the spiritual, emotional, and physical needs of others and has the ability to be of help in a cheerful way by bringing a little sunshine into a life that is trying to ride out a storm.

The Gift of Giving

Giving material or financial aid is the responsibility of every Christian in that he has been appointed a steward of the things of God. He is to give not grudgingly, or of necessity, but cheerfully. According to Romans 12:8, some believers have been given a spiritual gift to give in an unusual way in either a quantitative or qualitative way. The late Mr. R. G. Letourneau exemplifies a giver of this type. So also does the person who may not have been entrusted with as much material wealth, but who is still sensitive to the temporal needs of others and is able and willing to give without seeking earthly recognition.

The Gift of Faith

Faith, like giving, is experienced in some degree by all Christians. Just as every believer is a steward, so every believer lives by faith in the Son of God (Gal. 2:20). However, there are some believers who have been endowed by God with an unusual ability to exercise faith in the power and the wisdom of God to meet needs and give direction. The gift of faith is demonstrated in a man like Hudson Taylor, the great missionary statesman, who claimed the land of China for God.[3] Another example is manifested in the life of "God's Smuggler," Brother Andrew, who daily exercised the gift of faith in his work of taking

---

[3]Howard and Mary G. Taylor, *Hudson Taylor's Spiritual Secret,* (Chicago: Moody Press).

Bibles behind the Iron Curtain. In either case, it was an unusual capacity to believe God while serving Him which characterized the actions of the two Christians.

THE DISCOVERY OF SPIRITUAL GIFTS

It is one thing to know what the spiritual gifts are. It is another thing to know where they are. Every Christian who desires to be useful and effective in his Christian service must ask himself, "What is my spiritual gift?" It is not being presumptuous to claim that we have a special endowment from God for service, since the Word of God tells us that every single Christian has received a spiritual gift in order to do the work of service (Ehp. 4:7, 12). Since this is the privilege of every believer, it is important for him to know what his gift is. This salient question therefore arises: "How can I know what my spiritual gift is?"

There are a number of very practical tests that we can apply in order to determine our spiritual gift. None of these individually is conclusive, but collectively they can be used to determine the gift of the believer to give him boldness in order to use it. The tests include:

(1) A *desire* for a particular gift. In 1 Corinthians 12:31 the apostle Paul exhorts the believers to seek or desire eagerly the best gift. This plea does not condone jealousy or covetousness, but is a realistic way of creating interest in the lives of believers to help identify their spiritual gifts. If the desire for a particular gift is there, it should be pursued with the other steps in order to see if it is a legitimate bestowment of God's grace. The initial desire for teaching or evangelism or exhortation or administration should not be cast aside or discouraged by others, but should be regarded as a tool of God in the primary steps toward developing our gifts.

(2) The next step in the identification of a spiritual gift comes in the area of the *use* of that gift. If there is a desire to teach, then one should definitely find an opportunity to teach and to sharpen his teaching ability through study and the use of aids and techniques which are available in abundance. The principle is true for the use of all spiritual gifts. If they are to be discovered, they will be discovered while in operation.

A very important ingredient in the discovery of a spiritual gift through use is the matter of results. If I have a desire to teach and put that desire into operation, but find that there is little or no learning that takes place on the part of the student, then I should be realistic enough to recognize that the gift of teaching is not present. The same holds true for the gift of evangelism, or the gift of administration, or any of the other gifts available to the body of Christ today.

(3) The third test in discovering a spiritual gift is that of *recognition by others*. This simply means that we should allow mature, spiritual Christians to observe our ministry in operation and to evaluate it honestly and realistically with us. If the gift is recognized, that recogni-

tion should cause us to continue to develop it. Failure to have it recognized should not produce resentment but reevaluation.

By putting these three ingredients together — desire, operation, and recognition — one should be able to determine what his spiritual gift is. For some, this may take only a brief period of time; for others, it may take years. However, once the gift is discovered, every effort should be made to develop it through preparation and use. Discovering one's spiritual gift should by no means create a sense of pride, but rather a true sense of humility. We must remember that it is a gift, something that we did not earn or deserve, but which was freely given to us. It should also be kept in mind that there is no room for bitterness or hostility toward others should they observe that we do not possess a particular gift. In fact, we should be very grateful to anyone who would be willing to examine our lives honestly and realistically and help us determine what our gift or gifts are.

THE DIFFERENCE BETWEEN GIFTS AND NATURAL ABILITIES

One must keep in mind that spiritual gifts and natural abilities are not synonomous. A person may be a professor in a university and have much knowledge and be able to instruct in the realm of secular subjects, but may not be able to teach biblical truths because he does not have the gift of teaching. Another may be talented musically, but this ability does not necessarily predetermine his effectiveness in the ministry; apart from the gift of helps, his musical ability may be wasted. On the other hand, we must recognize that God does not allow our natural abilities to go to waste, but very often does endow us with spiritual gifts in order that the natural abilities might be used effectively in His service. Thus an opera singer like Jerome Hines possesses both natural ability and a measure of God's grace to use that ability in an effective way to carry out the ministry of Jesus Christ.

THE USE OF GIFTS IN THE MINISTRY

After outlining the meaning of gifts and some of their characteristics, we can come to a logical conclusion. Men are to be placed in positions of ministry and responsibility, not on the basis of popularity or availability, but on the basis of their spiritual gifts. The work of the ministry would be greatly enhanced if all of our men in positions of church leadership possessed the gift of administration or the gift of pastor-teacher as compared to the many men who are on the board of a church simply because they have social status and financial resources. It is staggering to think what goes unaccomplished in the Lord's work simply because the truth has not been made known that every believer has a spiritual gift that is to be exercised, that there is no room for spectators, and that every believer should be on the first string, actively playing in the ball game.

4

Selecting and Training
Church Personnel

$\mathbf{T}$he fact that every believer is invested with a spiritual gift (1 Cor. 12:7) and is called upon to do the work of service (Eph. 4:12) provides the local church with a tremendous resource of personnel. The cry that is heard from First Average Church, "We don't have anyone to do the work," is both true and false. It is true in the sense that churches are desperately in need of people who are willing and trained to minister, but the statement is false in the sense that everyone is a potential worker, needing to be selected and trained for the right job.

SELECTING PERSONNEL

Some people are always finding a bargain and others never seem to run across one. The difference is that those who find the bargain have been looking for it, and those who don't find it have not taken the time to look. The same is true in locating the right people to do the work of service.

It is a very small percentage of the people who come and volunteer their services. The average churchman feels unqualified and unprepared.

He is often afraid that if he volunteers for a task, it will involve him in a lifetime assignment or he will be thought of by others as being presumptuous. Even though he wants to be involved, he isn't.

It seems that as churches grow larger numerically, the percentage of participating workers grows smaller. This problem can be overcome only by implementing the philosophy that every saint is to be involved in the work of the ministry through proper selection, enlistment, and training.

Selecting and enlisting potential workers is a never-ending task. In small congregations of less than a hundred it may be the responsibility of the pastor to be a committee of one in selecting and training others to do the Lord's work. In larger churches a personnel committee of three to seven members, depending on the size of the church would be necessary. The name "personnel committee" identifies its mission. It should be composed of at least one elder and deacon, a member of the board of Christian education and others who would be representative of the total church program and acquainted with the majority of the people. Members of the personnel committee must, by the very nature of their responsibility, be spiritually mature, emotionally objective, well-informed, and themselves willing to work. Their task is behind the scenes and often thankless, but it is of ultimate importance.

The work of the personnel committee is basically twofold: research and recruitment.

Most churches have an unleashed potential of many megatons of spiritual achievement, but do not make the effort to locate it. The primary task of the personnel committee is to do careful research on people who have identified themselves to the body of believers, to know each individual in the congregation well enough to recognize his spiritual gift, to learn of his past experience, and to be aware of his abilities and training. The items necessary for conducting this research are (1) an up-to-date list of the membership, (2) a membership profile questionnaire (such as shown on pages 57-61), (3) a program for obtaining the information, and (4) a system for keeping it available and up-to-date. From experience it has been found that the most satisfactory means of gathering information is through a personnel interview. To do this, the members of the personnel committee must be trained in taking the survey and recording the results. There is no substitute for a personal interview, for it reveals feelings as well as facts.

The second area of research has to do with the jobs that are presently available as well as future needs. To do this research, make a list of the job opportunities presently available in the church. This would take in elected officers, such as deacons, elders, treasurers, Sunday school superintendents and leaders in Boys Brigade, Pioneer Girls, music ministries such as choirs and musicians, committeemen, and special forces such as vacation Bible school, gospel teams, ushers, nursery workers, and organizational officers. In other words, obtain a complete

MEMBERSHIP PROFILE

Name ——————————————————————————————————
        last   first   middle   (maiden)

Address ——————————————————————————————————

City ——————————————————————— Zip Code ——————————

Telephone: Home ————————————— Business ————————————

Birth: Date ————————————— Place ———————————————

Baptism: Date ————————————— Place ———————————————

Previous Church
    Relationship ——————————————————————————————

Other Family Members — Only one member of a family, preferably the head, should list the children.

Names	Age	Birthday
1.		
2.		
3.		
4.		
5.		
6.		

Occupation:

    Employer ——————————————————————————————

    Job ————————————————————————————————————

Education:

    High School ————————————————————————————

    College ————————————— Major ————————————

    Additional Training ————————————————————————

57

MEMBERSHIP PROFILE (Cont'd)

Bible Training _____

_____

_____

1. Church Offices Held:

_____

_____

_____

_____

_____

_____

2. Committees:

	Have Served on	Interested in
Missionary		
Evangelism		
Publicity		
Worship		
Property		
Christian Education		
Youth		

3. Would you be interested and willing to take training to equip you for a place of service?

_____Yes _____Not at this time, but after _____
                                                    date
_____ No

4. Remarks and/or other ministries to which the Lord has called you to serve:

_____

_____

_____

_____

_____

_____

MEMBERSHIP PROFILE — SERVICE ABILITIES

Prayerfully fill out the following. Your check mark in the "willing to help" column will indicate your willingness to serve in that area for one year.

5. Christian Education	Have Done It	Willing to Help
Teacher		
Substitute Teacher		
Clerical		
Music		
Youth Advisor		
Board of Christian Education		
Administration		

Areas of Service

Sunday School			Children's Church		
2s - 3s			2s - 3s		
4s - 5s					
6s - 8s			4s - 5s		
9s - 11s					
12s - 14s			Grades 1st, 2nd, 3rd		
15s - 17s					
Adults			4th, 5th, 6th		
Boys Brigade					
Pioneer Girls					
Vacation Bible School					
Camp					
Other					

6. Office Help		
Type — at Home		
at Church		
Dictation		
Filing, Mailing		
Telephone		
Mimeographing		
Other		

MEMBERSHIP PROFILE — SERVICE ABILITIES (Cont'd)

7. Music	Have Done It	Willing to Help
Song Leader		
Choir Member		
Instrument:		
Piano: Will Play for:		
Church Services		
Sunday School		
Children's Church		
Vacation Bible School		
8. Youth Worker		
Evening Groups		
Athletics		
Scouting		
Camping		
9. Visitation		
Church Members		
New Church Members		
Evangelism		
Shut-ins		
Every Member Canvas		
Other		
10. Child Training		
Nursery		
Cradle Roll		
Special Education		
Other		
11. Gardening — Maintenance		
Work on Grounds		
Landscaping		
Other		

MEMBERSHIP PROFILE — SERVICE ABILITIES (Cont'd)

12. Building Maintenance	Have Done It	Willing to Help
Carpenter		
Electrician		
Painter		
Plumber		
Other		

13. Groups	Office Held		
Youth or Single			
Married Couples			
Mens Organizations			
Womens Organizations			
Teacher of Home Bible Class			
Discussion Group Leader			
Other			

14. Special Services		
Provide Flowers		
Decorate		
Usher and Greeting		
Sewing		
Transportation		
Other		

15. Publicity		
Writing		
Editing		
Posters and Arts		
Layout and Printing		
Other		

16. Hobbies, Special Interests		
Photography		
Woodworking		
Electronics		
Stamps, Coins		
Camping		
Cooking		
Others		

roster of jobs to be done for the work of the ministry to be carried on effectively.

The personnel committee must also anticipate the needs of the future so that they are prepared to fill them when they arise. To do this, they must work hand-in-glove with the long-range planning committee so that they will know where the church is going and what to expect in five or ten years. If the long-range planning committee is anticipating a ten percent growth each year for the next ten years, the personnel committee must not only keep pace with the plan, but stay ahead of it so that the anticipated growth may take place through qualified and trained leadership.

One way the personnel committee will be highly motivated to do its task is to turn up one of the jewels that Cromwell writes about in his famous story "Acres of Diamonds."

Take the case of Bob. Bob and his wife had been attending the church for several years. They were faithful at the services, but were simply among the spectators. Bob was quiet and reserved and very unassuming because of the nature of his personality make-up; he would not volunteer for anything, yet inwardly he wanted to be used in the ministry. One day while visiting in his home, I learned something of his background and interests. He was an engineer for a fiberglass manufacturing company and also had an interest in art. I learned too, of his desire to serve the Lord, but he did not know exactly where or how. Not long after the encounter, I asked Bob to help in making a poster for an upcoming function in the church. Much to everyone's delight, his training, talent, and ability were revealed in the outstanding job that he did in making the simple poster. But that was just the beginning, for the seed that was planted was soon to grow and to mature. Bob found that he had not only a natural ability in the graphic arts, but also the gift of helps in using his ability for the glory of God. He began to develop his spiritual gift and soon found himself working in a children's-church program. It was here that he realized he could use his spiritual gift in visualizing Bible stories for the boys and girls and in making them come alive through means of chalk talks and take-home papers that he prepared for the boys and girls. Today Bob is a different man. He has a holy confidence in God's ability to use him in the work of service. He has found his spiritual gift and is in the process of developing it. He is no longer a spectator, but a participant. He is a brilliant diamond, just one diamond of the acres of diamonds, who could have gone through life without being uncovered because no one took the time to search and research.

Following the research, the next step is recruitment. This is one of the most abused activities in the local church today. The abuse comes in that for so long the church has been willing to put up with mediocrity that we have given the impression that the job is not important and the only thing that counts is that we have someone to fill the position, regardless of his performance. This is reflected in the persuasive arguments that are so often used to enlist people for service. Some of them are these: (1) "We cannot get anyone else to do it, would you do it?" (2) "It really won't take much time and not much is expected"; (3) the pressure approach: "We have a class of eight boys who are climbing the walls. We need a teacher *today!*" and (4) "Just do it until we can get someone else." There is no better way to minimize the task and to promote mediocrity in it than to use the wrong methods of enlistment.

If we believe that the Lord's work is of the utmost importance, we must begin to treat it as such by magnifying the office. What a difference it makes when we encourage others to serve the Lord on the basis of their love for Him (2 Cor. 5:14), rather than doing a favor for an individual. We magnify the office by showing that every believer, as part of the body of Christ, has a necessary function without which the whole body suffers.

A number of things should be kept in mind when recruiting people for service on the basis of the research and recommendation of the personnel committee. The prospects should first have been contacted by one or two members of the personnel committee. This contact must not be a casual meeting in the hallway as you are passing from one service to another, but should be a businesslike interview during which time ample clarification is given regarding the task and then accurate job description is presented so that the prospect knows exactly what is expected of him. Remember: magnify the position; don't play it down. Let the prospect ask questions concerning the assignment. Answer the questions honestly and completely. Be aware of the fact that excuses will be offered, but counteract the excuses by stressing the spiritual opportunities of the ministry and inform the individual that you and others have prayed about this need and felt led of the Lord to contact him.

In enlisting people for service never ask for or expect an on-the-spot decision. After you have clarified the job 'and have gone over its responsibilities, through the use of a job description, ask the prospect to take ample time to pray about the possibility. Give him a date when you will contact him again to find out his answer, and assure him of your continued interest and prayer during this decision-making time. It may be that during this time he may wish to observe the class or the group for which he is being considered. Remember, the more he knows about the position, the more likely it is that he will make the proper choice. Keeping people in the dark and letting them find hidden obstacles themselves will only hinder the ministry of enlistment in the future.

TRAINING CHURCH PERSONNEL

People who volunteer, or those who are drafted, have a right to expect training in the job for which they have been selected. In the military this is referred to as "boot camp." In industrial arts it is called "apprenticeship," and in medicine it is known as "internship." However, when we come to Christian service, this area of training is often bypassed due to the pressures of expediency, shortage of time, and the little value placed upon the office to be filled. At best, the training the average Christian receives who serves on a volunteer staff is minimal. We entrust the formidable responsibility of influencing the lives of our children into the hands of an untrained teacher and the business of the local church into the hands of men who have never been trained to be businessmen.

The problem in leadership training is not necessarily the lack of tools to get the job done. Reading materials and the latest in self-teaching aids, such as those provided by the Evangelical Training Association of Wheaton, Illinois, are readily available. Teacher-training sessions, either weekly or monthly, are not new ideas; nor are workers' conferences or Christian education seminars. The biggest problem is not one of telling, but one of showing.

The biblical imperative of leadership training is found in Matthew 28:19, 20: "Go ye therefore and make disciples of all the nations . . . teaching them to observe all that I commanded you. . . ." This divinely inspired program rests on the word "teaching," which in Matthew 28:20 comes from the Greek verb *matheteuo,* which is more properly translated "to disciple." The final mandate of the Master is to disciple men. Leadership training is not giving a lecture, it is making a disciple.

It seems incredible that the Lord Jesus would choose twelve men with varied backgrounds and abilities, many of them unschooled and all of them unprepared for the momentous task to which they were called. Yet He set out to train them so that in His absence they could carry out a work that would change the world. That being the case, there should be little question that we can improve on His methods.

Discipleship was based on invitation. Christ chose them (Luke 6:13) and He invited them to follow Him (Matt. 4:19).

The invitation led to an identification. In inviting men to follow Him, Christ was seeking a commitment, but in return He also committed Himself to them. His commitment is seen in His promise in Matthew 4:19: "I will make you fishers of men." That meant that He was willing to identify Himself with them in their failures as well as in their success. If we are going to expect people to respond to the invitation to serve, we must also be willing to commit ourselves to them in the area of preparation. This will require time and sacrifice and oftentimes heartache, but it is an absolute necessity.

Making disciples also involves instruction. One has only to read the Gospel accounts to see that the Lord had a system of continuing education. He taught His disciples in precepts and also in practice. An example of the precept is found in Matthew 5 in what is called "The

Sermon on the Mount." This can be likened to the lecture method of our present day; however, the instruction did not stop with words but there was also the demonstration or instruction by practice. Jesus *said,* "Greater love has no one than this, that one lay down his life for his friends" (John 15:13), and He also *gave* His life.

If we want trained leaders, we must train them. Every method possible should be used in teaching precepts. In teaching by practice or demonstration, there is no substitute, however, for the personal example. Again, this means an involvement and investment of our time with the one being trained. This process may be brief and simple in some cases, or, on the other hand, it may involve substantial time and effort.

Beyond the need of our own words and example, there is the need of the learner to both hear and do. The making of a disciple is like teaching persons how to swim. One can give them all the information from the textbook, he can personally show them how to do the various strokes in the water, but they themselves will never learn how to swim until they get in and themselves get wet. The Lord Jesus chose His disciples and after adequately teaching them, He sent them out to put into practice what they had learned. Here is the principle of involvement; to train a leader adequately one must give him the opportunity to make mistakes and to learn from those mistakes. This will demand proper supervision as well as an accepting attitude in the case of failure. Keep in mind that no person ever learned how to swim without sinking a few times.

The final step in discipleship is to realize that it is not an end in itself, but only a means to an end, and that those who are committed disciples are to reproduce themselves in others. This principle provides an unending supply of trained leadership. It alone can put an end to the cry "We don't have anyone to do the work," for it is God's appointed way to do His business.

PART TWO

The Work of Service:
The Challenge of Leadership

5

Choosing Your Leadership Style

"I prefer to handle important decisions through my group; we meet regularly and waste little time in getting to the heart of our problems. So you see the emphasis is on team work. I spend most of my time in looking ahead and planning the course of action that we are to take." (Group Achievement and Order)

"The most important ingredient of an organization is its people. If you keep the people satisfied, other things will take care of themselves. I make a special effort to get around and talk to my people. I listen to their problems, and that seems to mean a lot to them. Most of these guys are my close friends. That's the way I like it." (Personal Interaction)

"Most leaders spend too much time in worrying over a decision. In the process they waste their own time and everyone else's. People usually fail through indecision. I believe in making a decision, right or wrong, and going ahead with the action. I don't waste my time coddling my people because I know they are capable of making their own decisions. I believe in action and cannot tolerate procrastination. I stress the adage 'Do something even if it's wrong.' Believe me, my approach works." (Dynamic-Achievement)

"The problem with leaders today is that they do not command respect. They think that you have to get everybody's okay before you make a decision. In my group there's no doubt about who is in charge.

Sure, I listen to what others have to say, but first I expect my men to listen to my ideas and I make the final decisions. I was given this job to get results and I intend to do just that." (Personal Enhancement)

"You know the kids today have a saying I like — "Cool it." A lot of leaders run around in circles as if there is no tomorrow. I find that a person can get along all right without getting all hot and bothered about things. Life is too short to waste it in tension and worries." (Secure and Easygoing)

Each of these statements reflects an approach to leadership. You may have found yourself agreeing with one or more of them. It should be helpful to you at this point to clarify the leadership beliefs and practices that you hold. In the following survey chart are found a number of statements that are related to leadership behavior. Place a check by "yes" if you agree with the statement, and by "no" if you do not agree with the statement. There is no right or wrong answer to these questions; they simply survey your own opinions. To get the most from this chapter, complete the survey before reading further.

SURVEY OF LEADERSHIP OPINIONS

(Check One)

_____Yes _____No 1. A leader should expect to accomplish much of his decision making through regular group meetings.

_____No _____Yes 2. A formal list of specific items to cover makes a meeting too stiff to be really effective.

_____Yes _____No 3. Group goals are more important than individual goals.

_____Yes _____No 4. A leader should plan with great care and thoroughness.

_____Yes _____No 5. My work is neat and well-organized.

_____Yes _____No 6. I am highly systematic in my approach to my work.

_____Yes _____No 7. I am very tactful to others.

_____Yes _____No 8. A leader should spend much time in planning and organizing his work.

_____Yes _____No 9. If someone asks a question about the work, I give a firm and conclusive answer.

_____Yes _____No 10. A leader should persist until he gets all related information before making a decision.

_____Yes _____No 11. Group meetings should be informal and should involve much casual conversation.

_____Yes _____No 12. A leader should spend much time chatting and counseling with his people.

70

SURVEY OF LEADERSHIP OPINIONS (Cont'd)

(Check One)

_____Yes _____No 13. A leader should make close friends of those whom he leads.

_____Yes _____No 14. A leader should be engaged in about the same activities as the other members of his group.

_____No _____Yes 15. When a person comes to me with a problem, I almost always have a specific recommendation for him based on the Bible or on experience.

_____Yes _____No 16. When conflicts arise among people whom I know, I try to resolve the problem by talking with them.

_____Yes _____No 17. A leader should often give in to the people in his group when they disagree with him.

_____Yes _____No 18. A leader should always back up what the persons under him do.

_____Yes _____No 19. A leader should get the approval of the persons under him on important matters before going ahead.

_____No _____Yes 20. A leader should always be careful to review the decisions of others so that poor-quality decisions do not get past him.

_____Yes _____No 21. People think of me as being aggressive.

_____Yes _____No 22. In reviewing the work of others, a person should be aware of major progress points and ignore specific activities that they employ along the way.

_____Yes _____No 23. A leader should provide broad assignments to his people with the knowledge that they will do a good job.

_____Yes _____No 24. A leader should encourage his people to set specific goals rather than broad general ones.

_____No _____Yes 25. I usually schedule my work more than a week in advance.

_____No _____Yes 26. People in my kind of job are usually well-paid in view of their background and contribution.

_____Yes _____No 27. Group meetings should be formal and to the point.

_____Yes _____No 28. I believe that taking quick action is more important than lengthy planning.

_____Yes _____No 29. People consider me to be rather a tough-minded leader, compared with others in my line of work.

_____No _____Yes 30. A leader should support his men, even though he may feel that they are probably wrong.

_____Yes _____No 31. A leader should frequently employ the authority of his position to assure that people follow his instructions carefully.

71

SURVEY OF LEADERSHIP OPINIONS (Cont'd)

(Check One)

_____Yes _____No 32. A leader should take the center of attention during a controversy.

_____Yes _____No 33. A leader should insist that his people try his ideas first.

_____Yes _____No 34. A leader should require compliance to his wishes.

_____Yes _____No 35. A leader should pressure those who perform poorly.

_____Yes _____No 36. A leader should give his group much direction and control.

_____Yes _____No 37. A leader should be critical of substandard work by his people.

_____Yes _____No 38. A leader should insist on his group following to the letter the standard routines that he receives from those higher up.

_____Yes _____No 39. A leader should assign specific tasks to those under him.

_____Yes _____No 40. A leader should often rule with an iron hand.

_____No _____Yes 41. I often spend idle hours thinking about my work.

_____Yes _____No 42. An insurance plan should be of no importance to a person in accepting a job.

_____Yes _____No 43. Job security is of much less importance to a person than his pay.

_____No _____Yes 44. I view the work group as just one component in the total system.

_____Yes _____No 45. If one of my people "goofs" in his work, I just stay away until he gets it straightened out.

_____Yes _____No 46. I am very patient with others.

_____No _____Yes 47. Most leaders would be likely to become angry if someone "goes over their heads."

_____Yes _____No 48. I take things as they come with little concern.

_____Yes _____No 49. Others think that nothing seems to bother me.

_____Yes _____No 50. I live each day to the fullest and do not become concerned about the failings of myself or others.

According to the recent research of Wofford, five distinctive dimensions of leadership behavior can be identified.[1] These leadership dimen-

---

[1] J. C. Wofford, "Factor Analysis of Managerial Behavior Variables," *Journal of Applied Psychology,* 1970, vol. 54 (2), pp. 169-173; and J. C. Wofford, "Managerial Behavior, Situational Factors, and Productivity and Morale," *Administrative Science Quarterly,* 1971, vol. 16(1), pp. 10-19.

sions are analogous to the dimensions of a desk. The desk has height, width, and depth. It may be narrow or wide, but any desk can be measured in terms of the width dimension. This is true of leadership. A leader's behavior is measured along the five basic dimensions. He may be oriented toward one dimension or he may emphasize all five dimensions. Most of us fall somewhere between these extremes. Now, let's evaluate the survey and see which of the dimensions you emphasize. Count the number of times that you have placed your check in the left-hand choice for each of the following blocks of statements:

		Total	High*	Low**
Group Achievement and Order				
1-10	No. of check marks in left column	____	____	____
Personal Interaction				
11-20	No. of check marks in left column	____	____	____
Dynamic-Achievement				
21-30	No. of check marks in left column	____	____	____
Personal Enhancement				
31-40	No. of check marks in left column	____	____	____
Secure and Easygoing				
41-50	No. of check marks in left column	____	____	____

*If you have 7 or more check marks, place an X under high.
**If you have 3 or fewer check marks, place an X under low.

You have a strong emphasis of a leadership dimension if you have checked seven or more times in the left-hand column for the set of ten statements for that dimension. It is possible that you use all of the dimensions of leadership with high frequency; in this case you will find that you score above seven in each set of items. Conversely, if you score below seven on all sets of items, you do not emphasize the behaviors of any of the dimensions. If you score as low as three or fewer on any set of items, you place emphasis on behaviors that are directly opposite of those for leaders who score high on the dimension.

A series of research studies has been conducted with secular leaders, using 219 statements of this type. The statements of each set of ten given in the survey are variations of statements which were most frequently agreed upon by leaders who emphasized each of five different dimension of leadership.

THE DIMENSIONS OF LEADERSHIP

By now you are beginning to feel some familiarity with the five dimensions. In the opening paragraphs of this chapter you read a typical statement for leaders who emphasize each of the dimensions. In the survey you have seen statements that reflect the beliefs and behaviors of leaders who emphasize the dimensions. We will attempt to solidify these impressions by briefly describing the behaviors of leaders who are high on each dimension:

DIMENSION	TYPICAL BEHAVIORS
Group Achievement and Order	Behaviors of a leader associated with team action, group leadership, group goals, and group success. Orderliness of behavior is emphasized, i.e., careful planning; neat work; systematic, thorough, and organized approach to problems.
Personal Interaction	Behaviors of a leader who desires a close, personal, cordial relationship to his people. He is informal, casual, and talkative. People that he leads in the church readily become his friends.
Dynamic-Achievement	Behaviors of a leader who is forceful and active. He spends a minimum of time in planning or in decision making, perferring instead to be on the firing line of activity. He delegates authority to his people to make their decisions and then leaves them alone to accomplish the desired results. He has confidence in the people that he leads and in himself.
Personal Enhancement	Behaviors of a leader who enjoys the use of power. He depends heavily on his authority in directing others of his church group. He enhances his own position in his church group above that of others by trying out his own ideas first, by requiring compliance to his own wishes, and by closely controlling the work of the others in line with his own judgments and decisions.
Secure and Easygoing	Behaviors of a leader who is highly secure and free from anxieties. He does not worry about the work, about looking bad to other church members, or about his group doing poorly. He takes things as they come, with little concern for the consequences of the future. He does not pressure people that he leads. In fact, he does not demand much from them.

Perhaps the dimensions are best represented by the points of a star (Figure 4). With some leaders the dimensions operate independently with little interaction. Thus a person may emphasize a single dimension to the degree that it is far removed from interaction. Such a person would be placed at the point of the star. On the other hand, the dimension may be wedded to the behaviors of other dimensions toward the center of the star so that its influence is not clearly recognizable. Unless you were extremely high in one dimension and low in the others, it is doubtful that you can identify yourself as wholly within a given camp.

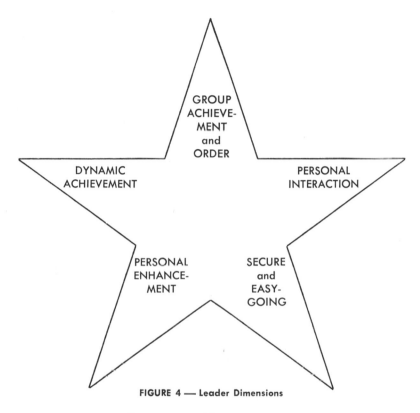

FIGURE 4 — Leader Dimensions

LEADERSHIP EFFECTIVENESS

To each of us who would like to improve our leadership effectiveness, the question immediately arises, "Which dimension should I emphasize?" To answer this question, we shall look first to the Scripture and then to research.

The Scripture has much to say about the importance of leadership and the personal characteristics of a leader. The leader is to be just and fair (Col. 4:1), above reproach, temperate, prudent, respectable, hospitable, able to teach, the husband of one wife, not addicted to wine, gentle, uncontentious, free from the love of money, able to manage his household, a mature Christian of good reputation, a man of dignity,

75

honest (1 Tim. 3:2-12), and an example in speech, conduct, love, faith, and purity (1 Tim. 4:12). He should be patient and kind (2 Tim. 2:24, 25), possessing qualities of power, love, and sound judgment (2 Tim. 1:6, 7).

But how is he to lead? What behaviors should he exhibit as he works with his people or guides an organization? On these questions the Bible has little to suggest. Perhaps the reason for this silence is found in the results of recent research on leadership.

In the last decade research with secular leaders has indicated that there is no "best" dimension or group of dimensions of leadership. The effectiveness of a particular leadership style is dependent upon a combination of situational factors. The characteristics of the people being lead, the nature of the tasks performed, and the type of organization are among the situational factors which determine the success of leadership behaviors. The important point is that a person should use those behaviors of leadership that are appropriate for the situation in which he is operating. A pastor may need to use a different leadership style in dealing with other staff members from the style that he uses with lay leaders of the church. In order to identify which of the dimensions of behavior you should use or the type of leader you should select, you should question yourself concerning the nature of your leadership situation. If you lead two different groups, you may wish to place an X for one group and a check for the other for the statements below.

(If the statement on the left is more nearly correct, place a check in the left hand column; if the statement on the right is more nearly correct, place a check in the right hand column.)

_____The people that you lead are independent-minded.	Your people prefer to be given_____ a lot of guidance.
_____The people that you lead are intelligent and experienced in their work.	The people that you lead_____ lack the ability to assume responsibility.
_____Your people prefer and expect to be involved with you in decision making.	Your people prefer and ex-_____ pect strong, firm, and decisive leadership.
_____The group that you work with directly is smaller than thirteen people.	You lead a group of more than_____ twelve people.
_____You have frequent contact with those whom you lead.	You have infrequent contact_____ with those whom you lead.
_____It is convenient for you to hold group meetings.	It is difficult to get your people_____ together for group meetings.
_____Your group performs very flexible tasks.	Your group's tasks are highly_____ structured.
_____Your group's tasks are complex.	Your group's tasks are simple._____

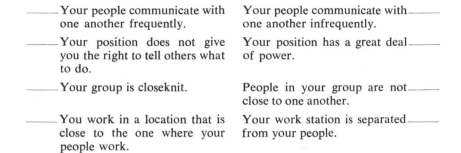

_____ Your people communicate with one another frequently.

Your people communicate with _____ one another infrequently.

_____ Your position does not give you the right to tell others what to do.

Your position has a great deal _____ of power.

_____ Your group is closeknit.

People in your group are not _____ close to one another.

_____ You work in a location that is close to the one where your people work.

Your work station is separated _____ from your people.

In light of these situational factors, let us consider which of the leadership dimensions is most effective. First, suppose most of your checks were placed in the left hand column; then you will be most effective in accomplishing the desired goals if you emphasize the group achievement and order dimension. If you are also concerned with maintaining a close-knit group with high morale, the personal interaction dimension should be given a secondary emphasis. You are leading independent, intelligent, and responsible people who prefer to be involved in the decisions and important activities of the group. Consequently, they are capable and willing to work as a team in setting goals and carrying out responsibility. Since you have a small group that can meet conveniently, the team work orientation can perform the complex tasks with maximum efficiency. Your personal activities can now center upon higher-level problems of planning, organizing, and coordinating of efforts. Thus the group achievement and order dimension is most effective.

Let us suppose that you lead this same type of people but that you are unable to work with them closely and you cannot hold group meetings; you will need to replace the team work actions with dynamic-achievement. Rather than working with the group as a unit, you can delegate important decisions to individuals and allow them to carry out the activities. Since you see the people only rarely, an aggressive, positive, and forceful approach will serve well. However, the personal interaction behaviors become more important to bring loyalty as well as inspiration into the relationship.

If your situation has resulted in your placing most of the checks on the right-hand side, you are leading people who are either dependent or inexperienced, and who prefer strong, directing leadership; the personal enhancement and personal interaction behaviors should be blended for effective results under these conditions. The use of power and the direction of others in an aggressive and controlling manner provides the secure guidance that these workers have grown to prefer. However, even with these people, the restrictiveness of personal enhancement behaviors tends to produce low morale unless their effects are diminished by offsetting situational factors, i.e., contact between the leader and the people should be infrequent; tasks should be sufficiently structured and simple so that the number of directives and commands are minimized; the work is performed by a person working alone so that frequent contact between the workers is not required. It is only in this narrow range of circumstances that personal enhancement behaviors are effective in achieving group goals and even here the workers will be dissatisfied unless the leaders also perform personal interaction behaviors.

Research results indicate that the personal interaction and the secure and easygoing behavior dimensions have little influence upon actual performance; most of their influences are with the satisfaction of those led. In the church situation, satisfaction with the work is very important even if it does not tie in with short-term effectiveness. If a church leader is to be truly effective, he must build a close fellowship within the body. The workers must be stimulated to work at least in part by their enjoyment of the experience, their feeling that they are making a contribution, and their appreciation of their leaders. Surely they have enough unpleasant experiences with their bosses in business that they do not wish to be pressured and subordinated in their church.

If the person is to lead a fellowship group, in which the satisfaction and closeness of the members is the basic purpose for the organization, then he should emphasize the personal interaction dimension. The secure and easygoing dimension is also useful if the group meets for a long period of time. A leader who emphasizes the personal enhancement or the dynamic-achievement dimension will be a disaster in this situation. The leader who emphasizes the group achievement and order dimension will be of moderate success.

Suppose a pastor works primarily with two groups — a small well-trained staff group and a group of laymen of the church who have historically been dependent on strong leadership and have little experience in taking responsibilty. For effectiveness in obtaining the goals of the church, the pastor needs to use the group achievement and order behaviors in leading the staff and he needs the personal enhancement and personal interaction behaviors with the laymen. If, on the other hand, the lay leaders of the church are independent thinkers, experienced in responsible positions in the church and in their businesses, interested in the work of the Lord, and willing to work, the pastor should emphasize the group achievement and order behaviors with these lay leaders as well as with his staff.

To be most effective, the leader should be able to adapt his style of leadership to the people and the environment in which he operates. Most of us have grown up under the assumption that one best approach to leadership exists; thus, we have tended to become rigid in our behavior. Once we have shucked this view, we may proceed toward a more versatile and a more effective ministry of leadership.

6

Motivating People for Action

Why does a person take responsibilty in a church?

Why does Jim put forth so many hours of effort in church work whereas Harvey does not? Why does John work so hard in preparing for his Sunday school class and yet do so little as the church treasurer? Why does the new pastor spend so much time with the people when the last one spent most of his time preaching and teaching?

The answer to the question "why?" is found in human motivation. Motivation is the energy and the direction of our lives. It determines both the path that we will take and the force with which we will pursue it.

The effectiveness of a person in performing a job will primarily depend on three personal factors: capability, spirituality, and motivation. These personal factors must be properly fitted to the environment and tasks of the job in order to obtain optimal performance effectiveness.

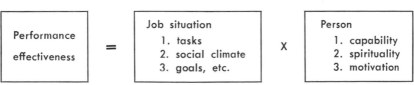

FIGURE 5 — Performance Effectiveness Equation

We can predict the effectiveness with which a person will perform a job if we can assess the many elements of the job situation and the personal factors. In this chapter we shall focus attention upon motivation.

When we say, "I am trying to motivate Ralph to perform his job better," we are showing a lack of understanding of the nature of motivation. This statement suggests that we can change the motivation of Ralph by our actions. Motivation is a characteristic of the person who is developed in large part early in the formative years of life. If one's motivation changes at all in adulthood, it is a gradual change coming only in small increments. Ralph is already motivated; so our task is to find a way of tying this motivational structure to the tasks to be performed in such a way that his energy will be directed toward the desired results.

Our problem becomes clear if we ask the question in this way: "How can I create the environment that will channel Ralph's motivation toward performing the job effectively?"

The Nature of Human Motivation

Motivation operates as a continuing cycle of activity. This cycle can be represented in terms of the following model:

FIGURE 6 — Motivation Cycle

Each need of the person produces an array of physiological and psychological reactions which we refer to as a drive. This drive energizes the person toward attaining a goal; once satisfied, the need subsides or is satiated. Thus, as we use up food nutrients in the body, we develop the *need* for food and the hunger drive appears. In addition to the increase in digestive secretions and blood flow to the abdominal region, the person becomes alerted to food. If he is reading a magazine, he will notice the food ads. If he is walking down the street, he will be particularly aware of the restaurants. Finally, he will respond to his impulse and attain the goal by eating. Thus he is satiated and the need is temporarily removed. The need is the key to all of this behavior; therefore, let us examine the need structure of the person more closely.

Human Need Structure

In order to tie a person's needs to the job environment so that he is motivated to perform effectively, we must recognize the nature of the need structure. Needs may be structured into seven categories: physiological, security and maintenance, order, personal interaction, achievement, personal enhancement, and group achievement. Although other categories can be used, these seemed to be most appropriate for understanding behavior in the church. We shall describe these categories of needs in terms of the goals and behaviors which reflect them.

Physiological needs are those which are basic to bodily processes and physical survival. A person is satisfying his physiological needs as he eats, drinks, breathes, adjusts the temperature of a room, or engages in sexual activity. Although these are the most significant of our needs, they have little relevance to our behavior in the work of the church.

Security and maintenance needs lead to behaviors which avoid fear and which protect or maintain our physical possessions. Fear of failure, embarrassment, punishment, or injury are among the threats which produce the anxious attempts to perform well and the worried concern for the future that we observe so frequently in the church. We also see the manifestation of this need in a more positive way as people clean, repair, and maintain their work and worship areas.

Order needs are satisfied by promptness, neatness, and thoroughness of work. Those who have strong needs for order are highly systematic and detailed in their work.

Personal interaction needs are highly active in the church setting. They determine the readiness to participate in social activities. A person who has a strongly developed set of needs in this area will prefer to be with people rather than to be alone. He will seek others to help him to perform his work. He will enjoy talking with others and performing in a group.

Achievement needs stimulate a person to set challenging goals and to strive for their attainment, to persist in the pursuit of desired ends, to work hard, and to enjoy purposeful activity.

Personal enhancement needs lead to the search for recognition, power, attention, and status. The person who performs a job for the power that it has to influence others or for the recognition and status he assumes among others is motivated by this area of need. These needs are not as acceptable to most of us as other motives for church work. However, the semantics may be deceptive. Seeking personal gain for personal achievement is no more virtuous than seeking personal enhancement. Is lust less a hazard than pride? All needs and behaviors must be yielded to the leadership of the Spirit.

Group achievement needs grow out of early affiliation with others in the family, in small groups, or in clubs. Those who have a strong need for group achievement will engage in team work; they will enter into

81

group activities when these groups have valued goals; they will cooperate and work actively as a group member or leader. They prefer church activities that require them to hold group meetings in order to make decisions or to carry out action.

While we all have needs in each area, certain areas of need are more highly developed than others. The area of need that is strongest for a person is dependent upon his culture, family, and experiences. Members of more primitive cultures tend to be stronger in their need for security. The need for achievement and personal enhancement is strong in the core culture of the United States. Some families show close affection and interaction whereas others emphasize individual achievement. Still other families build group achievement needs by doing important activities as a family unit.

MOTIVATION AND PERFORMANCE EFFECTIVENESS

A close examination of the relationship between the work of the Spirit and the motivational forces producing effective performance of church work indicates that the motivational structure of a person is used by the Spirit in the same manner as one's capabilities are used. When the Spirit chose a man to carry the Gospel to the Gentiles, He chose a man of wisdom and a man of great zeal — Paul the apostle. Peter was strongly motivated for personal enhancement and achievement long before the Spirit entered his life. John possessed deep human love before his love through the Spirit was developed. As one's life with its unique need structure is yielded to the Spirit, it is not only molded to conform to the will of God, but one is also led into those situations and responsibilities in which his motivational energies (which conform to God's natural law) are made compatible with His plan for the life.

Achievement, personal enhancement, and group achievement are the need areas that are most readily associated with performance effectiveness. The research of Frederick Herzberg has indicated that although security and maintenance, order, personal interaction, and bodily needs lead to dissatisfaction, they are not the key determinants of the motivation to perform effectively. Effective performance occurs as the person sees the opportunity to achieve meaningful goals, to be recognized or given status and position for his efforts, or to enjoy the success of a well-executed team effort.[1]

Surprising as this may seem, Herzberg found that a person's salary was not a source of performance motivation. It kept him on the job, but it was not an effective carrot to be held in front of him as an incentive. Actually, we are now finding that the traditional reward

---

[1]Fredrick Herzberg, *Work and the Nature of Man,* (Cleveland: The World Publishing Co., 1966), pp. 93-102.

incentives such as coffee breaks, retirement benefits, social groups, rest stops, and the like have little or no motivational effect on performance.

Several approaches may be used to tie the performance requirements to need structure for increasing effectiveness. Perhaps the most successful approach used in business has been job enrichment. This approach avoids artificiality or superficiality and at the same time involves a wide range of changes which make the job more challenging, more interesting, and more fulfilling for the person who performs it. It requires the leadership of the organization to look at the jobs and substantially change their content.

For the church, job enrichment will mean giving the workers a greater latitude for decision making, more responsibility in the areas of planning and policy making, greater authority to spend money or take other actions, and a greater influence in those activities of the church which concern them. This action may take the form of a budgeting system that allows each Sunday school department or each youth group to have a budget that they may spend at their own discretion rather than going to their director for authorization. It may mean that teachers and workers at the lowest organizational level will be able to choose material and supplemental aids with no "watchdog" surveillance. It may mean that leaders at any point in the church will have the freedom to choose their own personnel and create their own programs. It will invariably mean that the church or denominational leadership must loosen the strings of control and allow greater freedom and responsibility throughout the local church.

A second approach to directing the motivation of our church workers toward effective performance is by *goal setting* and *review*. The essential ingredients of this approach are the establishment of goals for future performance and the recognition of the successes in achieving these goals. Concrete and specific goals for improvement should be established by the person who is to carry them out. An example of the use of goal setting is that of a certain youth director who recognized several areas that needed improvement in his areas of responsibilities. The young people of the church needed to develop a greater awareness of the needs of others and a greater willingness to be of service; in addition, they needed to increase their ability to assume responsibility in church activities. Consequently, he established the following specific goals for the spring quarter:

1. To lead a youth training hour group, and plan and develop a religious program for the LaVilla Nursing Home, giving the young people the primary responsibility.
2. To lead the senior high group in planning a program for youth of the Stanley Orphanage.
3. To give responsibility for planning and conduct of the weekly youth time activities on Sunday night to the youth leaders.

4. To hold an Easter retreat for the high school youth that was totally planned and led by the youth.

At the end of the spring quarter, the minister reviewed the results in these areas with the youth director, who discussed at some length his successes and failures. He finally set forth his goals for the next quarter. It is important that the youth director take the lead in discussing his own achievements. The review must not resemble an inquisition; the emphasis is on sharing our burdens and encouraging one another in the work.

A third approach is oriented toward the personal enhancement area of motivation. This approach involves the *recognition and honoring of service*. Not only do recognition and honor tend to motivate people toward service; they are also commanded in the Scriptures. 1 Timothy 5:17, 18 says, "Let the elders who rule well be considered worthy of double honor, especially those who work hard at preaching and teaching. For the Scripture says, 'YOU SHALL NOT MUZZLE THE OX WHILE HE IS THRESHING,' and, 'The laborer is worthy of his wages.' " Methods for such reward include personal notes of appreciation, honor for outstanding service, public recognition of a job well done, and selection for a more esteemed church position. However, a word of caution is needed. Too often church leaders have succumbed to the appeal for using contests, awards, and public recognition as a means of stimulating their people to do things which the people have not been willing to do through the leadership of the Spirit. They fall prey to the tendency to recognize matters publicly that should be kept private. Perhaps stewardship is the ground of greatest offense. Christ in His wisdom cautioned us to present our alms in sercret that the Father alone might reward us (Matt. 6:3, 4). Yet we so often arrange our giving program so that it becomes almost impossible to keep our giving secret. Christ cautioned us to pray in secret (Matt. 6:5); yet we are not cautious in assuring that the prayers in our churches are not chest-beating displays of empty platitudes. Christ cautioned against displaying our intimate worshipful experiences (Matt. 6:16-18). Do we give proper attention to private worship? We must be careful to assure that our recognition and honoring of others does not encourage empty hypocritical performance.

The fourth approach is the use of the *dynamics of the small group*. This bases the motivation for performance on the individual's group achievement needs. The groups should be organized into action units to carry out important responsibilities. They should be encouraged to establish goals and to work cooperatively in meeting them. These groups may become keys to motivating church workers. The operation and dynamics of small group behavior will be discussed in the next chapter.

We must emphasize once again that the motivational forces within the person must be yielded to the Spirit of God. In whatever approach we use to stimulate a person to effective performance, we must be sure that he has the spiritual maturity to respond and perform in the power of Christ. Care must be taken that we select workers whose goals are not for simple personal gain, who do not work for the praise of others, and who do not seek to please their group rather than God.

MOTIVATION AND SATISFACTION

We have discussed motivation as it relates to performance; now we will consider the satisfaction of the church worker. Human satisfaction is commensurate with the degree to which a person is able to attain the goals which meet his needs. Satisfaction occurs as one actually attains goals and as he adjusts his goals to the will of God. We become satisfied and gain an internal peace from an awareness that God is in control of our lives and that as the loving Father he will gratify the needs in a way that will be truly satisfying. But few of us are able to find full gratification of needs or a complete and continuous yieldedness to God: thus, we fail to achieve the perfect peace of the completely satisfied life.

Failure to gratify our needs, for whatever reason, leads to discomfort, anxiety, and distress. The extent of this dissatisfaction may range from the very mild and brief to the extremely severe and prolonged. The effects on our lives parallel this expanse. When we suffer mild temporary dissatisfaction, we usually handle it by increasing our activity in the attempt to reach the goal. But there may be a roadblock in our path denying the success of our efforts. Frustrated in the attempt to gratify our needs, we use a psychological defense that will handle the anxiety until we can either reach the goal or erase the need.

June is a young lady with a great desire for status in her church family. This desire is matched by a strong fear that she will fail to gain the desired position. Becoming a Sunday school teacher constituted one of her goals. When she was given a class, her feeling of inadequacy soon produced hostility on her part for the class. As she revealed her emotions through her expressions and tone of voice, the class rejected her by using the most powerful weapon any class can use on a teacher, viz., their absenteeism record. Finally, in desperation, June asked to be relieved. Her need for status was unchanged, but her attempt to fulfill this need by teaching in Sunday school was frustrated. She reacted to this dissatisfaction in several of the typical approaches that people use in psychological defense. She became *hostile* to the members of the class who led in the mini-rebellion, she *blamed* the class for her failure, she showed signs of *guilt feeling* about her perceived failure, and she *rationalized* that this was really not the age group to which she was best suited. Finally, she *repressed* the incident and soon requested another class as though nothing had happened. Though her repertoire of reactions to dissatisfaction was rather broad, she did not use some of the typical approaches in this situation. She did not show *projection* (the tendency to attribute one's own weaknesses to others). She did not

85

withdraw from the situation as a means of escape. It did not appear that she used *fantasy* to imagine herself the heroine of a situation in which her class was conquered by her charm. And she did not use *compensation* which would have involved taking another job in the church "on the rebound" as a substitute goal. These are normal reactions which everyone to a greater or lesser degree uses as methods of handling dissatisfaction.

DYSFUNCTIONAL MOTIVATIONAL REACTIONS

A sizable minority of people in almost any church family are reared in an environment in which psychological stress is a way of life. They learn to respond to this unpleasant situation by forming a pattern of behaviors which grant them temporary relief from the perceived, severe stress. The patterns of release are useful mechanisms to relieve stress, but they may be dysfunctional in Christian service. Such patterns of defense result from neurosis. It is particularly important that the church leader be able to recognize neuroses so that he can use the proper caution to avoid selecting the neurotic person for responsible positions.

The *obsessive compulsive* reaction involves a neurotic person who is so frustrated in his attempts to perform the normal routine of life that he feels compelled to repeat the act for fear that a greater anxiety will befall him. The bank teller who must count and recount the money at the end of the day and the college student who reties his tie seven times each morning are caught in the trap of compulsion. In most instances, these compulsive tendencies are accompanied by obsessive ideas. Some have the obsession that they may harm a loved one or that they may contract a dreaded disease. These are mechanisms of defense which prevent greater anxieties for the person.

A *phobic reaction* is a persistent fear of some object or situation when little or no actual danger exists. Phobias often involve an exaggerated fear of things which most of us fear to a lesser extent. The list of phobias includes acrophobia (high places), agoraphobia (open places), claustrophobia (closed places), pyrophobia (fire), and nyctophobia (darkness), to name a few. These phobias may have a negligible effect upon one's effectiveness in performing church work.

The *anxiety reaction* is the most common of the neurotic reaction patterns and is typified by a recurring severe anxiety that cannot be associated with any particular situation or threat. The person is in a relatively constant state of tension, restlessness, and general dissatisfaction, but is unable to pinpoint the basis of the dissatisfaction, the nature of the fear, or the type of goal that is the key to the problem.

Other less common neurotic reactions include the *asthenic reaction* (characterized by experiences of weakness, fatigue, aches and pains, and lack of enthusiasm), *conversion reaction* (characterized by physical symptoms such as paralysis or loss of hearing or sight), *neurotic depressive reaction* (characterized by extreme and prolonged depressions and discouragements), and *dissociative reaction* (exhibiting amnesia, somnambulism, or multiple personality).

These neurotic reactions are manifestations of a tense and dissatisfied life. The church leader should be aware of them in order to handle them properly. Neurotic behavior represents the extreme use of psychological defenses which occur as a result of enduring roadblocks to satisfaction of important needs. Many people with mild neurotic reactions perform their responsibilities in the church well in spite of the reaction. An outstanding example of this is a girl's Sunday school teacher who shows mild obsessive-compulsive symptoms. Mary is so afraid of failure that she works far in excess of the "normal" teacher in preparing for her class. She attends all teachers' training courses and diligently applies the new methods that she has learned. Her classes are full of interesting and involving activities. This should not be taken as an appeal to place persons with neurotic reactions in responsible positions, but it would be a great loss if Mary were not a Sunday school teacher. A leader must take care that he does not place a person with neurotic patterns in a job that will cause greater frustration and distress both to the person himself and to others. A person with neurotic patterns should be encouraged to take only those positions which will not yield greater roadblocks in his life, but will offer an avenue of service and beneficial influence.

A psychotic disorder is a far more extreme reaction in which the person manifests severe and bizarre behavior patterns. The psychotic person is unable to adjust to his work or to other people and usually must be hospitalized. Psychotics manifest delusions, i.e., they hold false beliefs which are absurd and extreme. They also typically experience hallucinations in which they see, hear, or feel objects and events which do not exist in reality. Other symptoms of extreme irrationality, fear, suspicion, dependency, or depression are typical of psychotic disorders. Although it is clear that brain deterioration is the cause of psychotic disorders in the case of senility, brain tumors, cerebral syphilis, or meningitis, the origin of the nonorganic psychotic disorders has not been identified at this time. Early psychic trauma, frustrations, and excessive stress on the one hand, and brain chemistry on the other, have been suggested as the bases of the disorders. In any case, the evidence of dissatisfaction and failure in goal attainment is unmistakable as either a cause or an effect of the disorders. We can state unequivocally that a person manifesting psychotic disorders should not be placed in a position of responsibility in the church. Pastoral counseling with the psychotic will be of little value. It is best to make referral to a hospital for intensive treatment once the psychotic symptoms are identified.

7

The Dynamics of Small-Group Behavior

The most powerful force within any human organization is the small group. The small group not only contains a composite of the forces within the individual but augments these with the dynamics of the group itself. The small group was given a special place in the New Testament Church, according to Christ's promise: Where two or three have gathered together in My name, there I am in their midst (Matt. 18:20). Out of the multitude of followers, Christ chose twelve in whom to invest the depth of His ministry and whose message and work were so essential to the building of the early church. The structure of the early church as well as much of the operations of the contemporary churches place emphasis upon the activities of Christians working in small groups.

What makes the small group such a powerful force in the church? The answer is found in the impact that the small group has on the psychological and spiritual life of its members. Among the basic areas of human need are the needs for personal interaction and group achievement. The small group augments the satisfaction of the personal interaction need through the close fellowship of group members and the group achievement need through success in coordinated activities. The dynamics of a group grows out of certain of its key characteristics. We can predict the effectiveness of a group by knowing such factors as its structure, goals, norms, and cohesiveness.

GROUP STRUCTURE

Each group has a definable form or structure consisting of its membership, roles, pattern of authority, and communication network. Take one of the church groups with which you work and analyze it in terms of the structural elements. Each group has *membership*. It may be a large or small group with consistent or changing membership. The members may be heterogeneous in beliefs, values, characteristics, and style of life or they may be homogeneous. These factors have a significant impact upon the dynamics within the group, for if the group is small with a consistent, homogeneous membership, each person in the group will be spurred or restrained with much greater force. All of the psychological pressures that one person can apply on another are enhanced by the conditions of these groups, for small groups are able to satisfy the personal need of their members most adequately. Large groups in which members are hardly acquainted or groups in which the membership shifts from week to week have little potential for gratifying the needs for personal interaction or group achievement.

Looking further at the structure of your group, you can see that people within the group take on distinctive *roles*. Some of your group members will take certain of the leadership roles. They will initiate planning and decision making, coordinate the efforts of others in the group, and have the greatest influence on the group. These leadership roles may be performed by a single member or by several, depending on the degree of centralization of the power toward a single person. The person who has the greatest influence on the activities of the group may be viewed as performing the role of the informal leader. This person may or may not be the designated leader. Where the most influential member is not the formal or designated leader, rivalry often emerges between the two individuals. The formal leader may not even be viewed as a functioning member of the group. As, for example, the deacon in charge of Christian education who does not attend meetings or actively participate in the children's church ministry is not perceptually identified as a member of this program and consequently has little influence on it. A worker in the youngest age department who is aggressive, insightful, and active in the children's church meetings may in fact be the leader of the group. Other roles commonly found within a group include the jester who creates comic relief at tense moments, the scapegoat who receives the brunt of criticism and scorn, the gatekeeper who signals for others to speak, the expert who brings a bag of information and knowledge to the problem at hand, the rebel who defies the authority of leaders, the slave who is excessively acquiescent, and the hero who is a person of influence and honor. As the group becomes established, the roles stabilize for various group members. This stability in the roles adds to the security and order of the group process.

Irrespective of the desire and intent of the group members toward equality, groups evolve a *structure of authority* based on differences in the influence patterns of the members. The attempts at influencing others range in strength from highly authoritarian to relatively permissive; they range in style from harsh and vociferous to calm and soft tones. If we study the number of times each person in a group influences others, we will find an orderly pattern that is not dissimilar to the pecking order of chickens in a barnyard: one chicken is king and pecks all others, a second-order chicken pecks all except the "top dog." Finally, there is the scrawny little hen at the bottom of the order who is constantly being pursued but never pecks another chicken. In a less dramatic pattern, we have those in each group who influence others but whose manner discourages others from influencing them and those who are frequently influenced but rarely cause a colleague to change behavior.

The *communication networks* are structured in terms of direction and content. Whether the communication is oral or written, it follows a fairly consistent direction of flow. In the next group meeting that you attend, take note of the eye movements of the people as they speak. You will find that each person directs the bulk of his remarks to only two or three people, no matter how large the group may be. Since communication is our mode of influence, the direction of its flow is a clue to the pattern of influence as well as the interaction network. Individuals tend to direct communications toward people of higher status and toward people who share their values. The networks of communication have much to say about the underlying process of the group.

The content of communication conveys social and emotional qualities as well as task-related material. In his study of hundreds of problem-solving groups, Robert Bales found that about 62 percent of the content of communication related to the problem under discussion and about 38 percent involved emotional content.[1] The task-related content is obviously of significance in movement of the group toward its goals; the emotional content has a less obvious but equally as profound an effect. When negative emotions arise, they must be expressed and dealt with or they will continue to have a disruptive effect upon the group. A person who is hostile because of a previous event will often interrupt or display negativism toward every issue that arises in the meeting.

In the composite these elements of group structure provide essential functions in the process of the group. They allow the group to develop in time toward a more effective operating unit. Whereas the early meetings of a group may involve the expenditure of much energy on building structure, later meetings can give more attention to core group tasks.

---

[1]Robert Bales, *Small Groups,* (New York: Knopf, 1955), pp. 424-456.

Without the stabilizing forces of group structure it would be necessary for members to feel their way along in identifying membership, roles, patterns of authority, and communication nets for each individual meeting.

GROUP GOALS

The stimulant for action in a group is its goals. Since a group is a collection of individuals, its goals are a hybrid consensus of the needs and wants of its members. The strength of influence of each individual determines the influence that his personal needs will have upon the goals of the group unit. The influence upon goals may be so narrowly distributed that the opinion of only a single member determines the goals or so broadly distributed that virtual equality is maintained.

These are the informal goals in the sense that they may not be written down or even discussed; they are the goals that members perceive to exist. Thus, the group goals may be completely different from the ones for which the group was established. Some of the goals may even conflict with those of the overall organization. This can be the source of great conflict as when the board pushes an unpopular building program, a Bible study group draws a conclusion that conflicts with church dogma, or a youth group shocks the church with an unacceptable recreational activity.

The strength with which members will support the goals of the group depends upon a number of factors. A basic factor is the degree of compatibility between the goals of the group and the personal needs of the individual members. Group goals that are vital to an individual's need satisfaction will have great force upon that individual; consequently, if the group goals are directed toward the satisfaction of important needs for all of the members, the goals will be upheld tenaciously.

Groups in which the members are able to participate in goal settings will be supported more vigorously. Full participation of the members in goal setting is perhaps the most significant tool in assuming that the goals are related in a positive way to individual needs. Groups in which one or two members have a dominant influence upon the goals are not likely to have strong loyalty to those goals.

As we shall see more fully, groups which are highly cohesive are more likely to have strong support for their goals. These groups are able to use group pressure far more successfully. Factors which tend to increase group cohesiveness, such as the threat of external forces, tend to increase support of goals. The effects of this are seen most closely in the competition groups of summer camp. Competition for a trophy generates far more energy for group attainments than cooperative team work on an independent project. In a more subtle way, more permanent church groups tend to strive for their goals with greater thrust when they feel the threat of an external force.

In order to assure that a small group makes a positive contribution to the church as whole rather than becoming a devisive clique, the church needs to maintain a close fellowship among its total membership and to establish a firm tie between the members of each group and the official board. The members of the official board should be active in consulting with leaders of various departments and units of the church to assure a continuity of purpose and compatibility of church and group goals.

GROUP NORMS

Norms are the rules or standards of behavior for the group regarding procedure of operations, form of address, moral conduct, dress, speech, and key phrases, which are either explicitly or implicitly defined. Pressure will be applied to those members who dare to deviate from the accepted group norms. These pressures may come in the form of clearly delineated disciplinary procedures as in the case of the norms set out in a union-management contract, or the norms may be enforced by a gentle jab or nudging sarcasm. Church groups usually employ the less formal means.

Norms of a church or a church group serve valuable functions, but, at the same time, they create problems. The norms provide order and structure for the conduct of church affairs, as well as a consistency and a familiarity that makes the church seem comfortable to its members. The discomfort of the unknown is diminished. They also reduce the confusion and the necessity for repeated, detailed planning of routine events and programs.

The problems that norms create are largely for those who do not conform to them. Noncomformity occurs because of either lack of acquaintance with the norms or actual resistance to them. A church visitor has many questions that flash through his mind. How do they dress at that church? Where do you go when you arrive at the church building? When do you stand in the service? When do you sit? What do you say? A person who finds himself rising to sing a congregational hymn a few seconds before everyone else stands, will receive several gentle jabs from friends about being "quick on the jump," and "standing out in the crowd." No doubt, you have witnessed the discomfort of visitors who invariably use a phrase that brings forth a cool nod from those of the church who have developed other modes of expression.

How do we avoid these problems and quickly overcome the psychological threats to visitors and new members? Let's follow a visitor through his first visit to the church. The choice of a person to greet others as they arrive is of great importance. Some people have the knack, in a brief encounter, of making others feel that they belong. These people should be sought out for the use of their talent in this area. Assigning a person to greet everyone entering the church and a second person to give special attention to visitors is especially effective.

After the visitor enters the doors of the church, he is faced with the next threat to his security — that of finding his Sunday school class-room. Often he is required to give information that he is reluctant to present at this time, i.e., his age (or worse, her age), his address, his religious affiliation, etc. Since this is an uncomfortable experience for most visitors, it is best to prepare a brief chart showing the class name and age grouping. This chart can be handed to the visitor with the explanation that if he will indicate the class he wishes to attend, he will be accompanied to his classroom.

Each Sunday school class should be aware of the tendency to estab-lish comfortable little cohesive groups in which the members un-consciously exclude visitors and new members. The class should be reminded to be aware of new people coming into their group and to make a special effort to become acquainted with them. This is more than simply-making polite introductions. It involves becoming well enough acquainted that a member feels free to accompany a visitor to the church service and sit with him.

As the visitor reaches the auditorium before the church service, he is welcomed by a group of ushers. The ushers are busily handing out programs. As they see the visitor entering, one of the ushers can diminish his concern about the "proper" place for him to sit and the "proper" conduct during the service with a few simple steps. He should welcome the guest briefly, give him a program, and point out any unusual practices or standards of conduct for the service to avoid embarrassment. By having the norms made very clear to him at each phase of initial church contact, a visitor can quickly feel comfortable.

Norms are also a problem for members who cannot or will not con-form to them. It should be emphasized that our norms are products of our local traditions. Most of them have little to do with scriptural principles or theology. Yet it is the nature of groups that the person who deviates from these unwritten laws is pressured to conform. It is usually over issues of group norms that people are ostracized or that a church is split.

Here is a problem.

> You have returned to your hometown church for the summer. Last summer you went away to work in San Francisco to make some extra money. This year as you finish your sophomore year in college your father has located a summer job for you at home. As you enter your Sunday school class, you are suddenly struck by the feeling that some-thing has changed. You have trouble putting your finger on it, but it's different. In a very short time you begin to realize that the thing that's changed is you.

> For two years you have been at the State University. There you are seen as a respectable citizen who attends church regularly and even does some work with a church youth group. In your church near the campus all the college crowd wears blue jeans and T-shirts to church.

93

The fellows all have different varieties of hair length from long to very long. Yours hits a respectable happy medium.

You look over the Sunday school class and to your surprise all the fellows have short hair and are wearing a coat and tie. You shrug your shoulders and take a seat at the corner of the conference table in the center of the classroom. Some old friends come over and before you can express your delight at seeing them again, they have hit you with a barrage of kidding comments on your attire. "Okay," you say to yourself, "they'll get over this 'culture shock' soon enough."

The class session gets underway. Soon they come to a question of sexual immorality. The teacher begins to discuss the new concept of communal living. As the class enters the assault, it becomes very evident that they view all communal life as colonies of sexual perverts who live together to engage in sexual orgies, wear no clothing, pass around drugs, and steal for their income. Finally, you feel compelled to speak. You begin to explain that there are several types of communes, some of which hold practices in line with Christian beliefs. The others mention magazine and newspaper articles that describe communes. You make your point firmly and calmly that these represent only one type of commune. In others that you have seen, the people are happily married; they are highly moral; they are living together only for the added closeness of a small community, not unlike the community within the frontier forts.

You can sense what is coming next, they give you the pat-on-the-back routine. They joke and cajole in an attempt to win you over. But you do not budge. You even describe the Christian commune that you have read about that is operating in Arizona, but to no avail. Then it begins. The silken gloves come off to expose the iron fist. They begin to assault your ideas and finally your person with swift and powerful verbal blows. You continue to resist. Finally someone says, "It seems to me that we've wasted enough time on this question. Let's move on to the next topic." You notice others in the class turn their faces, bodies, and even their chairs from you to face the teacher and the other members. As the class continues, you attempt to add a few comments to the other topics. A couple of people in the group turn and listen to what you say, but they do not say anything in return. You have been ostracized from the class.

Groups follow fairly consistent patterns of handling those who will not conform. These stages of group pressure are used whether the group is dealing with a simple issue of little significance or a critical, fundamental question. The difference is usually one of degree. Fortunately for the existence of the group, most people will conform at an early stage and do not disrupt the cohesiveness of the group. The amount of pressure that the deviant feels at any stage will depend in large measure on the cohesiveness of the group. If it is highly cohesive, it becomes extremely difficult for even the most tough-minded individualist to hold to his position. The first stage is one of rational, reasonable argument in which the laws of logic are employed. If the deviant does not respond, the next stage is the use of charm. Smiles, jokes, and friendly persuasion are showered on our noncomformist. In the third stage, the group begins the attack. Every vulnerable point in the deviant's armor is hit in the hope that he will fall. But if he is insulated from attack, the group will take the ultimate step of psychologically eliminating the deviant. He will be ignored, ostracized, or excommunicated from the group. The church group must be careful to evaluate its norms and the pressures it is using. It must not drive away God's own people over matters of culture or tradition. If we are to survive as an instrument in the service of God, we must be able to adapt to change. We must reexamine our entrenched approaches, hold fast to those that are scriptural and be prepared to yield on those that are not.

"Group cohesiveness" is a term that refers to the warmth, closeness, and attraction of the group for its members. A group that is active, friendly, loving, and warm will be able to provide much satisfaction. The degree of the cohesiveness that will be found in a group depends on a number of factors. *Size* is an important one. The smaller a group, the more cohesiveness it will have. As we increase the size of the group, we decrease the opportunity for interaction among its members. Consequently, the members cannot be as close to one another; they cannot get to know one another as well; they may not even be able to remember the names of all of the others in the group.

A second factor in determining cohesiveness is the *homogeneity* of the members. The more similar the members are in experiences, values, beliefs, and characteristics, the more cohesive the group will be. For this reason, the local church holds great potential for establishing a close fellowship. People usually become members of a church because they share the beliefs and values of the church. What greater base for cohesiveness could be had than the fellowship of believers in Christ? This factor can produce cohesiveness where the other contributing factors are absent.

Cohesiveness of the group will also tend to reduce as *changes occur in the group.* A group may adapt fairly well to the addition of a few members, but their cohesiveness is threatened by a large increase. Rapid growth may represent a real conflict for a small congregation or Sunday school class that feels a threat to their warm fellowship but at the same times wishes to spread the Gospel to others. Groups should openly face the problem and avoid the tendency to close ranks and exclude others from their fellowship (if not from their membership) so that they can maintain cohesiveness without exclusion.

Special attention should also be given to the effects of *openness and frankness of communication* upon cohesiveness. If the participants in the group feel so loved that they are willing to share their thoughts, feelings, and personal life freely, the group will develop a strong cohesiveness. As each displays his confidence in, and love of, the others by sharing himself with them, they find a deep bond of acceptance and understanding built among them. In recent years many people have found a void in their psychological life created by the diminishing strength of the family unit. Unable to find a fulfilling personal interaction with others, many have been gripped with a sense of personal anxiety and dissatisfaction. The church now has the opportunity and the responsibility to fill this void by developing small, close, sharing groups among its members.

The impact of the small group on the spiritual life of its members can be of equal magnitude as its effect upon the psychological life. The importance of sharing openly with others is clearly emphasized in Scripture: "Bear one another's burdens, and thus fulfil the law of Christ" (Galatians 6:2) and "Confess your sins to one another, and pray for one another (James 5:16). We are able to encourage one another and to support one another in small groups as we grow spiritually and perform our areas of service.

GROUP EFFECTIVENESS

The more concrete the tasks of a group, the easier it is to measure the group's effectiveness. We can easily determine our success in achieving the goal for 1000 people in Sunday school, but it is quite a different problem to assess whether or not the members of a church are growing spiritually. We can easily judge whether we have successfully reached a stewardship goal, but it is much more difficult to determine how many lives have been brought to a personal encounter with Christ. It is unfortunate that our natural tendency is to strive for the measurable, yet the results of the most significant purposes of the church defy measurement.

Groups have a strong impact on the performance behavior of their members. Just as they apply pressure toward conformity to a norm, so they exert influence upon adherence to a performance level, the solution of a problem, or the achievement of a goal. Research indicates that group pressures have a stronger effect on performance effectiveness than do the financial incentives commonly used in business.

To fully appreciate the effects of the group upon its effectiveness, we must look at the problem as it relates to group cohesiveness. The more cohesive the group, the more effect it has on all aspects of individual behavior including performance. A group that is lacking in cohesiveness will have almost no effect on performance. Seashore has shown that in highly cohesive groups the performance levels of the members of a group will be rather close; i.e., each person will produce at about the same level as all others in the group.[2] This level may be high or it may be low, depending upon the group goals. For groups whose goals are

---

[2]Stanley Seashore, *Applying Modern Management Principles,* (Ann Arbor, Mich.: Foundation for Research on Human Behavior, 1963), pp. 18-36.

high because of a favorable relationship with organizational leaders, the performance will also be high. Among the various groups that oppose the higher level leaders, the highly cohesive group is the lowest performer. The ideal group situation for the church is one in which the goals uphold the finest ideals and practices, and the group is highly cohesive.

In most respects, groups are superior to individuals in problem solving. The question of group versus individual problem solving has been an area of research for the behavioral sciences for a number of years. Several areas of the research results are of importance for church leadership:

1. Groups are superior to individuals in the solution of complex problems. Problems which involve a wide range of knowledge favor the group over the individual.
2. Groups are superior in the quality of their solutions, but are not as rapid in arriving at a conclusion.
3. Groups generate a greater variety of ideas on a problem than does an individual.
4. Groups show a higher level of aspiration toward problem solution than individuals.
5. Groups are able to generate a greater number of alternatives for solutions to their problems and are better able to see blind alleys than the individual who pursues the task alone.

The superiority of the group in the quality of problem solving is probably a consequence of both the motivational forces generated by the group and the added expertise available in having several persons involved. It should be clear to the church leader that groups make an invaluable contribution to the functioning of the church. The leader can improve his chances for effective performance by integrating his ideas with those of others in the group process. Clearly, the effective leader must take advantage of the values of the group.

8

Interpersonal Conflict

As Karen Horney pointed out, we react to others in three basic ways: we can move toward them, away from them, or against them.[1] Not only do we have the need to affiliate with others (to move toward others), as we have emphasized so far in this book, but we also have the need to maintain our privacy and our autonomy (to move away from others). We need both the independence and the personal recognition that are fundamental to human life. Our motivational desires for power, dominance, and exploitation of others bring us into conflict with their desires for autonomy, resulting in moving against them in the form of hostility and aggressive behavior.

In the church the tendency to move toward others in the motivational realm becomes a unifying force. The tendency to move away from others or against them is perceived as a potential threat to the church body and the lack of involvement manifested in this moving away from Christian fellowship is usually met by church leaders with mild annoyance. Moving against another person evokes a fear of the destructive forces that can result. In order to avoid this threat, church leaders will

---

[1]Karen Horney, *Our Inner Conflicts: A Constructive Theory of Neurosis*, (New York: W. W. Norton, 1945).

98

use the tactic of silence, "patience," tact, humor, or passive resistance. The cover-up is often preferred to an honest confrontation. Unfortunately, our energies are so greatly expended in controlling and preventing the expression of hostility and in dealing with the underlying resentment that we have little opportunity to identify its source or to root out the cause. Church leaders often avoid overt hostility, fearing that it may become contagious and start a trend that will eventually destroy the church. Most people have little skill in dealing with hostility once it is expressed. We prefer to allow it to operate below the surface and to ignore it in the hope that the problem will disappear with the dousing of each new flareup.

BASES OF INTERPERSONAL CONFLICT

Our first step in learning to deal with interpersonal conflict is to identify its cause. Interpersonal conflict arises out of the three-dimensional nature of man. Most of the conflict occurs as a result of the frustration of personal needs; however, we can also enter into conflict because we are holding tenaciously to values of conscience that we feel are being threatened by others. Occasionally the motivational forces or even the inner law of conscience within one person comes into conflict with the leadership of the Spirit as revealed to another person. Let us examine these problems of conflict in a case that developed in an Ohio church between the pastor and the Christian education director. The relationship between the men started on a note of friendship and cooperation. The CE director had come to the church with high hopes of building the kind of educational program of which he had often dreamed. Since the church was involved in an ambitious building program, he enjoyed the responsibility of contributing many ideas. As he engaged in the work of training and counseling workers, he found that he was in disagreement with the approach used by the senior high school leaders. As he discussed his views with them, they reacted by becoming angry and more deeply entrenched in their ideas. In a later staff meeting the problem was discussed and he felt that he had the support of the pastor. However, on later contacts with the senior high leaders, he was informed that they had gone to the pastor and that he had agreed with them. As a result of this knowledge, the CE director's resentment for the pastor grew with each new grievance until even the smallest annoyance became a cause of hostility. The pastor failed to support him on other occasions; he did not like the pastor's habit of reading other people's sermons; he resented the lavish home that the pastor built and the way he favored the company of the wealthy people of the community. These feelings finally became so intense that they evolved into an open warfare in staff meetings. A few months later the CE director left the church ministry and took a job as a factory worker.

99

Conflict Viewed From a Broad Perspective

A broad perspective of the causes of interpersonal conflict must include the problems of role conflict, personality clashes, unjust treatment, and competition. *Role conflict* occurs when the beliefs or activities of a person in one church position seem incompatible with those of another. If a youth pastor and a CE director both feel that they are responsible for the Sunday night training ministry, each will resent the "interference" that he perceives on the part of the other. If a Sunday school teacher sees her role as including the acquisition of teaching aids for her lessons and the Sunday school superintendent believes that it is his job to get all materials, conflict will arise. In the above example of church conflict, the CE director perceived his role to be that of determining educational policy and practice; simultaneously, the high school leaders assumed the same role for themselves. The pastor perceives his role as that of counseling people who come to him with a problem — a role in direct conflict with the CE director's desire for autonomy and support.

Most observers of the conflict between the CE director and the pastor probably would detect a personality clash. The former is an idealist whereas the latter is a pragmatist. The former is direct and open; the latter is tactful and cautious. Their difference in approach and style aligns them in opposing positions. While the pastor is attacking a problem by hitting the flank, the CE director is opposing the same issue in a frontal attack. Bruises are bound to be suffered in the process. Personality conflicts occur when the activities of one person become barriers to the satisfaction of another. Thus, a brash, domineering person has few friends because he threatens the desire for autonomy and personal esteem on the part of most others.

Often conflict is attributed to *unjust treatment* of one person by another. A member feels that he is overlooked when important jobs are filled; a staff member feels that the pastor gets a disproportionate share of the church budget; a teacher feels that she gets only the obsolete equipment. In our example, the CE director felt that he was not getting the support from the pastor that he deserved. Just treatment is always difficult to evaluate, because it is not viewed in the same manner by different people. No doubt, events do occur where a person is slighted; another person claims his share, yet irrespective of the true fairness of the case, we feel unjustly treated when our needs and wants remain unsatisfied while the needs of others of comparable status are being met. This would seem to apply only to "selfish" people, but remember that the motivational nature of man is directed toward self-fulfillment.

Competition is a fourth major source of conflict between groups as well as individuals. Two parties seek a goal that cannot be shared. Nations have often fought over land that both claimed; companies compete for the largest share of a product market; candidates for office

100

become violent enemies because they cannot both be elected. Similar battlelines are drawn in the church over the allotment of budgetary resources, the use of rooms and equipment, or the placement of a new worker in Sunday school or children's church. We unconsciously compete for recognition of our efforts as we aspire to the class or church that will attract the larger membership or as we strive to appear the most spiritually mature.

These *differences between ideals and values* account for many of our conflicts and perhaps appear more evident in the life of the church than in any other organization. In the church life our ideals and values are often well-fixed by tradition, our family, and our society, as well as by the Scripture; consequently, they are often unrealistic and irrelevant to true Christian values.

The Motivational Root of Interpersonal Conflicts

While it is evident that we can understand interpersonal conflict from a broad perspective, a more basic level of understanding may be obtained by examining more deeply the underlying motivational forces which are at the root of most human conflict. Any of our needs — of the body, security, affiliation, status and esteem, achievement, or autonomy — may be thwarted by another person and a conflict will result. The CE director in our example possesses a strong need for achievement, esteem, and autonomy. The pastor also has strong needs for esteem, status, and achievement, but in addition, he feels the need to dominate others. Not only does the pastor's tendency to dominate conflict with the CE director's desire for autonomy, but their means of attaining esteem and achievement are also highly discrepant. The CE director expects to achieve and build esteem through building an effective program of Christian education, while the pastor seeks these same gratifications through affiliation with wealthy, prestigious men. Their differences in method bring them into conflict, but in addition to this problem, the conflict itself threatens their need for affiliation and adds more fuel to the flame.

Conflicts between church departments often emerge because the achievement and esteem of people become tied to the success or failure of the programs and activities of their departments. A person becomes upset or angry when faced with disagreement in a meeting because he fears a loss of acceptance and esteem. We grow to hate those who have had the highest potential for evoking love, but who did not follow through. One tends to hate the girl he would have married but who spurned him, the boss who ignores him and his efforts, the friend who breaks off a relationship for no obvious reason, the husband who is unfaithful or who begins to ignore his wife. Motivational needs are basic and are held to some degree by every person; consequently, none of us are completely immune from interpersonal conflict. It is as natural as eating.

101

The Inner Law and the Spirit As Sources of Interpersonal Conflict

The standards of the inner law of conscience differ from one person to another. For many people, they have become rigid, yet others of equally high standards attempt to apply them with flexibility to the situation at hand. The rigid standards and values of one church leader often come into conflict with the dreams and goals of another; the irresistible force meets the immovable object and the resistance produces sparks. The incompatibility between values of the CE director and the practices of the pastor feeds the friction of controversy. The Spirit also brings interpersonal conflict when He leads a person toward a certain action or belief that someone else opposes. Paul came into conflict with Peter over the issue of circumcision. Jesus Christ came into repeated conflict with the Pharisees and Sadducees, the money changers of the temple, and finally the Sanhedrin and the Roman rulers:

1. He was in conflict with the Pharisees who resisted his work of healing on the Sabbath (Matt. 12:9-14).
2. He came into conflict with the Pharisees who resisted His work of driving out demons (Matt. 12:22-25).
3. He came into conflict with the Pharisees and Sadducees who wanted Him to work miracles simply to show off His power (Matt. 16:1-4).
4. He came into conflict with the money changers in the temple (Mark 11:15-18).
5. He came into conflict with the chief priests and teachers of the Law because His message opposed their traditional methods (Mark 11:27-33).
6. He came into conflict with the Sanhedrin and Roman rulers because He refused to deny that He was the Son of God and the Messiah (Mark 14:60-63; 15:15).

Christ came into conflict with those who were hindering His work or destroying the meaning of God's commandments and teachings. We can also expect resistance and conflict today when we maintain the teachings and pursue the intents of Christ.

One who is being led by the Spirit will naturally come into conflict with others who are being led (at least for the time) by human motivational forces. It becomes a question of true spiritual discernment to identify the leadership of the Spirit in these issues. The tendency will be to yield to our desire for esteem and to conclude that our own position is the spiritual one.

How can we know whether our cause is directed by the Spirit or by forces of our human nature? Our position is likely to be one that is Spirit-directed if

1. we are clearly in close fellowship with God.
2. we are Spirit-filled.

3. our position was arrived at prayerfully.
4. our department or ourselves personally do not stand to gain from the position we have taken.
5. our position is clearly one of principle and one for which the scriptural support is evident. (Caution is required here because controversy often centers around the issue of whose position is the one of principle and scriptural support. When this occurs, an objective, outside person with Bible understanding and maturity should be consulted.)
6. on examining our personal, motivational needs, it appears that we are not taking the position because of needs that have not been fully yielded to the control of the Spirit; e.g., we are not supporting the position to side with a friend, to get recognition from others, to have the power of winning a controversy, or to show our superior knowledge and insights on the issue.
7. we are able to maintain our love and acceptance for the other person, while resisting his current belief or activity.

Effects of Interpersonal Conflicts

Conflict in the church is almost always unpleasant, and to the people involved, it usually seems deleterious to the organization. However, from the view of the effectiveness of the church in achieving its goals and purposes, conflict is often necessary and sometimes beneficial. We will consider both the negative and the positive effects of interpersonal conflict.

Deleterious Effects of Interpersonal Conflict

The effects of conflict on the feelings of the individuals involved are essentially negative. Conflict between people is unpleasant and frustrating because their needs, wants, and values are in jeopardy. If we are involved, our personal reaction will be one of offense or defense. We may become aggressive and hostile, backing up our position with a verbal or physical assault; depending upon our nature and the situation, we may take a defensive posture. We may withdraw into silence or even leave the scene; we may justify or rationalize our position; we may displace our hostility, removing it from the one who frustrates us but directing it toward an innocent third party (our wife or our children), or we may divert our energies toward controlling all of the feelings that are churning inside us so that the other person will not know of our feelings. It is a curious fact of human nature that we despise the person who lies when we ask him for his position on a question, but we admire the one who can lie by hiding his true feelings. Perhaps the admiration stems from our appreciation that he has not made us feel unpleasant by confronting us with the conflict.

From a human standpoint we prefer that people in conflict take a defensive position rather than an aggressive one in order to keep the frustration and turmoil at a minimum, but from a psychological and spiritual view, any conceivable reaction to conflict is equally deleterious except in its resolution. To show hostility, to harbor resentment, to withdraw into a shell — all break down the relationship that is basic to the Christian experience. The conflict must be brought to the surface and into the open in order to be resolved.

Conflict can also be destructive of the organization, tending to build and expand, if it is not resolved. A disagreement over a single issue can threaten the esteem of a pastor or church leader. He obtains the support of others and their grievances are added to his, until finally the majority of the church stands helplessly by as the leaders struggle against one another for victory.

Facilitative Effects of Interpersonal Conflict

Most students of organizational behavior view conflict as a natural, even necessary part of the conduct of organizational life. Moore indicates that interpersonal conflict is desirable within an organization, for without it the organization is either asleep or dead.[2] This statement seems to apply even more strongly to the church when members rally with renewed effort and enthusiasm in the face of external threat. The early church grew most rapidly during the time when its members operated under the threat of being killed by the Roman emperors. Even today, churches are quick to unite in the face of community or government opposition.

Conflict within the church body can also be beneficial. The church must endure conflict in order to change. Not all of the leaders or members of a church will accept a new approach or a new goal. You will find at least one person that will resist almost any change you might wish to propose; nevertheless, a church whose leaders are unwilling to press their goals or ideals against opposition cannot grow. The ability to face and to resolve conflict is an essential attribute of the effective church leader.

THE RESOLUTION OF CONFLICT

Behavioral scientists who have studied this field have developed a number of approaches to the resolution of conflict, with each approach recognizing the necessity of bringing the conflict into the open. Despite our fondest wishes, conflicts do not disappear with the waving of a wand. *Conflicts must be faced* and resolved. The problem of the resolution of conflict between two individuals differs from that of the problem of group conflict. Consequently, we shall examine these two types of situations separately.

---

[2]Franklin Moore, *Management Organization and Practice,* (New York: Harper and Row, 1964), pp. 311-313.

Resolution of Conflict between Individuals

The resolution of conflict between individuals is never an easy task. The easiest approach is often that of ignoring rather than resolving the conflict. By avoiding the problem, we take the option of maintaining an unexpressed resentment and a broken fellowship, rather than facing and experiencing its anxieties. In the church situation, conflict usually comes to light in the course of time with a much greater heat than would have been experienced had the conflict been faced earlier.

Another approach that we find appealing as an escape is one of telling a third party (and a fourth, and a fifth, and a sixth, etc.) of our grievance. Here we take great care to give only our side of the issue. This serves to get others involved in the problem but does not bring a solution. Recently, a church member approached the deacon in charge of Christian education to tell him of a grievance held by another member about the long hair and beard of a junior high Sunday school teacher. The emissary wanted the deacon to help him think through the problem, and more important, to talk with the teacher about his uncomely locks. As he considered such an interchange, the deacon realized that he would simply be giving the grieved member an easy way out. The member could stand in the wings and watch the action as he might view a TV adventure. Instead of taking on the assignment of conveying the accusation, the deacon suggested that the emissary take back the recommendation that the aggrieved member use the confrontation approach described below. Whether such a person will take the suggestion one can only guess. If he does, the problem will very probably never come to the general concern of other church leaders.

Christ initially acknowledged, and behavioral scientists of today have confirmed, that interpersonal conflict can best be handled by way of *confrontation*. Indeed, we have a responsibility as Christians to confront those with whom we have a conflict. "If therefore you are presenting your offering at the altar, and there remember that your brother has something against you, leave your offering there before the altar, and go your way, first be reconciled to your brother, and then come and present your offering" (Matt. 5:23, 24). We cannot maintain a proper relationship with God if we hold resentment toward another person.

If the confrontation is to be successful, it must be done with a true desire to overcome the conflict and restore the fellowship of love. In a recent conflict between members of a local church, an elder was appointed to go to a woman who held a grievance and to seek understanding and communication. He was a most inappropriate choice, for not five minutes before he left, he had called upon the board to "nail her to the wall," repeating the phrase on his return. We must have the desire and the intent for true restoration of fellowship reflected in our attitude toward the other person. Recently, a woman came to her pastor with a great burden of resentment toward him. In the proper spirit, she confessed her feeling and deep regret and admitted that she did not really know why she had held these feelings for so long. Then she went further to describe how she felt and how it had influenced her life. The pastor had not previously been aware of this resentment, but he accepted it and her completely. She went away from this confrontation feeling as though a great burden had been lifted from her shoulders. She asserted that the next Sunday morning she heard him preach for the first time in two years even though she had been in the congregation as he preached many times. Therefore, confrontation must be held in an attitude of regret, repentance, and openness. It must be approached prayerfully, with the anticipation that the Spirit of God will replace resentment with His love.

A slightly different approach involving *face-to-face problem solving* is more appropriate when the conflict emerges out of a problem situation rather than out of generalized feelings of resentment. The attitudes of the persons involved should be similar to those required for successful confrontation. They may also find it helpful to begin by acknowledging their regret and their desire for resolution of their differences. In this case, however, the discussion is centered on the problem which the people are attempting to understand. They attempt openly and honestly to relate their opinions and feelings about the problem and listen to the opinions expressed by the other person. It is the listening phase that is most difficult. It takes effort to hold your own thoughts, evaluations, and emotions in abeyance to try to see the problem from the perspective of the other person. Yet, it is essential to the resolution of the conflict. Once understanding is reached, the problem is either solved at that moment or with little additional time and effort.

Unfortunately, even our best efforts do not always yield fruit, in which case a *third party agent* is our "last best hope" for resolving the conflict. "And if your brother sins, go and reprove him in private; if he listens to you, you have won your brother. But if he does not listen to you, take one or two more with you, so that BY THE MOUTH OF TWO OR THREE WITNESSES EVERY FACT MAY BE CONFIRMED. And if he refuses to listen to them, tell it to the church; but if he refuses to listen even to the church, let him be to you as a Gentile and a tax-gatherer" (Matt. 18:15-17). The aid of a third party must succeed or the conflict moves out of the face-to-face level to become the concern of the total body. With each progression, the chance of reconciliation is greatly diminished.

The third party must be a person who is Spirit-controlled and of an even temper, exhibiting the attributes of love, concern, and wisdom. It is his responsibility to guide those who are in conflict to develop an attitude of forgiveness and a desire to resolve their differences. He must stimulate them to listen to one another by pointing out cases of apparent failure to understand as well as by patiently restating a point that is not being understood so that it becomes clear. The third party can further contribute by encouraging those in conflict to be open and honest, and to persist in their pursuit of a reconciliation. His responsibility is one of facilitating the processes of conflict resolution which did not work in the initial confrontation or face-to-face problem solving. In describing his theory of conflict, Boulding states that these approaches to conflict resolution are "intellectually and emotionally very demanding, and the achievement of consensus may be very expensive indeed."[3] However, they are worth the price.

RESOLUTION OF GROUP CONFLICT

The *confrontation meeting* is an effective means of eliminating conflict within a group and effecting a resolution. The confrontation meeting is useful when the group leader or the members recognize a hindering barrier of resentment and controversy within the group's operation. The meeting should be planned for a full day, preferably in a retreat or hideaway that will facilitate full and steady attention to the meeting. The meeting begins with a moderator (ideally, someone who is not a member of the group), who indicates the purpose of the meeting and the importance of its success, making sure to note the value of candor in the discussion. If the group is large, it is broken into units of about five, cutting across any departmental lines (assuming that the overall group may have several departments). The participants are asked to discuss the most significant problems they face in getting their job done. What are the things that "bug" them in their work? They are asked to return in one hour with a list of their problems and the causes of them. In the next hour the discussion units present their lists. These are written on paper for future reference and taped to the walls. The problems are then categorized to find common threads. The departments then go into group sessions for one hour to establish priorities on the problems and to recommend solutions. In the last session the departments reassemble as a total group and each in turn confronts the group leader with its recommendations. It is important to give plenty of time to this session, since the core issues and grievances should be forthcoming along with the recommendations for solution. Plans for implementations of recommendations or announcements of change should emerge from this session.

A second approach has been called *data feedback*. A survey of the church organization, activities, and interpersonal relations similar to that of Appendix A, page 231, is used to obtain basic information about the climate of the church. The results of the survey should be taken as expressions of opinion and feeling. Time should not be wasted in debat-

---

[3]Kenneth Boulding, *Conflict Management in Organizations,* (Ann Arbor, Mich.: Foundation for Research on Human Behavior, 1961), pp. 43-51.

ing the source or the motivation of the comments but the group should instead be concerned with the causes of negative opinions and how they can be remedied in order to improve personal attitudes. Although the surveys should be completed anonymously, the respondent should indicate the church department in which he is most active so that the results may be summarized for each department as well as for the total church body. Conferences made up of people from throughout the church should be held over the subsequent twelve-month period to provide feedback from the survey and to discuss methods of improving the operation of the departments and the total church.

The third approach to handling conflict within a group is the *T-group* process developed by the National Training Laboratories of Bethel, Maine, for increasing the human orientation among business managers. This approach attempts to provide a better understanding for the participant of his reactions to other people and of their reaction to him. Many churches are attempting to use groups of this type to increase the appreciation of their members for the human values of fellow Christians.

T-groups must be evaluated carefully before they are employed by a church. A professional trainer is required to conduct the groups. His approach should be examined thoroughly. If the trainer uses techniques involving various physical-contact or bodily "encounter" methods, he should be avoided. Although these approaches provide exhilarating experiences and build a real closeness and rapport within the group, they are based on human motivational and emotional forces rather than spiritual forces. Perhaps you can best understand the types of techniques used in encounter groups through two illustrations: (a) The group begins by forming a close circle. With each of the six to eight people facing the center of the circle, they move inward until the group is in a very tight cluster. They then bind themselves together by stretching their arms as far around the entire group as possible. They follow the physical contact with a discussion of concepts such as group unity or closeness. (b) A second method begins with the group standing in a close circle with their left shoulders toward the center. Each person puts his hands or arms around the person in front of him and they all sit at the same time so that every person is sitting in the lap of the person behind him and has the person in front of him sitting in his lap. After this exercise the group members discuss their feelings of closeness, trust, or dependency. These methods *do* stimulate emotional feelings of oneness while providing a feeling of release and affection that is not attained as quickly in any other human group experience. Yet they also prove to be sexually stimulating and often lead to extramarital sexual relationships. Clearly, the emotions aroused as we throw away inhibitions and allow a full and true expression of love provide wondrous human experience. But that experience is, in the final analysis, simply a *human* experience based on our *human* motivational forces.

The T-group process which has value in resolving group conflict involves a free and open discussion on the part of the participants as to the deep feelings that they hold about life, about people in general, and about one another. The discussion unveils the hidden fears and anxieties, and removes the masks that have separated people and have created conflicts; consequently, conflicts disappear. The approach is verbal but profound. It also builds interpersonal acceptance, understanding, and love without the physical and sexual stimulation. A major problem in applying the technique to the resolution of group conflict stems from the difficulty of getting a church leadership group to take the forty to eighty hours to participate in the sessions (usually in one or two weeks of intensive meetings). To be truly effective, the people involved in a T-group session should be ones who work together in the church — the official board, a staff group, etc.

The final approach for handling group conflict is that of *goal setting*. Conflict often occurs because people in the church have grown to see their own work or that of their department as of primary importance. The Sunday school superintendent may see his department as more important than the day school because his school is teaching the Bible. We tend to exalt our own areas of identification. Situations of this type may be improved through a process of group goal setting. Persons representing various departments come together to discuss (a) the goals of the church and (b) the goals for their department. As they hear others discussing the challenge and contribution that they are facing, they gain a renewed appreciation for the work of the other person. A valuable application of this approach is the board of Christian education. You may hold one meeting each quarter bringing together the Sunday school superintendent, children's church director, boys' group leader, girls' group leader, etc. Ask each CE board member to prepare a list of their accomplishments, current problems, and goals (three to five) for the next quarter to discuss in the meeting. This can enliven your meeting and tear down the barriers that have stood between departments.

Today's churches must learn to handle interpersonal conflict in order to survive in a rapidly changing society. Conflict is an inseparable companion of change. Deciding to take the path of avoiding conflict by ignoring the need for change may minimize the immediate conflict but will only serve to make tomorrow's problems more explosive. We must confront and resolve conflicts as they arise.

9

Reasoning Together Through Communication

Of all the activities that man pursues, perhaps the most difficult and most rewarding is communication. It is the basic human skill upon which we build the many other abilities that allow us to adapt to a complex society.

Communication within a church is fraught with many barriers. These barriers impede the fellowship and effectiveness of the church by directing our attention away from true and open expression of feelings and ideas. The path beyond the barriers follows the approach of listening and understanding. In the composite, the barriers and gateways to communication form the four styles — the developmental style, which builds communication; the controlling style, which uses communication as a means of dominating others; the relinquishing style, which is a responsive and dependency form of communication; and the withdrawal style, which obstructs the communication process by diverting attention away from the subject at hand. A person will usually use several styles of communications in a single discussion.

Pastor Truel has conveyed his point of view clearly to Walt, the board chairman. Walt is quite aware that the pastor wants to sponsor a youth tour of the mission field of Latin America, but has the pastor successfully communicated? No, he has not. Walt may completely understand what it is that the pastor wants but he may strongly disagree. If they walk away at this point, they do so without the pastor's understanding Walt's viewpoint, without settling a point of disagreement, and, thus, without mutual interpersonal communication.

We communicate for the following general purposes:

1. We would like others to understand our ideas.
2. We would like others to accept our ideas.
3. We would like to gain a favorable response to our ideas.
4. We would like to maintain a favorable relationship with others.
5. We would like to be able to change our ideas when they are out of line.
6. We would like to interact with others in the solution of problems.

In the leadership of a church the definition of communication must read: *Effective communication is the transmission and reception of ideas and feelings for the establishment of mutual understanding, agreement, and a favorable response.*

BARRIERS TO EFFECTIVE COMMUNICATION

We are surrounded by communication breakdowns. Church leaders will almost invariably mention communication as one of their core leadership problems.

Let's take a typical example of an incidental temporary communication breakdown. The members of a junior high Sunday school department drove sixty miles north of their hometown for a winter weekend retreat. During their Friday afternoon free time, money disappeared from the cabins of most of the girls on the retreat. The girls discovered their loss with alarm when they returned to their cabins after an exciting evening program. The counselors held a quick meeting and decided to put the matter squarely to the young people. An aggressive, brash lady counselor, whom we will call Jo Ann, went to all the girls and placed the responsibility on each individual to return the money to cans left in each cabin for the purpose. She approached one of the girls whom she suspected and with a forceful and accusing tone she asked, "Do you know anything about the money?" "No, I don't," the girl quickly responded. The issue was dropped; the next morning all of the money was recovered and the retreat was saved. The following Sunday Jo Ann was cornered by the girl's mother. "I want you to know that I do not appreciate your actions at the retreat," the irate mother declared. Surprised, Jo Ann answered, "Well, everyone else has praised my actions." "When you went to my daughter, you were way out of line. It upset her deeply," the mother declared. "I think you are far too sensitive," Jo Ann responded. "The problem is that you're insensitive to other people's feelings," retorted the mother. "I did what I thought was right; I still feel that my actions were justified," Jo Ann continued. And so the argument grew until they finally parted in anger. Obviously this is not effective communication.

Who was at fault? Jo Ann? The mother? Both? Perhaps this question itself provides a clue to the basis of communication breakdown. A major barrier to effective communication is the *tendency to evaluate* — to judge, to take sides. The mother showed little interest in understanding Jo Ann's point of view; instead, she immediately judged Jo Ann to be "out of line." But did Jo Ann attempt to understand the mother's feeling? No, she rebutted with an evaluation of her own: "You are far too sensitive." Then Jo Ann was accused of being insensitive, and the judgments and evaluations began to multiply.

Perhaps you are thinking that this is an unusual case. Let us look at a few other examples. Following a speech by Lawrence Richards on the need for small family groups in the church ministry, a group of pastors discussed his concepts on the way to lunch. The first pastor to speak said, "I believe Richards is going over to the United Brethren position." The others join in the attempt to decide which denomination Richards' views most closely approximate. We often pigeonhole people to avoid contending with their ideas. The president of the United States says, "We are handling our economic problems." Half the nation rises to applaud and half leaps forward to jeer. "I liked your sermon this morning, pastor," come the overworked words of praise. What better sign could we have that the pastor has not communicated effectively? He has been on trial; his sermon receives a high mark in the evaluation process. The conversation of Jo Ann and the mother is different only in the degree of the emotions involved; the two women are not at all unique in the tendency to evaluate.

In the argument of Jo Ann and the mother, another barrier to communication stands out — *interpersonal hostility*. The mother brought hostility to the situation and Jo Ann quickly became angry also. As the hostility grew, the messages became less and less coherent and the wall of resistance to the message grew higher. It was not an expression of hostility that was the barrier, but the feeling. Suppressing the feelings reduced the effectiveness of the communication even more. A great deal of energy was used up in this charade of calm; the true feelings certainly could not be understood, because they were not expressed.

Looking at the debate further, a third barrier emerges — *defensiveness*. Jo Ann began to defend herself immediately. "Everyone else has praised my actions," and "I did what I thought was right." Her ego challenged, Jo Ann quickly came to its defense. She upheld her actions both in her own eyes and in the eyes of others. She hoped to turn the tide with a strong show of force, but her defense did not aid in her understanding of the mother or the mother's understanding of her. She may have convinced herself that she was right, but she certainly did not convince the mother. We habitually jump to our own defense when we feel the slightest likelihood of losing face. If someone speaks of a topic that is unfamiliar, we quickly attempt to show our expertise. On the way to a baptismal service, I was attempting to tell my seven-year-old daughter the meaning of the ordinance we were about to witness. As I finished my first introductory remarks, she announced, "I know all about that." "Listen to me," I snapped; "you might learn something." My superior wisdom had been challenged just as I was about to fulfill my fatherly duty as the head of the household. Consequently, I missed the splendid opportunity to find out what her concept was and to help her ideas to grow.

At this point our list of barriers moves beyond our example — Jo Ann and the mother have not erected the barrier of *fear*. Yet this is a major problem in today's church setting. The pastor, and, to a lesser degree, other church leaders, are often viewed as superhuman judges of the fold. The laity regards their function as that of discerning sin and accusing the wayward; consequently, church members are on guard when talking to one of the leaders. They fear that they will expose themselves in their areas of weakness and thus provoke the reprisal of the standard-bearer of truth and justice. This reaction is usually subconscious and always unexpressed. Pastors sometimes contribute to this fear by smug and condemning sermons. "If they are so incensed by the evils of society, surely they will judge my weaknesses," the member reasons. Admissions of human weaknesses in the pulpit may be a help to reducing this barrier to communication. In any case, the church leaders must excel in their development of an attitude of compassion and acceptance.

Stemming from the same origin as fear, *status differentials* often present a barrier to communication. The wider the gap in the status of two people, the more difficult it becomes for them to communicate. John Kennedy lamented the fact that the day of his election to the presidency was the last day that he was able to get unblemished, true communication. Senators who were his seniors would go in to see him, irate over some abuse to themselves and their constituents, prepared to tell the president exactly what they thought, and find themselves in the big oval office saying, "Yes, Mr. President. No, Mr. President." Many business leaders describe reactions to a promotion they received: they go back the next day to their friends, but now as their boss, only to find them distant and ill at ease. The hierarchy of the church carries its status differentials as well. Each new title and element of attire adds a plank to the communication barrier — a barrier that can be destroyed only by close contact, openness, and warmth on the part of the leader. Status barriers can be eliminated only by fellowship. Church leaders must take every opportunity to talk with others in a relaxed, shirt-sleeve atmosphere.

The final barrier is of a different sort, but deserves our attention —

the parliamentary method. In board or staff meetings (or any meeting where fewer than twenty people are involved), Robert's *Rules of Order* provides a firm blockade against mutual understanding. The requirement that the chairman recognize the speakers chops up the discussion into a series of speeches, thereby denying free exchange. The necessity of a motion prior to discussion almost makes creative ideas illegal. The democratic majority system is built on the idea that the issues will not be resolved before agreement is reached. Small group meetings should be open discussions which seek free exchange, informality, and consensus agreement. Only by such an approach can we truly communicate in meetings.

Gateways to Effective Communication

Effective communication occurs when we listen with understanding and trust. None of these three ingredients — listening, understanding, or trusting — are sufficient of themselves; each adds to the total communication process.

Listening is an active process. One of the most striking characteristics about poor listeners is that they spend little energy in the listening process. In your next conversation, try listening intently for fifteen minutes; do not let your mind wander, but absorb every word. You will find yourself exhausted. The amount of energy that you will use in avoiding all of the hindrances to listening will surprise you.

Several talents go into the active listening skill. The effective listener is able to bring out the thoughts of others by the use of exploratory questions; he asks questions which aid the speaker in clarifying his meaning. Through follow-up questions, he pursues paths opened by the discussion. Effective listening also involves a search for ideas. A good listener is on the alert to open new vistas for his understanding through the knowledge and views of others. Because he is not simply tuned in to be entertained, he is stimulated by a wide range of material.

The good listener is able to sense his own conditioned emotional reflex and to avoid being thrown into pursuit of mental retravel of emotional thought paths. Words such as *evolution, red, pig, pervert, maimed, income tax, liberal,* and *fanatic* often stimulate a chain reaction of thought to an earlier emotional experience in which these words were used. We need to be aware of the words that "set us off" and avoid pursuit of their paths. We should use our mental capacity for the rapid exploration of ideas to open the way for our listening. Although we talk at an average rate of about 125 words a minute, we think at somewhere around 525 words per minute. The excess time in speaking should be used to anticipate, to summarize, and to integrate the words with gestures, inflections of speech, facial expressions, and body movements.

Understanding involves the ability to see an idea from the point of view of the person expressing it. We sense how he feels; we assume his frame of reference; we "walk for a day in his moccasins." A person comes to you for counsel and tells you that he hates his father. What is your response?

1. "Now, son, you don't really hate your father."
2. "You mean you hate him some of the time, but don't you love him some of the time?"
3. "Are you angry with your father, John?"
4. "How does your father feel about that?"
5. "The Bible says we should honor our father and mother."
6. "You feel that you have hate for your father."

Only the last statement pursues the understanding of your counselee's thoughts and feelings. But you say, my role is to *help* people, not just to understand. True, but to help assumes that you first understand. Most psychologists agree that the greatest help to a person comes from the communication of understanding. The speaker must sense your willingness to understand him rather than your eagerness to make an evaluation and give your advice if he is to feel free to relate his problem further.

A fundamental approach to gaining understanding in communication involves the reflective response. Suppose one of your Sunday school teachers describes his feelings this way:

"I'm just not able to relate to these junior children. I've got some boys in that class that are rude, disrespectful, and disruptive. They ruin the whole class. I know my attitude is wrong and I think I should give the class up."

A reflective response would be:

"You feel that some of the boys are disrupting your class and you feel your attitude is wrong." The listener has added nothing, but has shown an understanding of the teacher's feelings. In so doing, he encourages the teacher to clarify his feelings further. Such reflections or restatements convey understanding without threat or evaluation.

Another fundamental approach in encouraging the speaker to elaborate is the understanding statement, such as "I see," or "Tell me more," or "Yes, I understand." These statements assure the speaker that we are with him and want him to explain further.

Of equal importance in communication is *trust*. Effective communication is based on a mutual feeling of trust and acceptance between the persons involved. We cannot reach an agreement or make a proper response to the communication unless we feel that we can rely on what the other person says, confident of his honesty. Effective communication requires the openness and warmth that is the basis of trust. It may appear to you at this point that such communication would be very one-sided and highly receptive. But remember that we are discussing the process of opening gateways to others in communicating with us. It is hoped that they will reciprocate and listen with understanding and trust when we become the speakers. Let us consider the styles used by communicators.

Four Communication Styles

In his conference on *Developing Communication Skills,* Malcolm E. Shaw describes four styles typically used in communications — the developmental style, the controlling style, the relinquishing style, and the withdrawal style.

The Developmental Style

Developmental communication involves a mutual sharing among equals. The communication flows back and forth, with each person attempting to convey his ideas and to understand those of others. Each person remains open-minded and receptive to new ideas. The communicator attempts to inform and to stimulate others. His goal is to arrive at an understanding that will challenge others and build commitment to the solution that they develop. The developmental communicator seeks out the ideas of others and explores these ideas with interest by asking questions, reflecting the opinions that he hears, and showing support. Examples of the comments of the developmental communicator might be:

1. "I saw that our attendance decreased during the sermon series on the *Book of John.* I'm sure that this has something significant to say about the needs of our people. What do you think?"

2. "I wonder if we shouldn't look at other alternative causes of the problem before we settle on this one. Do you see any other reason for these results?"

The Controlling Style

In the controlling style, one person assumes the primary role as communicator. Most of the communication flows from him out to others. He assumes that his own ideas are best and tries to sell them to others. His assumption often leads him to force his ideas on others and to dominate the situation. Examples of controlling statements are:

1. "If we follow my approach we will have fewer youth problems and will develop more mature Christians in adulthood."

2. "I'm sure my plan will work. Remember, you didn't go along with my view on the material last time and we wasted two hundred dollars."

The Relinquishing Style

The relinquishing communicator and the controlling one get along together fine since the former prefers to stay in the background and shift the responsibility for the conversation to the other person. Assuming that others have more to contribute, he readily accepts their alternatives and gives up his own convictions. These are typical comments of the relinquisher:

1. "Could we work together on this project? I'll try to cooperate with you on it."

116

2. "Okay, if that's the way you think it should be done, I'll go along with it."

3. "Tell me how I can help out. I'm willing to do anything you think is best."

The Withdrawal Style

Here the person avoids contact with others. He quits contributing or soliciting suggestions, often withdrawing by way of flight or fight. In choosing flight, he pulls away from the entire situation and the other person. But by staying to fight, he is withdrawing as well if his attack is on the person rather than the problem. The board member who

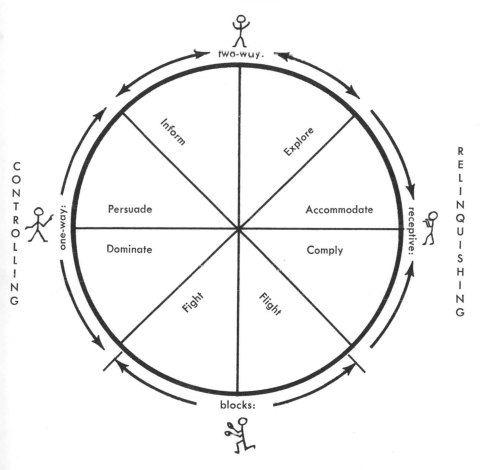

FIGURE 7 — Four Communication Styles

attacks another for his mishandling of a project and then refuses to talk about it further is using both fight and flight to avoid the issue. Some withdrawal statements are:

1. "I see no reason to pursue this problem further. We are wasting our time."
2. "Look, James, if you don't have anything positive to contribute, shut up."
3. "That was a stupid statement."
4. "Let's forget this problem. No one here knows enough to talk about it."

When any pair or group of people are involved in problem solving, analysis or results, counseling, casual conversation, or any other communication, one or several of these styles will be used. All of them may be used by a single person in the process of a discussion.

Figure 7 illustrates the styles and flow of the communication process.

For the developmental style, the communication flows both ways as individuals attempt to share the process. The person with the controlling style does not receive the flow but pushes out with his communication flow through persuasion or dominance. The relinquisher is strictly receptive in his communication, while the withdrawn communicator is essentially rejecting of the process.

How would you classify each statement in the following discussion of the church board? (Circle C, D, W, or R for controlling, developmental, withdrawing, relinquishing for each person's statement)

1. CHAIRMAN: Well, next let's look at a bittersweet problem. Attendance in Sunday school has been growing rapidly in the past few months and it appears to be a continuing trend. But the growth creates problems of spacing. We simply are running out of unused classroom space. Mike, why don't you bring us up to date on this and see what alternatives you would like for us to consider.   C   D   W   R

2. MIKE, SUPERINTENDENT OF SUNDAY SCHOOL: All right, here's the way things look. We have gained an average of fifty people in our Sunday school in the past six months, a spurt of 10%. Most of our classes are now too big for the rooms. I've studied this thing quite a lot, and there is only one alternative. The only thing to do is to build a new wing on our education plant.   C   D   W   R

3. KEN, BOARD MEMBER: We've talked about this before. What's the point of dragging through it again? Let's turn it over to a building committee.   C   D   W   R

4. GORDON, BOARD MEMBER: Now hold on a minute, not so fast. I think we ought to think about this more. Are we sure that this is the only solution? How about holding elective classes and allowing them to meet in homes? What about buying a trailer-house type building — one of these prefab type structures? Maybe we can use the auditorium or the kitchen for rooms. Let's talk about some of these possibilities.   C   D   W   R

5. KEN: Well, okay, whatever the rest of you want to do is all right with me.   C   D   W   R

6. RICHARD, BOARD MEMBER: My opinion is that we should avoid a building program right now. We've got too many things going already. Let's move a class into the auditorium and divide one that's too big and put half of it in the kitchen area. That's the way to handle this problem.   C   D   W   R

7. MIKE: That's no good and you know it. You and your stupid conservatism. You're always against progress.   C   D   W   R

8. RICHARD: I resent that. Okay, it's your problem; you solve it yourself.   C   D   W   R

9. JAMES: Now men, let's not get upset about this thing. We all need to look at it, get everybody's views, and see if we can come up with a solution. Clay, you're in charge of property; what do you think?   C   D   W   R

This gives us a sample of communications to look at.

Statement 1 by the chairman is a developmental comment. He is encouraging others to talk, to seek mutual understanding of the problem, and to look for new approaches to the solution of the problem. This style is usually the best, particularly in opening a discussion.

In statement 2, Mike is using a controlling style. He assumes that his approach is best and tries to impose that position on the group, rather than pursuing alternatives. The controlling style is usually second best when compared with the developmental style. It may be an appropriate style for use at the end of a discussion when commitment is needed to the decision that the group has made.

In statement 3, Ken uses withdrawal comments. He desires to avoid the issue by giving it to a committee. He is not interested in discussing the problem. This style rarely contributes to a solution; however, it may be necessary on occasion when time is short and more important items need attention.

Gordon (statement 4) shifts the discussion back on track with a developmental comment that is very effective in continuing progress on the problem.

Ken comes back in statement 5 with a relinquishing comment. He is prepared to let others take over the problem. Relinquishing is a style that contributes very little to the communication process.

In statement 6 Richard assumes the controlling style in opposition to Mike, but seems equally forceful.

Mike retorts by withdrawing from the topic of discussion to "fight" Richard.

In statement 8 Richard joins him in the withdrawal. Now the discussion is totally away from the topic at hand. No direct contribution can be made by these comments. However, when the feelings are there, it is much better to get them out and deal with them rather than to have them smolder beneath the surface. If the men had stewed in private, they would have lost the ability to contribute meaningfully because of their unexpressed resentment.

In statement 9 James takes the usual reaction to get the discussion back on course with a developmental statement. A developmental statement is needed, but this one does not seem to be the best possible. A new problem involves the conflict between Mike and Richard. James should have directed a developmental statement to that problem, brought it to a resolution, and then continued with the classroom issue. In solving the resentment problem, he might have averted many future flare-ups and augmented the closeness and fellowship of his board.

As we see from this discussion, the developmental style is the most beneficial to the communication process, and is an indispensible tool of the church leader. This style should be used when a joint commitment is important, when there are differences of opinion, or when innovation is needed and no one person has all of the facts. The controlling style is useful when one person has most of the information and experience on the problem, speed of decision making is important, and unity is not necessary to the issue. Relinquishing is useful only when a problem is being discussed on which a person has no knowledge or interest. It is doubtful that withdrawal is ever directly helpful in the solution of a problem. However, if one is frustrated and hostile about a situation, it is usually best to deal with that feeling rather than merely suppressing or trying to hide it.

From our discussion it should now be obvious that communication is no simple process. It involves almost every facet of human motivation, perception, and ability. The leader needs to take careful note of this process and attempt to develop his communication skill.

10

Overcoming Resistance to Change

$\mathbf{A}$ny organization must change if it is to survive. This has been an accepted fact of business for fifty years. Churches of today are beginning to recognize that their survival is now in question, for in recent years, almost all of the major denominations have experienced a reduction in membership and contributions. Our youth are dropping away from the church, and unlike those of former generations, they are not returning.

CHURCH ADMINISTRATION DEMANDS CHANGE

Handling change is an integral part of the job of leadership. The success of an organization is dependent in large part upon its ability to innovate. Change is definitely a part of the basic fabric of the operation of a church. Operational problems require the church to change from the approach that produces the problems. Gaps between the performance level of the church and its performance objectives call for a change in performance in order to meet these objectives.

Some churches are required to change as their increased growth produces greater complexity, more diversity, and greater formality.

These are unplanned changes that occur as a natural outgrowth of increasing size. In order to avoid the detrimental effects of growth on the personal and spiritual fulfillment of its members, the church must be innovative in changing its forms of worship and study. Its leaders must establish an organizational structure that will handle complexity; the church must build strong fellowship groups; it must establish a free flow of communication throughout the congregation; it must involve all members; it must increase its full-time staff. It must take every possible step to build a fellowship of love and closeness in spite of growth.

A church must change in order to overcome the insidious stagnation that can grip a program or an entire church body. If such stagnation develops, change becomes more difficult. With each passing week and month, the members become more entrenched in the sluggish mode of operation, sometimes requiring a window-shattering blast to arouse them. But they are more likely to respond only to a diligent, patient leader who will seek out those who are alive to a challenge to action. He must build dynamic programs around them: as these programs make their impact, other people will begin to awaken and assume a vital role. Every church of every age has found the necessity for change in its forms (while holding fast to foundational principles), but never before has the need been so apparent as it is today.

Change or Perish in a Changing Society

Today, the church stands as a rock in a stream of social change. The rush of change is wearing away its surface at an ever-increasing rate as changes in society create new demands on the church. Our attention has recently been drawn to these changes because of the rapid rate of change in the last decade. Because most of the forms and traditions of today's churches were formulated about a century ago, they rarely meet the needs of Christian worship and study within a society that is so vastly different from that of a century ago.

Suppose for the moment that you have the opportunity to live two lives, one typical of life a century ago, and the other typical of contemporary society. You were born in 1845 into a large family of eight children. Your family lives on the farm and you work long hours in the fields together. Your father supervises the work as well as the home and spiritual lives of the family with a firm but gentle hand. Your family spends many hours together, forming a close loving unit. As your father reads from the Bible aloud to you each evening, you realize that he has a sincere regard for the Scripture and a respect for God, even though he does not verbalize his feelings.

You expect to go through the eighth grade in school after which you will work on the family farm until you are married. By that time you plan to have enough saved to buy a small acreage and to begin building your own farm. You probably will always live within this same community, not having thought much about any other arrangement. The community seems closely knit and everyone has his particular social position. The community and church leaders are one and the same; consequently, their authority and judgment are rarely challenged.

Since the population of your community and your state is sparse, your church is small, consisting of one room in which you all gather on Sunday morning at ten o'clock. By this time your chores are finished for the day and you can enter into a relaxed worship. Since your own education is limited, you particularly enjoy the sermons. You know that you could never understand the Bible by yourself with its difficult phrasing, but the pastor has studied it for many hours. Everyone in church knows everyone else; visitors are rare, with the exception of a sporadically attending neighbor who will occasionally get up on a Sunday morning with the urge to go to church and surprise everyone.

Now, examine the properties of your second life. You are the only son in a family of four. Your dad is an accountant for a large corporation and your mother is a nurse in a local clinic. They met while in college and were married shortly after graduation. You were born two years later. Your family has moved frequently during your life as the result of transfers or job changes. When Dad finds time to be with you, he will usually play a game that you like or will take you on an outing. Sometimes he is a firm disciplinarian; at other times he ignores your antics or plays along as a chum. In your family, everyone has a part in decision making. If you are deciding on where to spend a vacation, everyone can give his suggestion. As a matter of fact, if you and your sister can agree, the two of you will probably win out.

Your dad has already started your college savings account and you will be able to go to the school of your own choosing. The community is not important to you. You rarely see your next-door neighbor. In fact, you have little interest in returning to this location after college. As a teenager, the most important people to you are your school friends. Later when you are in college, your family will become very remote from your life.

These changes in society demand a new role for the church — not new theology or doctrine, but new methods and practices. As the church methods and traditions of the last century were oriented to the spiritual and personal needs of its people, so today's church must also structure its practices to be compatible with the nature of contemporary man. It must build an environment which will stimulate today's Christians to grow in spiritual maturity. Let's look at the changes reflected in your two lives in terms of the implications of the major areas of change for the church.

A major area of change in society in the past century has been the *change in the family*. The working mother, the separation of the work life from the family life, the diminishing influence of parents upon the lives of their children, and the early separation of children from the home are factors which have an impact upon the needs and lives of the individual. We do not experience the depth of love and mutual respect in the family or the community that was characteristic of the earlier society. Yet in order to truly understand the nature of God's love and to find a deep devotion for Him, these experiences are essential. Churches today must help to fill this void. They must provide a focal point in which the family will be brought together in a close fellowship of love. As Lawrence Richards has explained, we must place the family at the center of the church structure. We must build our church on the sharing relationship of its people.[1] A church that is "fitted and held together by that which every joint supplies, according to the proper working of each individual part, causes the growth of the body for the building up of itself in love" (Eph. 4:16).

People in our contemporary society have much greater *mobility* than individuals of a century ago. We have few roots. Companies move their employees to suit the needs of the enterprise; career ambitions keep many on the move. This mobility erects a barrier to a "full maturity in love," for love develops only as we share the life we have in Christ with others. Time and continued sharing help it to blossom and mature. The church must provide a basis for rapidly integrating new families into its fellowship and functioning. It must build depth involvement of small groups exploring the Bible and sharing their burdens.

Increased education and social complexity add to the demands for change. As people become more highly educated they become more confident of their own judgment and less tolerant of those whose actions assume that they are inferior. They demand to be involved, and to have a stronger voice in the church. We are no longer satisfied with a church service or a Sunday school class in which one person is assumed to have all of the valid ideas worth sharing with us. We seek to enter into study as equals, mutually sharing our insights and problems.

The form of leadership is in the midst of change. Warren Bennis points out that the irrepressible tide of our social structure is dissolving bureaucratic forms of organization and replacing them with democratic ones.[2] Likert, in a report of his survey of top executives of many of the nation's major corporations, disclosed that although they are not currently practicing the participative management style to its fullest, they prefer that style and are attempting to develop it in their companies.[3] The authoritarian rule of the last century is passé, yet our churches of today are based on an autocratic model. If you find yourself thinking

---

[1]Lawrence O. Richards, *A New Face for the Church,* (Grand Rapids: Zondervan Publishing House, 1970), pp. 121-131.

[2]Warren G. Bennis, *Changing Organizations,* (New York: McGraw-Hill, 1966), pp. 16-34.

[3]Rensis Likert, *Human Organization,* (New York: McGraw-Hill, 1967), pp. 27-38.

as you read this, *Our structure is democratic; our people vote on every-thing,* you must ask yourself the honest question *Do they?* Is it not more accurate to say that our people vote to accept or reject decisions of their leaders? They are rarely involved on the ground floor in the process of discovering that a problem exists, analyzing the problem, or selecting from among alternative means of solution. But you say, "How can 500 people get involved in all of this activity; how can they know what is going on in the same way as the leaders who work with the situation daily?" Does not this thought confirm the point — the church is structured on an autocratic model. As most churches are currently organized, the people cannot possibly become involved in setting goals, making decisions, or constructing programs. They are not even aware that most of these events are occurring. Church functioning must be structured around small groups which take responsibility for their own problems, with each group being involved at every level in the decisions for which they are responsible. (See chapter 18 for a development of this concept.)

The *concept of the community* as a close, active unit is disappearing. With it we lose the affiliation and love of others outside the family, as well as the feeling of responsibility for the well-being of others. Our human need for personal interaction is frustrated. We must build the church into an overall community structure that defines limits and bounds for the small groups. Each person must come to see his role as one of caring for the needs of all others in his church community.

The almost overpowering thrust of the concept of these demands for change is that each of them necessitates a return to the fundamental structure of the early church. The change must truly be a renewal. We are compelled to renew the fellowship of love, the small sharing groups, the bearing of one another's burdens, and the fitting together of each part of the body of Christ.

PROFILE OF AN INNOVATIVE CHURCH ORGANIZATION

If we are to meet the needs for change, we must weave into the fabric of our church organization an innovative environment. Let us look at a church which provides such an environment. Unfortunately, we are not describing elements which have been found in any one church. These elements are collected from many churches which contain certain aspects of this environment.

Our ideal church might be found anywhere in America. It might be a rural, suburban, or inner-city church. We shall call it the Brandom Community Church.

As a visitor at BCC you cannot really appreciate its core innovative structure, but you do notice that it is engaged in many creative pro-grams. Most noticeable, however, is the congregation's closeness. They have a sincere and deep-felt love for one another that expresses itself in the quiet greeting of the members as though they were sisters or brothers returning from a few weeks of estrangement. As you talk to them you discover that they are simply brothers and sisters in Christ who have been apart for a week. But as they come together, their feeling of Christian love finds clear joyous expression.

Another thing that strikes you about this church is its regard for its leaders and their concern for the body. You listen to the leaders and you hear two themes of concern laced as a binding thread through every area of decision. They are openly and persistently seeking the mind of God regarding their decisions, but at the same time, they are concerned about their own ministry to the body. Apparently the members have become aware of this attitude. Perhaps it is a natural reaction; in any case, they respond with a show of confidence and respect for their leaders.

Now, you are curious; you want to learn more about this unusual church. You begin talking to the leaders of BCC and find them delighted to talk about their church. As you begin to ask them how they have been able to conceive and implement so many new ideas, you find that they are well aware of the ingredients that have allowed them to bring about change. It readily becomes clear that the innovative environment was a matter of design and not an accident.

The chairman of the board, Dick Richardson, reaches into a desk drawer and pulls out a typewritten document. He describes the content of these pages as the basic beginning point. It represents the means by which the church leaders become alerted to the need for change. Thumbing through, you find several sets of material: (1) first is a concise statement of the general purposes of the church, and (2) next come statements of the specific objectives of the church. Dick points out that the most important thing that they have learned about setting objectives is to do so with careful attention to the guidance of the Scripture. "It is from this basis that I became aware of the necessity for tightening our requirements for the deaconship," he points out. "We had never really considered talking to each candidate about his devotional life until we examined the Scripture as we set our leadership objective." (3) The third section of the document is entitled "Standards." It contains signals of the needs for change. If at any time the leaders find that the church is not measuring up to these signals, they swing into action to see what can be done to bring the church up to the standard. Dick describes a time when they discovered that the youth of the church were falling into open immorality. "On closer examination, we found this to be a symptom of our failure to bring the complete message of Christ to our youth," he explained. "Some of the youth winter camps and family retreats that are going today grew out of the efforts to solve this problem." In effect, the church has a complete alarm system that allows its members to identify needs for improvement. In a few areas they admit they've never been able to bring the church up to their standards but they have never stopped trying. Of course, in their personal Bible study, they will often find an area in which they have not yet established a standard for the church and will discuss it at the next leadership meeting so that the document is in a constant state of renewal.

You soon discover that BCC has borrowed from business leaders in their concepts. Dick explains how they discovered another vital ingredient of the innovative environment — total participation in decision making. Harwood Manufacturing Company has disclosed the key role of total participation in the innovative environment. In an actual situation, work procedures were developed and installed, using three different methods. In the first method a carefully developed work change was introduced to the workers through expert staff people. The people were given ample instruction, but were allowed no participation. The second group was allowed to participate through representatives selected from their members. In the third group, all members participated in the development of the change. All of the group members met with staff men and learned of the need for change, at the same time discussing methods of improving operations. The responses of the three groups to the change were strikingly different. In the first group, results of the change were devastating to the operations. Productivity dropped by one-third of the previous output and remained at this level throughout the thirty days of observation following the change. Aggression against management, conflict with staff engineers, and hostility toward supervisors were in evidence; 17% of the group quit in the first forty days. The results in the second group were only slightly better. In contrast, the total participation group had a rapid recovery of the output rate that had been lost during the adjustment period; they continued to improve to a final level that far exceeded the previous performance level. No signs of resistance or hostility were in evidence and no quits were experienced in the experimental period.[4]

Full participation also in the church is essential to the change process. Any problem or need for improvement that a member discovers can be handled at the level of the responsible worker. If a problem or need is found by BCC board members, the group responsible for the area in which it occurs participates in analyzing the problem and working out solutions. Whenever resistance to change occurs, it is resistance to someone else's ideas. People never resist ideas that they themselves have conceived and nurtured.

Another aspect of the BCC innovative environment is the key role of its change agents. The change agents are of two types: the staff and an innovation and improvement group. Each staff member is viewed as a change agent in his area of responsibility. If an area is functioning

---

[4]Lester Coch and J. R. P. French, Jr., "Overcoming Resistance to Change," *Human Relations*, 1948, vol. 1(4), p. 512.

at an optimal level, he does not get involved. However, if the area needs change, he is a catalyst to that change. He stands as the consultant, expert, stimulant, trainer, or whatever is needed to provide guidance and impetus to change.

The second type of change agent, the innovation and development group, is set up in the organization specifically for the purpose of stimulating innovation and progress. It is the responsibility of this group to discover areas of need for change, focus attention on those needs, and assist those responsible for the specific function to overcome the problems and improve. Like the staff, this group identifies the need for innovation and stimulates it.

The people at BCC have become accustomed to the pattern of innovation and change. To them change is a way of life at the church just as it is in their work and home. They expect it in the same way that many churches have a pattern of resisting it. Not advocating change for its own sake, they nevertheless have come to realize that the fruits of change at BCC produce a church in which they can find warmth, love, fellowship, spiritual guidance, involvement, and a meaningful, challenging place of ministry.

Through this model church we hope that you can identify the key ingredients of a church that possesses the innovative environment. In summary, the church has the following characteristics: (1) It has warmth and closeness among its members. They feel loved in a manner that reduces their concern about change. (2) Theirs is a mutual trust between the leaders and the members that eliminates any fear on the part of members that they might be exploited for the needs of the church leaders. (3) The church has a change system by which its leaders are able to identify the direction in which they should progress. They have guideposts that signal areas for needed improvement. And the church focuses its creative energies toward creative improvement. (4) The members of the church participate fully in the process of change. (5) Change agents in the person of the staff and an innovation and development group are actively pursuing the challenge of innovation. (6) The church body has become acclimated to a pattern of innovation and change.

Overcoming Personal Resistance

Having examined the approaches by which an organization may bring about systematic change, let us now explore the phenomenon of resistance to change from the standpoint of the individual. We have often heard the comment "People naturally resist change." This comment is false. People do not resist change by nature any more than they accept change by nature. The concept of a natural resistance to change stems from the observation that people do in fact quite often reject change. In the church the resistance to change may stem from the idea that the existing forms and traditions were structured by the New Testament; of course, many of them were, but many were not. Many in the church are unwilling or unable to distinguish between these.

As we have seen in chapter 8, our attitudes, perceptions, and behaviors are our means of gratifying our basic needs. As human beings we tend to react to proposals for change in the way that we expect will produce the greatest satisfaction and minimize our frustration. If the change offers greater gain for us, we are strongly inclined to accept it. It is as simple as that. The preponderance of the tendency to resist change grows out of the fact that the *status quo* offers familiarity and removes risk. The present situation was chosen at some time in the past because it had certain positive features for us. We hesitate to give it up for an unknown. If we are basically insecure, our fear of failure will heighten our resistance to change.

How do we deal with such resistance? Many leaders who have assumed that resistance is a natural characteristic of man have resorted to force, pressure, or gimmicks. Actually these tactics only raise hostility. They may gain a public acquiescence, but privately the person will subtly sabotage the change with passivity or hidden retaliation. Paul Lawrence tells of a manager who boasted of a foolproof gimmick for gaining agreement to change. He would leave an obvious flaw in his proposal to his men, and, as predicted, the men quickly pointed out the error. The manager made the correction, and the change was accepted. However, later he discovered that the men were aware of what he was doing and had no trust in him. They exhibited hostility and aggression toward him.[5]

The salesman's bag often includes an array of such gimmicks designed to manipulate, disarm, or deceive the one to be influenced. Although they may work for the one-time contact, they are disastrous in the continuous church setting. Playing dumb, getting the other person to think that it was his idea, appealing to the fear of embarrassment, or using your friendship as an inducement are examples of gimmicks that provide a poor basis for a true support of the change or a lasting relationship with the person influenced.

Overcoming resistance to change in a person is not simple. We need several things going for us. Perhaps the most crucial is that the person whom we wish to accept the change must trust us. He must believe that we are sincere and honest in proposing a change that will benefit him or his group, having confidence that we will not deceive or trick him. He must clearly understand the consequences of the change and their effects on him. If possible, the change should be made so clear to him that he can visualize the effects that it will have. He should be able to

---

[5]Paul Lawrence, "How to Deal with Resistance to Change," in G. E. Dalton, et al., *Organization Change and Development,* (Homewood, Ill.: Irwin-Dorsey, 1970), pp. 181-197.

"try it out" in his imagination. The environment for change should be secure and nonthreatening. An individual is more likely to accept change if he feels secure. Relationships in the church should build his self-confidence in his ability to handle the unknown.

Another valuable asset is the support of a reference group. If the group of friends or associates of the individual accept the change and recommend it to him, he is likely to accept it as well. He is even more likely to accept the change if his reference group is so convinced that they apply pressure for his acceptance.

In a long-term relationship the person will be less resistant to change if he has found that such proposals in the past have supported the gratification of his personal and spiritual needs. With each new success his resistance to the next proposal is diminished.

PART THREE

The Building Up of the Body of Christ:

The Challenge of Guiding the Church Organization

11

The Church Organism and Community

As church leaders we are instructed to build up the body of Christ — to assure that the purposes of the church are fulfilled to the maximum. Three questions immediately arise: What is the church? What are its purposes? How can these purposes best be fulfilled? The scriptural church is an organism rather than an organization; it is a community rather than an institution.

THE CHURCH AS AN ORGANISM

The church organism "fitted and held together by that which every joint supplies, according to the proper working of each individual part, causes the growth of the body for the building up of itself in love" (Eph. 4:16). The church has been supplied with members and each member has a function in ministry — mutually interacting with others in the work of the church body. All of the members are joined and knit together into a complex unit. If each part of this unit is working together, it flourishes and builds itself toward maturity; however, if certain members withdraw into inactivity, they become atrophied and the body becomes handicapped and weak. No doubt the human body was taken as an analogy for the church organism because it is the most complex, efficient, and beautiful mechanism known to exist. The properly functioning church has a complex of working parts and functions — intricate, deep in meaning and purpose, vital. When it is operating properly, the church body is efficient in its work: its energy is directed toward significant needs; few resources are wasted; it is able to focus on areas of maximum need. Most striking of all is the beauty with which each element is integrated into a whole, serving not its own isolated ends but the common interests of the entire church community.

The church of today is failing to fulfill its purposes largely because it has ceased to be an organism. A church in which one person preaches, a few teach, and a few others work in an administrative ministry, but the vast majority simply listen, learn, and follow without becoming functioning members of the body, is not an integrated organism. Too many of the members are forced to become parasitic, taking energy from, rather than contributing to, the life of the organism. In addition, the parts that are working in the church are all too often not integrated into an operative whole. Each is doing an act of service quite independently of other workers. The deacons may be unaware of the work in Christian education or youth activities, or the teachers of youth may be oblivious to a family relations program. As a consequence, each worker may be only incidentally or even negatively affecting the whole body. In the face of the demands of today's society, the survival of the church is dependent upon its being "fitted and held together by that which every joint supplies, according to the proper working of each individual part" to fulfill its purposes in Christ.

THE CHURCH AS A COMMUNITY

The scriptural church is a distinctive community of closely bound believers. The early church was distinctive in the love of its members for one another. Christ had told His followers, "All men will know that you are My disciples, if you have love for one another" (John 13:35). No one who has read the New Testament can doubt that this love was indeed a mark of the Christian community. Theirs was a beautiful relationship in which the strength of inner Christian love poured forth not just to a few, but, as Paul expressed in his epistle to the Philippians, it was *felt for all.*

The community is unified into a common bond of faith "with all humility and gentleness, with patience, showing forbearance to one another in love, being diligent to preserve the unity of the Spirit in the bond of peace" (Eph. 4:2, 3). We are unified not only in Christ, but also in caring for one another. This is not to be limited to the emotional or intellectual realm but extended to the level of mutual needs and interests. "God has so composed the body, giving more abundant honor to that member which lacked, that there should be no division in the body, but that the members should have the same care for one another. And if one member suffers, all the members suffer with it; if one member is honored, all the members rejoice with it" (1 Cor. 12:24-26). We are to be bound so closely in Christian unity that we are one in suffering and in joy. This is true communication in the deepest sense of the word.

The church is a community with concern and mutual sharing in which people become involved in one another's lives. "Let us consider how to stimulate one another to love and good deeds, not forsaking our own assembling together, as is the habit of some, but encouraging one another; and all the more, as you see the day drawing near" (Heb. 10:24, 25). In our concern we "bear one another's burdens" (Gal. 6:2), not eager to find another Christian in sin, but desiring to build one another up in the faith. Like the early church, we are to meet frequently with each person, encouraging and exhorting one another as a body of equals as we confront common problems.

The church community is distinctive in that its fellowship is not only on the horizontal level — with others — but also vertical — with God: "that you also may have fellowship with us; and indeed our fellowship is with the Father and with His Son Jesus Christ" (1 John 1:3). By this means our fellowship becomes complete, as we fellowship with God. This close community is not only teaching and exhorting but sharing in fellowship as we sing "psalms and hymns and spiritual songs, singing with thankfulness in [our] hearts to God" (Col. 3:16).

The community of believers is distinctive in its values. Its values are on things that transcend the earth (Col. 2:2, 3; 3:2, 3) and are antithetical to those of the world (Col. 2:5-25 and Galatians 5 and 6). The values of the community are lofty even in the eyes of those who make themselves enemies of the Cross. The church community is to maintain these values clearly in perspective, to keep themselves true to the values, to teach them in truth, and to discipline those of the body who transgress them.

The church community is to encourage and train its members in carrying forth the Gospel of Christ. The community holds a partnership in the Gospel (Phil. 1:5), provides mutual support in presenting the Gospel, (Phil. 4:14-17), and encourages and instructs one another in the work of spreading the Gospel (Phil. 1:27).

THE CHALLENGE OF TODAY'S CHURCH

This, then, is the church: a dynamic, integrated, complex body of believers bound together in a beautiful fellowship of love, sharing the hardships and trials of the Christian life, supporting and exhorting one another, rejoicing in a relationship of deep devotion and worship for God, holding fast to our common values, and doing all this through the hope and love of Christ Jesus.

The church must not become a social institution whose goals are embodied in the accomplishment of some visible, external ends. It must not become enmeshed in its own organization and property. It must not yield to the impulse to strive for an abstract pan-human good. Rather, it must conceive its purpose, organize itself, set its goals, and handle its resources in such a way as to fulfill its true meaning and essence in the twentieth century as it did in the first century.

Our problem today is to bring a renewal of these basic forms into the church life. Each church must do so within its own environment and with the people that are uniquely its own. Each church is supplied by God with particular joints and parts to make up the total working body within His plan. The members may be well-educated, professional people or people of lower education; they may be wealthy, poor, or in-between; they may have an abundance of administrative, teaching, and other gifts for full church functioning or only a few gifts. The church may be large or small. It may be an inner city, suburban, or rural church. The local citizenry may be stable or mobile. It may be located in a cosmopolitan region with an intellectual focus or in a pragmatic, working society. These factors are compatible, in the providence and purpose of God, with the work that He plans for the church as a close, loving, functioning body.

Whatever the particular environment or people of the church, it must stay true to the scriptural form of the church as an organism and a community. It must define its objectives with the intent of fostering these church attributes in its unique manner. If the church is small and rural, it will find less difficulty in establishing the community atmosphere than the larger urban church; however, it may have greater difficulty in developing the church as a fully integrated body in which every member is contributing to the whole. The large church may find that the truly close community atmosphere will be obtained within smaller units such as prayer groups, Bible study groups, and sharing groups. The total church will grow closer as community is established in this way, and as the effects spread among, as well as within, groups to finally include the entire congregation. Each church should recognize its own needs and establish its objectives to build itself up in its areas of weakness. In previous chapters of this book we have been primarily concerned with building the church as a community. In the remaining chapters we will direct our attention to the organismic problems involved in integrating the members into a working, unified whole. We will deal with the objectives, plans, and goals which bind the church into a total unity; the structuring of the organization that will allow all of the members (parts) to be knit together into a smoothly working body; the proper scriptural form and freedoms for church authority, power, and decision making, and the handling of supportive financial and physical resources.

12

Objectives of the Church

The objectives of a church are its means of translating the scriptural purposes into directions. In Wonderland, Alice said to the Cheshire cat, " 'Would you tell me, please, which way I ought to go from here?' 'That depends a good deal on where you want to get to,' said the cat. 'I don't much care where,' said Alice. 'Then it doesn't matter which way you go,' said the cat." As with Alice, so with the church: without objectives, we may find ourselves moving in any direction.

Objectives focus upon the unique roles that a church should take in its place and time. Whereas the organismic and community purposes of the church are within the constraints of basic scriptural forms, the specific directions of a local church are within its freedoms. Many of the problems of churches today arise as they establish objectives that are tangential with the scriptural forms. Certain of its objectives, such as those to make a contribution to the social welfare of our secular society, to have a large attendance in congregational worship service, and to have beautiful and functional facilities, may be of value at a secondary level, but they must never be placed as primary church objectives. As a church establishes its objectives, it must keep in focus its fundamental purposes so that each objective will be totally integrated with these scriptural forms. Every church should examine these forms

137

and analyze its own objectives to determine whether it is striving toward the New Testament concept of the church.

PRIMARY OBJECTIVES

In order to maintain a proper perspective, a local church must distinguish between primary and secondary objectives. Primary objectives are statements by your church of the manner in which it should pursue its organismic and community purposes. Secondary objectives are statements of the kinds of supporting functions and resources that it must have in order to fulfill its primary objectives, viz., physical resources, financial resources, organization and personnel, and public responsibility. No matter how important these secondary objectives may appear to be, they must not take our attention away from the primary ones. We may have the best possible church staff, superb facilities, and a huge budget, but if they are used for the wrong purposes or if they become ends in themselves, they are meaningless and ours is a most pathetic situation.

Although we cannot prescribe the primary objectives for your local church, perhaps it will be helpful to suggest the following as some areas in which objectives are needed:

1. *Spiritual growth of Christians.* What are your objectives as a church to help one another to grow toward spiritual maturity?
2. *Recognition, development, and use of spiritual gifts.* What are the objectives of your church that are directed toward the spiritual gifts of all of your members?
3. *Unification of the body in fellowship and service.* What are your church's objectives in bringing unity among the many parts of the body of Christ?
4. *Growth of Christian love.* What are your objectives for building love and mutual concern among members for the well-being of one another?
5. *Mutual sharing and involvement in one anothers' lives.* What are your objectives for the interaction and involvement of your church community into one another's lives?
6. *Maintenance of Christian values.* What are your objectives to assure that Christian values are maintained by your members?
7. *Spreading of the Gospel.* What are your objectives for encouragement, training, sending, and supporting members who witness locally or abroad?

These are the bases for our existence as a church; we should direct our efforts, our resources, and our time totally to these primary objectives.

SECONDARY OBJECTIVES

Secondary objectives have no inherent value beyond their contribution to the attainment of primary objectives. While it is true of primary objectives, it is even more emphatically true of secondary objectives that they are unique to the environmental and internal characteristics of each local church. Secondary objectives may be organized into four useful categories, viz., physical resources, financial resources, organization and personnel, and public responsibility. In a small church of one-hundred or fewer members, these areas may be handled very informally. As a church grows in size, the amount of attention that must be given to these factors rapidly multiplies.

The *physical resources* of the typical church are a crucial factor in its strategy in fulfilling its basic objectives. Often this role is given a sacred status. We often consider the expansion of the church building program to be both a symbol of church life and an essential component of an effective church. In contrast, the early New Testament churches were able to fulfill their purposes with amazing success without a form of permanent physical structure. Thus, at the outset it is important for a church to determine clearly whether it will build its approaches to fulfilling its primary objectives and purposes around a large physical complex or establish a home-based approach.

The present system evolved in part from the Roman Catholic traditions of the large cathedral and in part from the public education systems. It is interesting to note that in his innovative treatment of public school education, George Leonard predicts that the educational program of youth in the twenty-first century will be based in the home. He points out the contribution of mass communication and self-instruction techniques as a basis for gaining routine facts, and the discussion and exploration approaches as a basis for gaining creativity, judgment, and social development.[1] If such a trend develops in the public school, church schools will very probably fall into a similar pattern. The success of the early church and its obvious advantage in fostering Christian love and fellowship speaks strongly for the home-circle ministry. Yet there are several reasons why this approach might not succeed in the present age. People expect a large structure; they associate smallness with an initial phase of church life, a denominational characteristic (e.g., United Brethren), or failure to grow. It seems quite likely that such attitudes are so firmly fixed that most established churches would not be pleased with the results of shifting to a home-circle church; however, they might choose to establish more of their programs in this way, including activities such as Sunday school, prayer meetings, youth activities, and family worship. On the other hand, a new church would be far more ready to pursue a home-circle plan if it follows this concept from the beginning. It hardly seems appropriate to bring division and conflict over the question of how best to build a unified community. Nevertheless, we must avoid at all cost the con-

---

[1] George Leonard, *Education and Ecstasy,* (New York: Delacorte Press, 1968), pp. 174-228.

clusion that a large physical church complex is an end in itself and that it should be the focal point of objectives.

After the basic approach has been established, objectives regarding the type of physical structure for fulfilling the primary objectives should be considered separately to determine the facilities that each of the objectives will require.

Financial resources are also critical to success in reaching primary objectives. Financial considerations have a great impact upon the emphasis that will be placed on each primary objective. Your manner of allocating financial resources and determining the method of obtaining the resources has a strong influence on the attitudes of the members. Once again it becomes important to establish the best approach to fulfilling the primary objectives as a preliminary step to consideration of this secondary one. Certain approaches to fulfilling primary objectives are more expensive than others; yet the cheapest approach may not be the one that is most desired. Foreign missions are more expensive than local witnessing of members; still, both are essential purposes of the church.

Organization and personnel objectives should be helpful in guiding the church in the coordination of its efforts toward the recognition, development, and use of spiritual gifts and toward the activities of church members in fulfilling other primary objectives. We are concerned with the establishment of an organization and the development of people who can most effectively fulfill the purposes of the church. The approaches to church organization will be discussed in the next chapter.

Public responsibility includes two important areas. First is the question of the responsibility of the church as an influence on the moral and social influences confronting society. The church should clearly delineate its stand on such public issues as: (1) poverty, (2) racial discrimination, (3) pollution, (4) population control, (5) crime and the law, (6) civic rebellion, and (7) moral decay. It may choose to take no stand at all, but it should do so as a matter of decision and not as a result of apathy. A second area is that of publicity, the means by which the activities of the church are communicated to the secular community. As such it is basically of value in supporting the spread of the Gospel at the local level.

How Do We Set Objectives?

What should be our objectives? Who should set the objectives? These are questions that face the church as it begins to establish objectives. Objectives should be specific, concrete, and unique to each church. No two churches will have objectives that are identical. Real direction and a foundation for future actions and decisions will be provided if objectives are sufficiently concrete in nature. The objectives should be sufficiently clear and succinct in order to establish a backdrop for determining whether or not a particular program is within the desired direction in which the church wishes to move.

In deciding what the objectives should be, the church has a distinct advantage over other organizations, for it has the Scripture as a master plan within which it can carve its rightful place. Able to provide a permanence and applicability to both today's and tomorrow's problems, the Scripture establishes the authority and stability that are valuable characteristics for any set of objectives.

The persons developing the objectives should have time to devote much effort to the task and to understand the operations of the church. The group who would be most capable of developing the objectives would be the official board of the church, since it establishes policy and makes major decisions. Small board or church groups study each primary objective area and arrive at a set of recommendations for the board.

Upon approval of primary objectives, the board should establish similar groups for the development of objectives in the secondary areas to be integrated with the primary objectives as they are developed. The board's objectives are then taken to the congregation for approval. The review of these objectives by the congregation should help to bring unity to the fundamental concepts of the church's mission and to avoid future controversy about whether a particular program or decision is appropriate. The objectives should also help to resolve differences of opinion about future issues as they arise. Church objectives become the focal point for establishing long-range plans, annual plans, church goals, and organization structure.

13

Building the Organization Structure

Now that you have decided where you are going, it is time to decide how to get there. You must determine the proper deployment of people, functions, and resources to accomplish your objectives effectively. This requires much more than drawing a clean and systematic organization chart or describing well-designed jobs. We are confronted with a far more complex task — that of setting into motion an organization that works smoothly and efficiently toward its desired ends. It is not enough simply to lay out in theory how the organization should function, i.e., who should make particular decisions and who should perform certain tasks. We must go beyond that to anticipate how the organization will operate on a day-to-day basis and to be of influence in that operation. We must attempt to build an organization that is not simply well-structured, but one that will function effectively, as well.

In the middle ages the practice of surgery was left in the hands of the barber. The physician prescribed the treatment and was often on hand for the treatment, but he had neither the mental attitude nor the sharp knife required to perform the task. Indeed, his oath not to inflict bodily harm was often interpreted literally so as to prevent the physician even from watching. Following the prescribed procedure, he would station himself well out of range of the struggle and read instructions to the barber from a Latin text. Not understanding a word of Latin, the barber would inflict whatever tortures seemed appropriate to the occasion. If by some twist of fate the patient survived, the doctor claimed the credit. If he died, the barber received the blame.

As we begin to write about the structuring of a church organization, we seek to avoid the role of the physician, that of writing concepts which cannot be applied, recommending practices which have no relationship to the reality of the situation, and of remaining aloof from the struggle of structuring the organization. We shall attempt to emphasize the practice rather than the abstract theory.

Some of the most critical characteristics of effective organizations and of ineffective ones are outlined below. Our task in establishing the organization structure requires that we emphasize effective characteristics and move away from those that are ineffective. The following list of characteristics was developed by the authors from a review of the research done by the Institute of Social Research under the direction of Rensis Likert.[1]

CHARACTERISTICS OF INEFFECTIVE AND EFFECTIVE ORGANIZATIONS

Organizations which are ineffective in that they tend to have low member involvement and interest and lack of performance results hold in common the following restrictive characteristics:

- General meetings are large and formal.
- There is little candid personal interaction of the leaders with the membership.
- There is little board participation in departmental meetings.
- Leaders are more active than in effective organizations.
- Some members are not personally familiar with others, thus reducing the warmth and openness of the interaction.
- Board members are often viewed as visitors of departmental meetings rather than as members.
- Members feel that leaders have little interest in their ideas.
- Members feel little influnce upon the organization.

Organizations that are effective in that they have high member involvement and good results have the following characteristics:

- Members feel more influence and encouragement to be involved in the work from other members than from the board or the organization leader.
- The basic unit for action is the small group.

---

[1]Rensis Likert, *New Patterns of Management,* (New York: McGraw-Hill, 1961), pp. 140-161.

- The optimum size for an effective small group is twelve to twenty persons.
- The board is the basic unit for holding ultimate responsibility for the organization's various functions.
- Communication flow is sustained by having committees and departments linked by common members and by board members.
- Each unit has a person on the board as a member.
- Face-to-face interaction within groups is the basic mode of operation.
- Group meetings are warm, close, and candid with feelings freely expressed in preference to formal meetings where standard rules for motions and discussions are employed.
- There is free flow of communication from the leader of the organization to individual members.
- The organization sustains a minimum number of organizational layers.
- Members feel that the leaders and board members have an attitude of acceptance and support.
- All groups are directly linked to the board by having a board member as its leader or as a member.

Structuring the Official Church Board

What are the implications of these characteristics in building the church organization? The official church board holds a critical and pivotal role that is a key to the total success of the church. This in effect makes the official board directly and ultimately responsible for evangelism, spiritual growth, Christian fellowship and love, the fulfilling of the physical and emotional needs of members, physical resources, financial resources, cost and budgeting, organization and personnel, and public relations. These consitute a weighty group of responsibilities.

The Scripture provides two significant forms for church organization at this point. The first assigns certain responsibilities to elders and other responsibilities to deacons (1 Tim. 3:1-13 and Titus 1:5-9), the second prescribes the requirement for unity in the church (Eph. 4:1-16). Many churches emphasize the first form and have two church boards: an elders' board to guard the doctrine, to feed the flock, and to exert discipline, and a deacons' board to care for the material needs and problems. Even more commonly do churches emphasize the call for unity by assigning the total scope of responsibilities to a given board which has the duties of both deacons and elders. In one sense they are right, i.e., the unity of the church can be maintained only by having a unified church board that can bring together the various types of issues and problems and integrate them toward a unified solution. It seems that these forms taken together require that the church appoint certain men as elders with the responsibilities of this office and other men as deacons with their appointed responsibilities and that both the deacons and the elders meet as a unified official board. The elders will occasionally have to meet as a separate group (as an elders' board or council) to con-

144

sider issues that are uniquely their own, as will the deacons; but they should also assure the unity to the total church effort by periodically meeting as a single official church board.

While maintaining leadership of the church, the board members must avoid the tendency to do everything themselves. They should establish committees or departments through which the decisions and activities of each area are channeled. The question "What committees and departments are needed?" seems appropriate at this point. So that no objective is slighted, responsibility for accomplishing each objective should be assigned to an organizational unit. The number and size of these organizational units depend upon the size of the church. First the organization structure for a church of 250 or more members with a physical plant and a wide range of ministries will be considered. Subsequently, the structuring of a small church organization will be discussed. Figure 8, p. 146, depicts the array of committees which branch off the official board. The committees to be established are a matter of complete local church freedom; however, with the intent of stimulating your thinking regarding the needs of your church, we will describe some of the committees and departments that will have utility for many churches:

Evangelism Committee. This committee is responsible for the local evangelism activities of the church. Visitation programs, evangelism training, and evangelism teams are examples of activities which this committee may plan and sponsor in order to support personal evangelism among the church members.

Missions Committee. The foreign missions program is the evangelism effort that is the responsibility of this committee. It conducts missions emphasis weeks, special missionary visits, missions giving or faith-promise programs, missions prayer emphasis, and similar activities. It becomes the responsibility of this committee to make the missionary outreach of the church a vital and vibrant one that not only builds enthusiasm for support of missionaries, but also encourages young people of the church to consider the mission call for their own life.

Sunday School Department. The Sunday school is so well-established as a part of church life that its purpose in the scope of the church objectives is often overlooked. Its primary role is one of fostering spiritual growth, partially as an instrument for evangelism. In view of these objectives, the Sunday school should attempt in a direct way to build a daily prayer, Bible study, and devotional period, seeking to be an instrument for enriching the members in their knowledge of God. In addition, the Sunday school classes become a focal point for fellowship. In larger churches the Sunday school becomes more significant in this fellowship effort. The total congregation is often too large to be the basis for a meaningful, warm, and close fellowship. If the Sunday school classes are small enough, they can bridge this gap.

Children's Church Department. Children's Church serves a similar

145

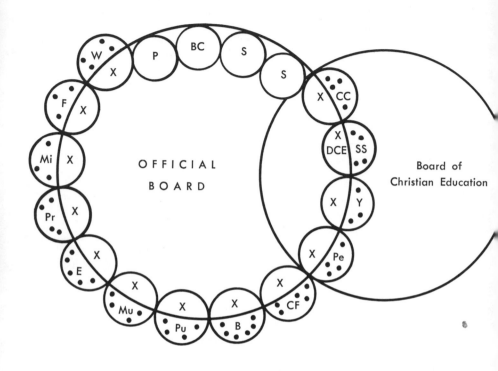

X	BOARD MEMBERS	Pu	PUBLICITY COMMITTEE
•	Department and Committee	B	BENEVOLENCE COMMITTEE
	Members	CF	CHRISTIAN FELLOWSHIP
BC	BOARD CHAIRMAN		COMMITTEE
P	PASTOR	Pe	PERSONNEL COMMITTEE
W	WORSHIP COMMITTEE	Y	YOUTH COMMITTEE
F	FINANCE COMMITTEE	DCE	DIRECTOR OF CHRISTIAN
Mi	MISSIONS COMMITTEE		EDUCATION
Pr	PROPERTY COMMITTEE	SS	SUNDAY SCHOOL
E	EVANGELISM COMMITTEE	CC	CHILDREN'S CHURCH
Mu	MUSIC COMMITTEE	S	STAFF MEMBERS

FIGURE 8 — The Linking System of Church Organization

purpose for children during the morning worship hour as the Sunday school. It also helps to prepare the older groups to enjoy and benefit from the regular worship service as they reach the age of going into that service.

Worship Committee. This committee is responsible for the arrangements for such aspects of the worship services as decorations, ushering, seating, materials, and similar items.

Christian Fellowship Committee. Men's fellowship, women's fellowship, church recreation, home Bible study groups, retreats, and other fellowship groups are the responsibility of this committee, which organizes and encourages these activities to give opportunity for the work of the Spirit in building Christian love.

Youth Committee. This committee is concerned with the many facets of youth activities and programs, such as training hours, fellowship activities, camp programs, and Christian youth organizations.

Music Committee. Responsibility for choirs, the choice of music, and music personnel is assigned to this committee.

Benevolence Committee. This committee is assigned the difficult task of aiding members of the church in areas of physical and emotional needs. They assume responsibility for the care of widows and orphans, the aged the ill and handicapped, the poor, and those who need emotional support, comfort, or counsel. This function goes far beyond the rather superficial activities that are usually dubbed "benevolence." It is the vital Christian function of caring for others in Christian love.

Property Committee. This committee provides for, maintains, and oversees the use of the lands, improvements, tools, and equipment that are required to fulfill the primary objectives of the church.

Finance and Budget Committee. Planning for determining the financial needs of the church and for obtaining the necessary financial resources is the function of this committee. Being responsible for establishing the type of budget that allows flexibility and control in making expenditures, the committee sets up a reporting system that provides reports to those who must make decisions about operating expenditures.

Personnel Committee. The personnel committee is very crucial to the involvement of members in church activities. The committee should survey the talents of members by questionnaires and interviews in order to plan a development program of service for those who wish to serve (a plan that begins at the individual's current level of experience and carries him into responsibilities that require increased spiritual depth). It should seek to involve a wider scope of people rather than placing a few people in a large number of jobs. The committee is concerned both with the development of the talents of members and the assurance that each job is filled by a capable person.

Publicity Committee. The publicity committee is responsible for making public announcements of those activities of the church that are

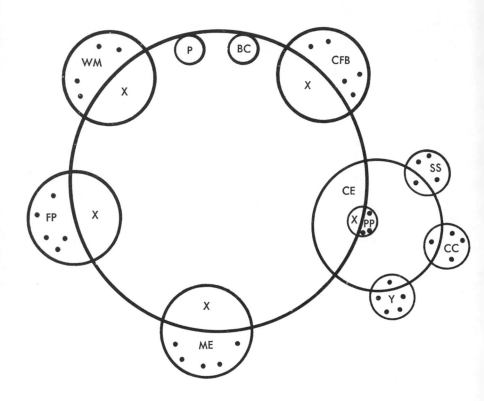

X	BOARD MEMBERS	CFB	CHRISTIAN FELLOWSHIP &
•	Department and Committee		BENEVOLENCE COMMITTEE
	Members	PP	PERSONNEL & PUBLICITY
BC	BOARD CHAIRMAN		COMMITTEE
P	PASTOR	CE	BOARD OF CHRISTIAN
WM	WORSHIP & MUSIC COMMITTEES		EDUCATION
F&P	FINANCE & PROPERTY	Y	YOUTH COMMITTEE
	COMMITTEE	CC	CHILDREN'S CHURCH
ME	MISSIONS & EVANGELISM	SS	SUNDAY SCHOOL
	COMMITTEE		

FIGURE 9 — The Linking System of Church Organization for a Small Church

of interest to the general public. It should seek to attract the interest of the community to the work of the Lord in the church, also concerning itself with communicating ideals, values, and purposes to the people of the community through attempting to present an accurate picture of the church. By this means, it assists the evangelistic efforts of the church.

These thirteen departments and committees may either seem like an excessive number to leaders of small churches or too few for those in larger churches. Some churches will need to combine the functions of some of the committees so that fewer are required. The number of committees is not so critical as the activities. If too few committees are used for a church of a given size, important activities will be ignored.

Figure 9 presents an illustrative organizational system for a church of approximately 150 members. Churches of this size and smaller have the same functions as larger churches, but with smaller numbers of people, programs, facilities, and other resources involved. This allows a single committee to assume responsibility for more than one of the functional areas. Insofar as it is possible, the areas of activity for a committee should be related and compatible.

As the titles for the committees of Figure 9 suggest, in the smaller church the following committees combine the functions of two or more committees for the larger church, the worship and music committee, the finance and property committee, the missions and evangelism committee, the Christian fellowship and benevolence committee, and the personnel and publicity committee. In this suggested structure, the youth committee remains a single unit. The Board of Christian education includes the superintendents of Sunday school, director of children's Church, the personnel and publicity committee chairman and the youth committee chairman.

You may very well ask at this point, "How do I know whether my church has too many or too few committees and departments?" As you were reading the functions of the committees described above, did you note important activities that are being neglected in your church? If so, you either need to assign that function to an existing committee or create another one. You can use an existing committee, provided you have one that is currently responsible for similar activities and is able to handle the increased level of work. The committee to receive the additional activity should have functions that are closely related to the new ones; for example, music activities should not be assigned to the property committee, just as fellowship could not be handled by the finance committee. These functions do not involve the same type of decisions or tasks and therefore they require people with different talents and interests. Unless the church is small (fewer than 200 or 300 active members), it is best to have a separate committee for each of the functional areas discussed above.

The Linking and Coordination of Functions

It is important not only that the vital functions be assigned to a permanent committee for planning and execution, but also that the committees be linked together. The activities must be coordinated through a sharing of problems and ideas among the committees. The best way to provide this unity is to have each committee chaired by a member of the official board. Thus the board is not only a policy-making body, but it also links together all of the activities of the church. This arrangement allows board members to keep their finger on the pulsebeat of the work of the church; simultaneously it allows the workers who have problems or ideas to get them quickly to the board without being lost or garbled by a long chain of communication. Figure 8 (page 146) illustrates the organization of the board in this fashion. In situations where a great deal of coordination is required between two committees, it is good to have one or two people serve concurrently on both.

The church staff carries out certain critical functions and serves in an advisory capacity, performing those functions which require special knowledge, skill, or work on a full-time basis. They should be members of the committees whose functions are related to their work. The work of the staff will be discussed in detail in chapter 17.

The departments and committees should be organized with the same concern for efficiency and smooth communication that has guided the overall organization of the church. We should avoid having too many layers in the organization hierarchy. If you can view the church organization as a hierarchy with each administrative position in a department as a layer, the reason for reduction of these layers may become apparent. Suppose a worker in the children's church decides that he needs an overhead projector. To purchase the item he must go up the organization hierarchy, getting approval at each stage. If there is a department director in his age group, he must gain approval there. Then the request must be taken to the division director by the department director. Assuming that neither of these directors forgets or garbles the message, it finally gets to the children's church director who takes it to the property or finance director for approval. Downward communications follow the same gauntlet. The number of these layers involving transfer of communication should be kept at a minimum. This is especially important in departments such as the Sunday school. Departments within the Sunday school are essential for a large or medium-sized church. However, it is not wise to structure divisions within departments. For example, having a young adult department, a middle adult department, and an older adult department is usually not as effective as simply having one adult department. Even though this department may have a large number of teachers, it does not provide the kind of communication gap and coordination problems that exist when divisional departments are operating. Some churches prefer these divisional departments in order to implement an opening assembly; usually these assemblies are of little value in contributing to the purposes of the church. The smaller Sunday school class seems to provide much better opportunity for study and fellowship than does the opening assembly. Ideally, the Sunday school teachers should be only one step from the board. In this way they can communicate their ideas to the Sunday school superintendent who is a board member via their department superintendent.

The accomplishment of church objectives through these organizational bodies is the next concern in building the organization; these goals may be influenced in some degree by formal, systematic approaches such as job descriptions and organization charts. However, most of the activities of a dynamic organization cannot be programmed or even anticipated. They occur informally. Formal means of building the organization are important; however, they must be viewed as only a first step which inclines a person to fall flat on his face unless other steps keep him in balance. Both formal and informal problems are discussed in the remainder of Part 3.

14

Authority and the Power to Influence

$\mathbf{T}$he scriptural form for church organization includes an authority structure. Those in authority are to rule well, to exhort, to rebuke, and to discipline (1 Tim. 5:17; Titus 2:15). This authority is to be exercised with gentleness, love, faith and purity (1 Tim. 3:3; 4:12). Those who are under this authority are to obey and submit to the leaders, imitate this faith, give them double honor, and are not to despise their acts of leadership (Heb. 13:7, 17). Obviously, the scriptural form places authority in a place of honor and respect. The freedoms regarding the exercise of authority and power are also in evidence. The amount and kind of authority to be used is dependent upon the individual leader, the requirements of the situation at hand, and his social environment.

One of the most pronounced trends of modern society is the movement away from the use of authority. Beginning in the home, the trend toward equalitarian leadership has moved into business and is now a force within churches. The human relations and behavioral sciences have followed this change in our culture since the 1920's. Research in the Hawthorne Electric Company announced the dawning of a new day in business in which people were found to respond to the reduction of authoritarian pressure and the opportunity for all workers to participate in the leadership process. Bennis states that the higher education level, mobility of workers, complexity of organizations, and humanistic values are mounting forces auguring for more participative or democratic leadership.[1] It seems that in today's culture, Paul's instruction to Timothy not to rebuke an older man, but to exhort him as you would a father and to treat younger men like brothers (1 Tim. 5:1), is an important point to emphasize in today's society. With a lessening of the use of authority (particularly harsh authority) in other avenues of society, church leaders will find it increasingly more difficult to use strong authoritarian rule. Gentleness and kindness must temper the use of authority today more than in any other generation.

A second type of freedom that is afforded the leader is in the type of power that his authority rests upon. The scriptural form has reference to the use of two types of power; viz., positional and referent. Positional power is the power invested in a person by virtue of the office that he holds — power of the office. Referent power is given to a person who is respected or held in high regard. According to Scripture, church leaders are to be given this type of power. The Scripture gives complete freedom for the leader in the use of three other types of power — reward, coercive, and expert. Let's see how each of these five types of power operate in practice.

The Use of Positional Power

Mr. Holt, the chairman of the deacon board, wishes to get Mr. Mack, the superintendent of Sunday school, to hold group meetings every quarter as a means of uniting, coordinating, and stimulating Sunday school workers. Holt meets Mack in the hall of the educational wing just before the worship service.

MACK: Say, Jim, we had a good showing in Sunday school today.

HOLT: That's good, Bill; that's a good sign we're growing. I've been thinking about our Sunday school organization. I've decided that it would operate much more smoothly if you call a workers' meeting every quarter.

MACK: Well, it just doesn't seem to me that group meetings are the best way to use the workers' time. Their problems are localized in their classes and departments.

HOLT: It can't hurt them to meet one night a quarter. The Sunday school could use some unification. Bill, as deacon chairman, I want you to start having those quarterly workers' meetings.

---

[1]Warren G. Bennis, *Changing Organizations*, (New York: McGraw-Hill, 1966), pp. 16-34.

In this situation, Holt is using the power of his position as chairman of the deacon board to get an activity going that he thinks is needed. His church constitution apparently gives him the authority to make this decision and to require compliance. If Mack had refused, he would have been at a loss to take further action. Actually, Mack is not likely to refuse to comply unless he is a true rebel. Most people accept positional authority. Yet of how much benefit would you expect the meetings to be? This depends upon the manner in which the authority is received. The responsibility rests with both Mack and Holt. If Holt follows scriptural form and directs in a gentle and loving manner, Mack will probably enter the meetings with confidence and enthusiasm, and they will be effective. But even if Holt's manner is not conducive to building enthusiasm, Mack still has a responsibility to obey and to submit, not only overtly but in his attitude as well. Mack has a responsibility to attempt to do the job well, and to follow Holt's direction out of a love for Christ who is the Head of the Church. Unfortunately, most church workers lack the Christian maturity to submit their attitude and will totally to this scriptural principle, so that it becomes even more imperative for leaders to have the proper attitude and approach.

THE USE OF REFERENT POWER

Referent power depends upon the leader's being highly respected by the one being influenced. We must assume that Mack holds Holt in high regard and wishes to emulate him in order to understand the next scene.

It is the same time and place as before.

HOLT: Looks as though we had good attendance in Sunday school today, Bill. Do you mind if I make a suggestion about an approach to operation of your Sunday school that I think would be good?

MACK: Of course not; please do.

HOLT: It seems to me that if you held quarterly meetings of your workers that these could help your operation.

MACK: Well, I had thought of those, but I don't know. Do you really think they would help?

HOLT: Yes, I do. Why don't you try them?

MACK: Okay. I'll start them this quarter.

Mack respects Holt's opinion beyond his own. In fact, once he knows Holt's view, he refrains from even giving his own side, in order to avoid disagreement with Holt. Many church leaders, particularly pastors, hold this power in their churches. Some leaders with referent power find this a real help in getting their ideas and programs across. Referent power is very effective and tends to get a positive reaction from others unless it is pushed against a strong, rigid position.

Leaders with referent power may also find that it is a handicap to their leadership. While they are really seeking an open, free exploration of problems, they find that their members are too quick to accept their ideas without challenge or consideration of alternatives. The leaders recognize that the problems are suffering from lack of analysis; mistakes are being made which, with the perspective of others, might have been avoided. They find that they must retreat into silence in order for a problem to get a fair hearing. A moderate use of referent power is desirable, but too much can stagnate an organization into becoming a one-man operation.

THE USE OF REWARD POWER

MACK: Say, Jim, our Sunday school attendance is looking pretty good.

HOLT: You're doing a fine job, Bill. It delights me to see the way you've taken hold of that superintendent's job. Surely, the Lord must be pleased at our progress.

MACK: Thanks. It's nice to hear you say that.

HOLT: By the way, your organization of the Sunday school is coming along well, too. There is one thing I think might make things go even smoother — that's the quarterly meetings of workers. I know it would be a lot of work, but I think you could accomplish a lot by having workers' meetings.

In this conversation, Holt is using reward power. He is not being obvious and offering money or promotional opportunities. People don't volunteer for church work for these reasons. He is rather offering recognition and a promise that he will be serving the Lord in a better way. The use of the promise of psychological reward, particularly in the manner used by Holt, can be quite effective. Not only does he gain agreement to carry out the activity, but Mack also enters it with the feeling that it might be a valuable method. He is much more likely to give the activity a fair chance to work.

THE USE OF COERCIVE POWER

Let's have a replay of this scene, but this time using coercive power.

MACK: Good morning, Mr. Holt.

HOLT: Mack, 483 is not anywhere near what we should be doing in Sunday school. Do you think the Lord is satisfied with such mediocrity? I'll tell you what I think is one of the problems. You're not having any meetings with your workers. You ought to have quarterly meetings.

MACK: Oh, I don't think that kind of meeting would help.

HOLT: Sure it will. That's part of the trouble; you're afraid to try out good ideas for improvement. The Lord calls for zeal among His workers. Surely, you can spare one night in the quarter for this effort.

Coercive power is the use of threat of punishment as a means of influencing others. Business managers often use threat of discharge, layoff, or demotion as a pressure point. Holt is threatening in the areas of self-esteem and pleasing God. He is saying that Mack will have low personal esteem and will displease the Lord if he does not hold meetings. The problem with this approach is also fairly predictable. If this approach is used often, Mack will begin to think to himself as a loser, eventually concluding that he is doing a disservice to the church by being a conscientious worker. He may be motivated for a time, but he will eventually do as little as possible to serve out his term. Clearly, coercive power is in conflict with the scriptural form for the use of authority.

THE USE OF EXPERT POWER

Now let's look at Holt as he uses the expert power.

MACK: Say, Jim, Sunday school is looking good today.

HOLT: Yes, you seem to be enjoying your work with the Sunday school pretty well.

MACK: Yes, I guess I do.

HOLT: Would you mind an old head giving you a little advice? I've been in a lot of churches and watched Sunday school superintendents both good and bad. You know one of the ways that the good ones always seem to operate is to hold quarterly meetings. They seem to build a real unity and enthusiasm in the workers that way. I believe this would work for you, too.

Expert power can be very effective for a person who has special knowledge or experience. Expert power runs into problems when the person being influenced feels he is being criticized, especially if he is insecure about his own ability. Unless such a person is approached very cautiously, he may bolt and defend himself to the end.

With this recognition of the existence of several types of power, the question of delegation of authority becomes a difficult one. Traditionally, it was believed that all one need do to delegate authority was to assign a responsibility to a person and give him the legitimate authority in a job description to carry it out. Now it is clear that we are dealing with a multi-faceted process. Even though the job description may give a person the right to decide and act, he may very well be controlled by other sources of power.

VALUES AND DANGERS OF THE USE OF AUTHORITY

The use of authority in the guidance of the activities of church workers has several organizational *advantages*:

– The use of authority facilitates the coordination of activities. If two or more persons or groups must carry out functions which must be phased together, a direct command or at least a strong influence is usually required to blend the functions. Suppose a special program is to be held on Wednesday night, and it is very important to the church that all other activities be suspended so that all the members may be able to attend this program. There is no other method worth consideration than the use of some type of power.

– The use of authority assures that there will be a minimum of confusion. The leader makes his point and the decision is clearly transmitted. There is comparatively little wasted effort or disorder.

– The use of authority assures uniformity. If you wish to have a consistency in educational materials, a decision to use material from a single press for the entire Sunday school can gain this end. Failure to use direct authority here leads to a wide range of approaches and quality of material.

– The use of authority provides security to the leader. With direct authority there is little questioning or disagreeing. The leader can get his decision accepted with little open argument.

– The use of authority is relatively simple. One doesn't need to be a psychologist to figure out how to give an order. Little understanding of people is required.

From these advantages it is apparent that the use of authority is an important tool in every leader's bag. He must use authority in many situations in order to accomplish a desired end.

Yet as we review the disadvantages of authority, it will become obvious that a church that uses authority as the primary method of leadership will reach only a small proportion of its total potential. The following are the key *disadvantages* of the use of authority.

– Authority tends to be met with resistance. Since the use of power places the person being led in a dependency role, he often resents this position. His self-worth is threatened. Although not exhibiting open hostility, he may often resolve to do no more than the minimum. In some cases, the member will even sabotage the operation because of his resentment. It is regrettable when sabotage occurs in the church, for it is directly contrary to scriptural principles.

– Reliance on authority also results in a stagnation of members. The dependency fostered by authority tends to cause the members to sit back and wait for orders or suggestions. Thus they lose confidence in their own ability and certainly do not grow in their ability to assume greater responsibility.

– Although conformity is desirable in certain situations, it is undesirable in many others. If there is excessive conformity, the creativity and spontaneity of the organization is lost.

– The use of authority can thwart or distort communication. The member may begin to feel pressured and will not feel free to state his position. He often states one position but believes another, contrary to indication.

– The full human potential is not being utilized. As authority is abused, a leader may exercise his power for the sheer desire to dominate. He assumes that he knows best how to do the workers' job. A caste system does not recognize the potential of most of the members.

– The authority system is not responsive to change. Since the members do not have a part in initiating change, they tend to be fearful of its consequences.

In view of all these disadvantages, you can probably discern that there is an alternative to the reliance on strong authority as the *primary* system of accomplishing objectives. The alternative is the *team-centered approach,* which is discussed in the next chapter.

15

Building a Team-centered Organization

Although the ability to use direct authority is an essential tool of leadership, it is not wise to depend upon this authority as the primary organization stimulant. Effective churches are built on an involved, active, and responsible membership, not merely on a membership that is involved by participation in programs that are conducted by church leaders. Involvement runs much deeper than that. An effective church is one in which the individual members are involved in each phase of the church activity into which they invest their energies. They set the objectives and goals, plan activities, organize, make decisions, take action, and evaluate those programs and activities in which they are involved.

How does a leader assure the success of this church in achieving its goals without using his influence in some direct authoritative manner? A leader may picture his congregation wandering aimlessly with no rudder to guide its direction and with no spark to ignite its engine. He says, "I can't get the congregation moving, even though I'm using every ounce of energy that I have. I have to keep pumping the people up constantly just to get the things done that we have going now. If I stopped pushing, our church would simply be adrift." How sadly true

159

these words are for so many churches. Strong direction from strong leadership often has, over the years, lulled the congregation to sleep. They begin to move only when pushed and to do only as much as they are instructed to do.

Another leader wonders, "Can I be sure that my aims, decisions, and plans will be fulfilled, if I do not use my full influence in getting things done?" No! If you have the wisdom to know what is best, if you are sure that your plans are the Lord's plans, and if you possess the charisma necessary to influence the congregation to follow your lead, then the strong and consistent use of strong authority is the only approach. At any rate, it is the only means of getting things done your way. Unfortunately, it tends to limit the success of the church entirely to the number of bases you can touch and the extent of your interest, ability, and creativity.

Ingredients of a Team-centered Organization

How does a church build its organization around effective member involvement and responsibility? First, consider the basic ingredients of a team-centered organization:

1. It is an organization in which the basic unit of communication is the group rather than a one-to-one relationship.
2. There is a high amount of mutual influence within each group.
3. Group members manifest their love and acceptance of one another. The group leader is especially warm and accepting of others.
4. The group possesses a high degree of responsibility for decisions and actions within its special area.
5. Communication links are assured among groups within the organization by virtue of overlapping memberships (i.e., individuals are members of more than one group, especially where coordination of efforts is important.)
6. The official board of the church has as its membership the leaders of all major groups; therefore, each group has a communication link to the board.
7. The organization sustains a minimum number of organizational layers.
8. Members participate actively in their areas of responsibility.

It would be simple if one could wave his magic wand and see these ingredients of organizational effectiveness suddenly appear; however, they can occur only through prayer and effort. We shall now look at the procedure that you might use in building this type of organization.

Steps in Building the Team-centered Organization

As a first step, the key leaders of the church must agree on the value of the team-centered organization. They must understand the major ingredients of the organizational approach and how they will operate when put into effect. They must consider and modify the existing policies and practices of the church that are incompatible with this approach. For example, if the choice of material for each children's church or Sunday school worker must be reviewed by the board, then the board must relinquish this authority so that the group directly involved can make decisions. The board may give the music committee authority to make final decisions involving financial expenditures which are within their overall budget limitations.

The second step is to make any necessary changes in the organization structure. If the official church board is not currently assigned overall responsibility for the major programs and departments as described in chapter 13, this becomes the first step. Examine the organization to determine whether there are excess layers creating subtle, but devastating communication barriers. You will need to eliminate these middle-level jobs carefully to find another important area of service for those displaced and to explain the basis for the reorganization. A side benefit is that you may find a brief relief for your personnel deficiencies and gaps through these changes. You should also form new groups for responsibilities that have not been handled in the current organization. For example, you may need to appoint a personnel committee if you do not already have one. Take care in any formation or change in groups to link them with one another and with the official board. This is done by having the leader of each committee and department as a board member. Also you will need to have overlapping memberships.

The next step is the development of the members' understanding of the team-centered organization. Members and leaders have acquired concepts and expectations under the existing organization which do not change with the stroke of a pen. Once the key leaders understand the concepts and values of team-centered organization, they should discuss them with their group members. They should discuss in detail the effects of this approach to their operation. If the leaders are sold on the change and can show its benefits to their group, they can expect enthusiastic response. Group members will see a broader opportunity to serve and glorify God through their work in the church. It may be helpful to work out a job description clarifying the new roles and responsibilities with the group members. Putting concepts into written form through a job description can help solidify the ideas or identify areas of lack of understanding.

The final step is one of initiating the process of team action. Regular meetings should be planned for each operating work group. These meetings may be held on a monthly or a quarterly basis, depending on the frequency with which their problems arise. As the focal point for carrying out the leadership functions, these meetings, in addition to an evaluation of previous activities, should include decision making, problem solving, the establishment of goals, and planning for action. The meetings should encourage the support and influence of members for one another.

The success of the team-centered approach depends on the effectiveness of these group meetings' sources of decision making and influence. The successful group will be one that develops a strong bond of Christian fellowship based on honesty and openness of expression, and so is able to bring out key problems and solve them. The successful group will find stimulation and interest from the opportunity and challenge of dealing with its problems. The members of the group will influence one another toward goal attainment and project completion by attending the meetings and by entering into the discussions.

COMPARISON OF TWO APPROACHES TO ORGANIZATION

Perhaps it will be helpful in clarifying this approach to organization if we compare a typical church Sunday school organization with team-centered organization.

Figure 10 illustrates the formal organizational structure for the authority-centered Sunday school. The Sunday school superintendent stands either as an autonomous person, reporting only to the congregation, or he may report to the board. He is assisted by the Christian education director in administering the Sunday school. At the next organizational layer are the superintendents of the various departments. At the final worker level are the teachers. Periodically, the Sunday school workers are called to a general work session in which announcements and progress reports are made, and future plans are discussed. Most churches find that only a small proportion of the workers actually attend these general meetings. Consequently, if anything important is accomplished, the many that are not present will become out of touch. In fact, very little is likely to be accomplished. Even in the most successful general meetings in which attendance is good and important matters are discussed, the size of the assemblage often prohibits frank and open discussion.

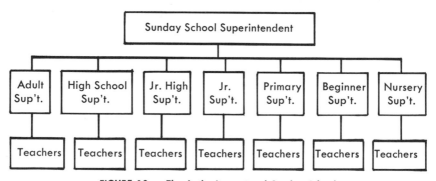

FIGURE 10 — The Authority-centered Sunday School

In the team-centered approach, as shown in Figure 11, the organization structure is in contrast to the reporting relationships indicated in Figure 10. In the former organization the Sunday school superintendent is a member of the official board. He is not an isolated person, but a member of a group at the broadest church decision-making level. In meetings of the board, he interacts on problems that are of significance to the Sunday school, coordinates schedules and plans, and perhaps most importantly, is influenced, encouraged, and given warm support by others. In this way, he receives stimulation and motivation.

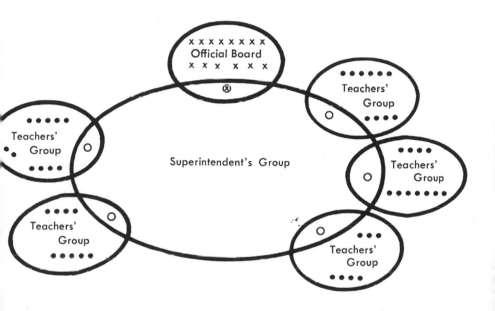

x   Board Members
⊗   Sunday School Superintendent
O   Department Superintendents
•   Teachers

FIGURE 11 — The Team-centered Approach

Notice that he is also a member of another group, viz., the superintendent's group. In quarterly or semi-annual meetings the superintendents discuss general issues of spacing arrangements, personnel needs, recreation plans, curriculum, materials, training, etc. Again, the interaction is close, supportive, and vital. The teachers, in turn, meet quarterly or monthly with their department superintendent to look at specific plans for the next period. Where teachers work in teams within a class, they may discuss their goals and approaches, and decide which of them will handle each segment of the lessons. Here again the key ingredient is the fellowship in love that develops as Christians meet to discuss their common interests and problems.

The team-centered approach can work with the same effectiveness in any unit of the church organization. The use of this approach throughout can produce a close and involved church, one in which all members work together in unity and with impact in fulfilling the purposes of the church.

16

Formal Organization Structuring

In Exodus 18, Moses was faced with the responsibility of leading a nation of 600,000 men plus their families and livestock out of Egypt into the land of promise. His responsibilities included judging the people. Any problem that they were unable to decide among themselves was brought to him. This central control of decision making in the hands of a single person seemed inefficient and placed demands on Moses that were beyond physical endurance.

In suggesting a solution to the problem, Jethro, Moses' father-in-law, outlined an approach to formal organization and pointed out some of the administrative functions that accompany it: "Furthermore, you shall select out of all the people able men who fear God, men of truth, those who hate dishonest gain; and you shall place these over them, as leaders of thousands, of hundreds, of fifties and of tens. And let them judge the people at all times; and let it be that every major dispute they will bring to you, but every minor dispute they themselves will judge. So it will be easier for you, and they will bear the burden with you" (Exodus 18:21, 22).

Following these suggestions, Moses organized the nation into divisions, sections, and units, selecting qualified men to manage each segment, training them, and delegating to them all but the most important of decisions.

As the early church exploded with growth in its initial phase, the apostles faced a similar problem in dealing with interpersonal conflicts among ethnic groups (Acts 6:1-6). The problem was not only one of having large numbers of people to lead, but also a question of the conduct of different types of functions. The apostles saw the proper form for their responsibilities as those of prayer and the ministry of the Word. Duties such as the serving of food were outside of their province; consequently, they established the office of deacon to handle these functions.

Today, we are faced with a similar problem of organizing a number of people and a set of functions that exceed the capabilities of one person. In the preceding chapters we have discussed the dynamic ebb and flow of the organization as it operates on a day-to-day basis. Now we shall give attention to the more enduring dimensions of the church organization which establish the framework within which action is taken. The effective accomplishment of organizational objectives requires both elements — dynamic team action and the underpinning of a well-structured formal organization.

Dimensions of Formal Organization

The dimensions of the organization determine its formal communication, delegation of authority, reporting relationships, and job content. These dimensions include the chain of communication, division of work, span of management, decentralization, and job description. Since the formal organization serves as a foundation for the flow of daily activities, we shall examine the dimensions in the light of their relationship to organizational objectives and their use for motivational and team-centered approaches.

Chain of Communication

"Who should I talk to about this?" "Should I clear this with Jim?" "Who would I see about getting this done?" We use questions like these to identify the chain of communication. It is advantageous to have an established and recognized channel through which the communications flow. A new worker should not have to stumble his way through the chain to get each message to the person that needs to receive it.

These channels should be as short and direct as possible. The maintenance of a minimum number of organizational layers is a principle that parallels this one. If a few layers of leadership come between the worker and the board, we can minimize the number of roadblocks and gaps in communication. Suppose you are a children's church worker who needs a flannelgraph for your next class and your director, who must approve all materials, is out of town. If, once he returns, you cannot reach him for another week, you have lost two precious weeks. With each additional barrier toward final approval, we have an added chance for just such a delay. When we were in our teens, most of us played the game of gossip in which each person in a chain was to relay to the next player the same story he received. Invariably, however, the story was highly distorted by the time it reached the end of the line — the longer the line, the greater the distortion of the message. The message may have picked up the biases of intermediary leaders, it may have had elements omitted; it may have contained less emphasis on the original expressions of concern. Whether we have reference to interdepartmental or vertical communication, we should keep the lines short.

Formalization with flexibility should be balanced in order to assure that persons in positions of responsibility are consistently informed and are able to make intelligently the decisions that must be made. Yet the flow must be flexible to be efficient. Much communication does not follow a prescribed route, nor should it. In practice, people usually go directly to the person who can answer questions or get answers. For most items this is the best procedure. As a general guideline, we might suggest that people should take the most direct route to get results, so long as their actions do not infringe upon the activities or the needs of another member of the organization.

Division of Work

Who should do what? The work necessary to meet the objectives of the church must be divided among the members in an efficient manner. Today's church should follow the scriptural form used by the apostles and initially divide the work according to the functions which must be performed. As the apostles noted, the work of ministry and prayer should be separated from that of "serving tables." This does not in any way imply that a church should have two governing boards. Having two boards is the equivalent of two company presidents; the church must have *one central governing board.*

When we speak of the division of work, we are referring to the assignment of the responsibility for various functions to the board members and in turn to the committees and departments which they lead. This division should place functions which are closely related to one another into the hands of one person. Unrelated functions should not be assigned at random to one man.

Below the level of the official board, the work may follow either the division by functions (illustrated by the apostles) or the division by numbers and attributes of people (used by Moses). The Sunday school, children's church, and youth departments are usually organized according to age groupings into workable size numbers. Men's fellowship, building committees, long-range planning committees, and choirs are examples of groups that are divided by functions.

The division should facilitate the coordination of related activities with coordinated activities being handled by one person or by a committee which meets regularly. By the same token, people who must work together closely should be in the same work team.

SPAN OF MANAGEMENT

Traditional management theorists have held that "no superior should have more than six immediate subordinates." A recent survey indicated that the average number of people supervised by each manager is nine. It is clear that the theoretical view is not the one that is found in practice. In fact, recent research has indicated that a broad span (having more than six immediate subordinates) tends to enhance the success of an organization by reducing the length of the chain of communication.[1] If each leader has a large number of people reporting directly to him, fewer levels of leadership are required. In addition, the broader span forces a greater degree of delegation of authority. With many people to lead, a person cannot get involved in doing the work of any one person under him. Likert has reported that in a voluntary organization of as many as 400 members, the board should consist of 12 to 20 members. In the more effective organizations, each of these board members has a similar-size committee or department with whom he works. This size of grouping increases the number of members vitally involved, without increasing the number of layers of leadership.

DELEGATION AND DECENTRALIZATION

As Moses divided the work of leading a nation, he concurrently specified the delegation of authority. Each leader was to have authority over his division of the people with the restriction that the most difficult problems were to be brought up for Moses' decision. The principle involved is equally important today. The authority for decision making should be placed as far down in the organization as the scope of the decisions will allow. The worker should be able to make final decisions about any matter that concerns his own activities. If a decision or action will influence others, those individuals should be involved. A few matters of a truly critical nature should be referred to the board. It should be emphasized that more important decisions are made at the top of the church structure, not because of inherent superiority of individuals, but because of the assignment of responsibility.

JOB DESCRIPTION

Job descriptions serve several purposes for the church. They provide a vehicle for the structuring of the organization by allowing the assignment of responsibility, the clarification of formal communication chan-

---

[1]Rensis Likert, *New Patterns of Management,* (New York: McGraw-Hill, 1961), p. 158.

nels, and the reporting relationships between leaders and workers. They can be used in selection to identify the qualifications required for the job and for the orientation of the person who is placed in the job, as well. The job description may be useful in training a person to do the job, motivating him to fulfill its demands, defining goals for future action, helping him to gain an understanding of the jurisdiction of his activities.

The job description may include the following items of content:

1. Job title
2. Formal communication lines
3. Other jobs with which the person in the job works; groups or boards of which he is a part
4. Statement of responsibilities for decisions and actions in the church
5. Statement of responsibility and privilege in carrying out extra-church services to the community
6. Opportunities for self-improvement
7. Statement of benefits such as vacation periods, days off, holidays observed, etc.

WHO DEFINES THE JOB?

The answer to this question varies with the nature of the job. Normally a staff person who specializes in an area will hold the responsibility for describing the jobs within that area. If the position currently exists, the person serving in it should make a heavy contribution to describing it.

Following is an illustrative job description. Appendix B, page 239, contains additional illustrative job descriptions.

JOB TITLE: DIRECTOR OF CHRISTIAN EDUCATION

Communication Lines and Interactions

The director of Christian education is responsible to the official board and reports to it monthly. He also meets weekly with the pastor and other members of the staff; serves as chairman of the board of Christian education and is a member of the committees led by each of its members. (Members of the board of Christian education include the director of children's church, Sunday school superintendent, director of boys' and girls' organizations.)

Responsibilities

The director of Christian education has general oversight of the program of Christian education with the following staff responsibilities:

1. Formulates policies for the education programs of the church.
2. Coordinates and unifies educational agencies in the church with respect to leadership, facilities, schedules, and materials in order to avoid overlap and duplication.

3. Coordinates the services of the department of Christian education with other departments of the church.
4. Provides service to department leaders in selecting training, placing, and evaluating workers.
5. Coordinates and assists in the selection of materials and curricula for the areas of Christian education.
6. Develops and conducts a training program for church workers.
7. Directs the summer day camp sponsored by the church, using high school and college students as staff.
8. Directs the vacation Bible school program.
9. Maintains a central filing system of personnel.
10. Assists department workers in formulating a Christian education budget.
11. Maintains and coordinates the operations of a church library and Christian bookshelf.

Extra-Church Activities

The director is encouraged to contribute to local and national education conferences and seminars and is given the time required to do so. He may serve as consultant to other churches requesting this service.

Self-improvement

During the course of each year the director is expected to attend training seminars and conferences which are designed to build competence in his field. His expenses to such activities will be paid, up to the amount of $400 for the year, as approved by the official board.

Statement of Benefits

The director has three weeks of vacation with pay at a time agreed on by the official board. In addition, he has time off for extra-church and self-improvement activities.

_____

Chairman of Official Board

_____

Director of Christian Education

17

The Vocational Staff

The pendulum of thought concerning the problems arising from church growth is in a state of flux. On the one hand, there are those who advocate the small church with its emphasis upon community, the total involvement of the laity, and multiplication that comes by dividing. On the other hand, there is the continuing increase of the large churches, following the pattern of a business conglomerate where there are specialities in every area and where the organizational structure looks like a blue-chip company. It is quite obvious that both of these extremes will continue to exist as long as there is the freedom of choice and the opportunity for worship in our society. In many cases, the choice will be determined by sociological and financial factors resulting from the concentration of population in small areas and the isolation which makes it difficult in many places for a small congregation to survive financially. The result of this philosophy and pressure has caused some rethinking in regard to a vocational staff to handle the complexities of such a situation.

THE STATUS OF THE STAFF

The history that perpetuated the gap between laity and clergy can be traced back to the first century. George Huntston Williams credits Clement of Rome for using the term "layman" for the first time in a written document. In a letter written about A.D. 95, Clement states "The layman [ho laikos anthropos] is bound by the lay [laikos] ordinances" (I Clement 40.5) as quoted in *The Laymen in Church History*. Though the term "laity" was used, it had no significance in separating responsibilities in the life and work of the church; all had a right to perform the services within the body. The one person most responsible for driving the wedge between laity and clergy was Cyprian (A.D. 200-258). Cyprian, a lawyer by profession, saw the bishop as head of the congregation with authority over the lesser clergy. He felt that the clergyman served as a priest who offered sacrifices and as a mediator between God and man. With Cyprian the idea of apostolic succession became a fixed doctrine of the western church. Bishops were apostles in the same sense as the first-century apostles. They represented Christ. In the lesser clergy, deacons and elders became assistants to the bishop — in a sense, his eyes and ears. It was Cyprian who set off the clergy from the laity with authority of office and adopted the dress of the government officials to signify the office of the clergy. Thus today the mode of dress, not only in the Catholic Church but in other churches as well, is the result of the distinction separating clergy and laity, made in the second century.

This distinction continued through the middle ages, and the wedge began to create a wider and wider gap. It was not until the Reformation with its emphasis on the priesthood of the believer that the gap seemed to narrow, but the damage had already been done and to loosen something already set in concrete became very difficult. In fact, it has not been until recent years that significant headway has been made in bridging the gap. The emphasis on the church as a body and as an organism rather than an organization has caused a reevaluation of the role of clergy and laity and in many cases has resulted in a divorce from the use of these unjustified terms.

Recognizing the priesthood of believers, the endowment of every believer with a spiritual gift, and the oneness that is ours in Christ makes the distinction between laity and clergy archaic.

The only legitimate distinction in Scripture is that based on the spiritual gifts (Rom. 12; 1 Cor. 12; Eph. 4). The other imposed distinction is of economic difference, which, because of spiritual gifts, has made it necessary that some carry on their work vocationally dependent upon other believers to supply their need. It is this vocational distinction more than any other which today separates and causes widespread confusion within the church.

Rather than using the terms "clergy" and "laity," it would be far more appropriate to refer to our church staff as "vocational" and "volunteer," the vocational deriving their livelihood from their ministry, whereas the volunteer staff members have other means of income to support their ministry. With the evolution of the vocational ministry, we find that the church staff has become more and more professional and specialized. Thus, there may be a senior pastor; a specialist in education, in youth, in music, and administration; and those engaged in support ministries such as a secretary, a receptionist, a custodian, a business manager, etc.

The vocational minister is not paid by the congregation to do their work for them, but his primary function should be to lead and train the volunteer ministers to develop their gifts to do the work of the ministry more effectively as God gives direction.

THE SIZE OF THE STAFF

There is no hard and fast rule which dictates the size of the vocational staff. There is a rule of thumb, however, which says that for every two hundred members there should be a vocational staff minister. This, too, may be altered, however, if there are specialty ministries which demand vocational staff, such as a Christian school that is part of the church ministry. A church of three hundred might conceivably have eight vocational staff members, although five may be directly involved in the school program. The same thing may be applicable to a church strategically located near a college or high school campus and desiring a speciality outreach to these young people.

The following guidelines are suggestions in determining vocational staff positions. These figures are based not simply on the membership roll, but on the actual number of people being ministered to in the congregation.

Figure 12 indicates the staff positions on the basis of the size of the congregation. You will note that the vocational staff is divided into ministerial staff and support staff. The ministerial staff is determined by the two-hundred-to-one ratio.

SELECTION OF THE STAFF

Selecting a church staff requires the faith of Abraham, the wisdom of Solomon, and the patience of Job. Choosing the right man to share the same yoke with others is of utmost importance. In a sense, it is a vocational marriage. A staff will spend more of its waking hours surrounding itself with the church family than they will with their own family. Even though they may be specialists in various fields, concerning themselves with one aspect of the ministry, they must be, as Peter exhorts in 1 Peter 3:8, "harmonious, sympathetic, brotherly, kindhearted, and humble in spirit."

The vocational ministry is different from any other occupation in the placement of personnel. There are no placement bureaus, employment offices, or professional counseling services such as there are in industry. In fact, caught in the rut of traditionalism, we have frowned on churches

173

Size of Congregation	Ministerial					Support		
	Senior Minister	Minister of Education	Minister of Youth	Minister of Music	Speciality Ministers	Secretarial	Custodial	Speciality
100-200	X					X*		
200-300	X	X*				X*		
300-400	X	X				X		
400-500	X	X	X*	X*		X	X	
500-600	X	X	X	X*		XX*	X	
600-700	X	X	X	X*	Intern X*	XX*	X	
700-800	X	X	X	X	Intern X*	XX	XX*	
800-900	X	X	X	X	Intern X*	XX	XX	
900-1000	X	X	X	X	X Associate	XXX	XX	
1000-1500	X	X	X	X	X Associate X Children X	XXX	XX	Business Manager X
1500-2000	X	X	X	X	X Associate X Children X College X Adults	XXX	XX	X

(*) Indicates part-time

FIGURE 12 — Vocational Staff

advertising their need for vocational staff. Likewise, we have been reluctant to consider men who on their own initiative make an application to fill a position: usually it has been the church that has made the initial contact with a potential staff member. In evangelical circles, the term "candidating" is used to describe the process of staff selection. Though the term "candidate" simply means "one who is selected by others as a contestant for office," it is usually shrouded with a pseudo-spiritual connotation, whereas what we are really looking for is a demonstration of the individual's qualifications and some indication between church and individual to determine if there is a mutual affinity. It is through this process that one must depend on the Holy Spirit to confirm the decision with His peace. Surely, it is essential that in the church "all things be done properly and in an orderly manner" (1 Cor. 14:40).

Because the selection of a staff member affects the lives of so many people, it is imperative that we exercise our responsibility in taking utmost caution to insure the proper choice. The following steps should be taken: First, determine your needs. Many churches make the mistake of looking for a director of Christian education when they really want a specialist in working with young people of high school age. Or they will look for a minister of music and expect him to do the work of a director of Christian education. The leaders of the church must determine where the church's greatest area of need lies and then launch out to find a man who can meet that need. Thus, it is good to have a job description finalized before the search begins.

The second step in selecting a staff member is a major problem; that is, where to look for a man to meet a specific need. Industry advertises for the kind of man needed to fill a certain position, and then, after screening numerous applications and résumés, narrows the prospects down to a few who are given personal interviews. This, however, is not the procedure for filling most staff positions in a church. For some reason it has become unacceptable for a man to apply for a position, for the attitude seems to be that a man who is looking for a job is unacceptable, since he apparently is not "cutting it" where he is. As a result, we are more prone to be dependent on a referral system by which contacts come through a third party involved. Since there is no ministerial employment service, we are pretty much at the mercy of friends, placement bureaus of colleges, Bible institutes, and seminaries, all of which have very inadequate information available other than the record of academic achievement made by the student while he was at the institution.

If and when a name is secured, the next step of vital importance is the personal investigation and interview of the person under consideration. This investigation should include a written résumé of the person's spiritual and educational qualifications as well as a brief history and description of his accomplishments. In addition, there should be a list of at least six people who know him well. By this time there should be enough indication as to whether the investigation of the candidate should be pursued at further length.

It is necessary, of course, to confer, either by letter or by phone, with each of the people whose names were given as a reference. More can be learned from them than from the candidate himself. It seems inconceivable that churches would hire a staff member without thoroughly investigating the references, but sad to say, it happens all the time. Things to look for in communication with the references should include the following: the candidate's spiritual life, his personal relationships with others, his family life, his attitude toward his wife and children, his physical and emotional health, his financial habits, and his effectiveness in the type of work for which he is being considered. Since most people give the names of their best friends for references, it is also wise to ask for one of the references to give the name of someone else who may know the candidate. If this person is not one of those whose names the candidate has given, he should be contacted and his evaluation weighed very carefully, for in most cases he will give an unbiased picture of the candidate's qualifications.

If the process is carried out as thus far indicated and there still seems to be a green light, the next step is to bring the candidate on the scene for a personal interview with the personnel committee and an honest exposure to the ministry for which he is being considered. If the candidate is married, it is essential that his wife accompany him. If ever it was true that a wife will either make or break her husband, it is surely true in the vocational ministry, and thus careful consideration should be given to her to see if she is in sympathy with her husband's vocational calling.

Following this investigation and exposure, both congregation and candidate should have ample time for prayer and evaluation, before having to make a decision. If and when both parties enter into an agreeable decision, a time should be set for the candidate to assume his responsibilities. The church will naturally be responsible not only for moving expenses, but also for traveling expenses during the time of candidacy as well as transfer to the new location.

LEADERSHIP OF THE STAFF

Though the principles of leadership have been covered in another section of this book, a few items should be given additional consideration at this time.

The leadership of the staff should be the direct responsibility of the pastor unless the size of the church allows for an executive pastor who would be responsible for the task. The goal of the staff leader should be to produce an esprit de corps. This is what makes a staff a team rather than an organization.

Developing an esprit de corps is not an easy task. It begins with the leader who sees himself not as an autocrat, but rather as one of the team members. He must treat his staff as colleagues and not as subordinates. In most cases, a staff member will be younger than the senior minister. A successful leader will appreciate a young man's abilities and potential. He must respect his abilities without jealousy and be patient with his limitations.

Keeping the lines of communication open is an absolute essential in good staff leadership. All too often staff members get on a little island of their own and set themselves off from the remainder of the operation. The youth minister thinks of nothing but youth, the music minister concerns himself only with music, and the CE director is interested only in education. And so the senior minister sits on a live explosive that is ready to go off at any minute. Communication is the only remedy to this problem. The wise leader will accomplish this through regularly scheduled staff meetings. These may take place once each month or, preferably, once each week. During a staff meeting there should be spiritual enrichment through the reading of the Word and prayer. The staff should be encouraged to share their blessings and burdens and to uphold one another in prayer. The freedom to talk must be present. Being able to express ideas, opinions, and attitudes freely is necessary to good communication. Staff members should feel free to express themselves or evaluate one another without fear of being misjudged or criticized. During staff meetings, opportunities should be given for each member to share accomplishments, goals, and failures in an atmosphere of acceptance. The senior minister must be willing to encourage the staff and to share his life with them. When offering suggestions or ideas, he must be willing to allow his staff to receive the credit in the event of success. Remember, the staff leader is a coordinator, not a dictator.

The communication lines are kept open not only through staff meetings, but also through casual and informal opportunities of meeting with staff members. The leader should be available for personal counsel and help at any time. A good staff leader will be sensitive to any areas of stress which may be present, either among staff members or between staff and congregation. These areas of stress should be dealt with immediately and not allowed to fester.

Fundamental to building an esprit de corps is the concept of "no responsibility without authority." In other words, if a staff member has the responsibility of the youth ministry of the church, he must also have the authority to carry it out. He should not have to report to the senior minister in order to get the "green light" on decisions. However, should he assume authority beyond his responsibility, then the matter will have to be taken in hand and dealt with accordingly. It should be kept in mind however, that proper leadership demands total mutual support between each staff member and the senior minister, and also among the family members of staff. This support will be based on the communication level and the understanding that each member of the staff has for the other members. It is imperative that the members of staff support one another before the congregation. One member of the staff should in no way undermine another; if there are areas of disagreement, they should be taken care of in the staff meeting and not outside in the congregation. (This holds true for staff members' wives as well.) Unless each member can support his colleagues in the ministry, he constitutes a weak link to the chain which soon breaks under stress.

An esprit de corps is maintained not only through communications and personal support, but also through informal opportunities of fellowship and fraternizing. "All work, and no play, makes Jack a dull boy" is an ancient and trite saying. Its ancientness and triteness, however, may add to its validity. A church staff needs to develop a spirit of community. It is an attitude that comes when people get to know one another in the context of their family lives, attitudes, and opinions. The staff fellowship should go beyond the traditional coffee break, and as far as possible, families of staff members should be included. Since the church is a family institution, the families of the church staff need to know one another on a fellowship basis. This type of work climate can do much to ease the tension of personality conflicts, disharmony, and misunderstanding. It is conceivable that wives of vocational staff members may even be invited to some staff meetings or study sessions and thus bridge the gaps that often exist in a staff.

If building an esprit de corps is the goal of a staff leader, he should keep in mind that it is essential to provide adequate facilities in which the staff can perform its duties. If a member of the staff is housed in an inadequate office, in a far-off corner of the church, he soon becomes discouraged and thinks that his job is unimportant. But if he is provided with an adequate office on a standard enjoyed by the senior minister, his position soon becomes elevated in his own mind and the result is accelerated self-motivation. Status differentials should be minimized.

A happy staff is a working staff and when they are working together, under the guidance of the Holy Spirit and the leadership of the senior minister, there will be no need to exhort them, as Paul did Euodia and Syntyche, that they live in harmony in the Lord (Phil. 4:2).

Leading people is never easy. It is often a thankless job. However, implementing the above-mentioned principles will certainly make the task more enjoyable for all those involved and more honoring to God.

18

Work Goals and Evaluation

"Roger, I asked you to come down to the church tonight because I'm evaluating the performance of everyone in my department, and, as superintendent of the junior high department, you are next in line. You've done a lot of good work, and I want you to know that I appreciate it. I do notice what is going on in your department. You are to be commended. Of course, there are a few areas in which you could improve, but let's start the evaluation with the good side. You've done a fine job of holding departmental meetings this year and attending the general meetings. Your department has held several good social activities which are valuable to the youth. I was glad you were able to attend the Sunday school workers' conference. . . .

"Now, Roger, let me tell you where I think you need some improvement. I don't want to hurt you. Rather, I hope this will help you to do an even better job for the next year. You've been rather uncooperative in superintendents' meetings. I think that your attitude could be better on these occasions. You also need to get to your department earlier. Sometimes I notice that the young people are mostly all there before you arrive. You should develop some plans for your department. I'm sure you agree that you haven't shown much imagination or creativity in doing your job and this is an area that is critically important. . . ."

I'm sure you recognize this as a frank and direct evaluation of the performance of a church worker. Evaluations of this type have been discussed and encouraged in Christian leadership circles for years; however, actual application of this evaluation procedure has been sparse. Human instinct or spiritual guidance has somehow spared us the atrocities of these devastating appraisals. Certainly their purposes are noble and their practitioners well-meaning, indeed courageous; but their value is often far outweighed by the anxiety, conflict, and poor attitudes that they foster.

WHY SUCH EVALUATIONS FAIL

Worker evaluation views a person as though he were a product on an assembly line ready for inspection, by assuming that he is an object to be judged and catalogued. The approach is based on the false position that a person can change his behavior by turning a dial or tightening a screw in his personality.

The evaluation often causes a person inadvertently to place interpretations on the person's behavior that go beyond his actual performance. In our illustrative interview, Roger is observed to arrive at his Sunday school department later than he should. This is an observation of performance. Conversely, when he is evaluated as having a poor attitude in superintendents' meetings, an interpretation or evaluation is made that is beyond the power of any person to make with accuracy. Yet the evaluator assumes that his perception is accurate.

Criticism is intended to provide insight into poor performance so that it can be improved. In fact, a research study undertaken a few years ago indicates that criticism yields the opposite effect. Persons who receive the higher number of criticisms in evaluation interviews become more defensive and show a reduction in subsequent performance. The lower the amount of criticisms, the higher the future performance is likely to be. Contrary to former opinion, this research also revealed that praise does not affect future behavior. Persons who received much praise were not essentially different in their level of performance than those who received little praise.[1]

Both the appraisee and the appraiser tend to approach the evaluation with anxiety and tension. The confrontation involved in the process, however well-conducted, is a threat to the personal enhancement needs of the person. The attitude following such an interview also tends to be low.

In spite of the pitfalls of traditional approaches to evaluation, its purposes are important.

---

[1]E. Kay, J. R. P. French, and H. Meyers, *A Study of the Performance Appraisal Interview,* (New York: Behavioral Research Service, General Electric Company, 1962) pp. 18-24.

What Purposes Should Performance Evaluation Serve?

An effective approach to evaluation will foster initiative, encourage imagination, develop a sense of responsibility, and intensify efforts to meet organizational goals.

Church workers who are volunteers to service usually want to do a good job. They are exerting effort which is not required for their livelihood. Christians usually assume responsibility in the church because of their belief in the value of the contribution that they will make. An evaluation assists the worker in appraising his performance. Therefore, information regarding performance effectiveness should be as precise and specific as possible. A person *must* have this information in order to identify his weaknesses and improve.

The church worker should also know what is expected of him. Again, the knowledge should be specific and clear. The General Electric Corporation conducted a study of the appraisal interview in which they observed that some of the managers set specific goals with their men, whereas others did not. During the following twelve weeks, the performance among the men who had specific goals increased more than twice as much as those who had not set goals. The goals provided a clear statement of expectations for the men and stimulated their performance.[2]

A person also needs to know where he stands in the eyes of other persons. In his poem "To a Louse" Robert Burns penned for all of us:

> O wad some Pow'r the giftie gie us
> to see oursels as ithers see us!

How often we have heard the declaration: "If only I knew what people really think of me!" In our fervor to hide our perceived faults from others, we also distort our own view of ourselves. We are then curious to know what our mask looks like from the other side. Unfortunately, others are busily adjusting their masks and dare not be honest in their appraisal of us. An evaluation can help us to see how our performance measures up to the standards of others. We have already seen that the evaluation as it has historically been performed is a threat. We must use an approach that will give information to others without being considered a threat. Let us look at some of the methods that have been developed to meet the purposes of evaluation while avoiding the pitfalls.

Self-Appraisal

Self-appraisal must be a primary ingredient of any evaluation approach. We must establish an environment in which a church worker can effectively evaluate his own performance. Heavy reliance on the evaluation of others is completely unacceptable. Who sees the performance of a person as continuously as he sees himself? Who under-

---

[2]*Ibid.*

stands his reasons for his actions as well as he does? Who has prayed about his responsibility as he has? Nevertheless, we must not abdicate our responsibility for evaluation with the conclusion, "Oh well, he can just do it himself." Our responsibility goes far beyond this. We must establish an environment and a vehicle that will support self-appraisal.

An archer stands poised to shoot at a target. He fires and sees his arrow pierce the outer circle at the top right. He aims again; the arrow hits farther to the left and lower. His third arrow strikes the center of the target. What has happened? Let us examine the situation.

First, we have a person who is motivated to persevere, who knows his responsibilities, and has the ability to perform well. Without the right person, we could not get these results. The church also must have motivated, capable workers who know what their responsibilities are. These we obtain through selection and training.

Second, we have a target — a goal that is clearly visible and un-ambiguous in its design, conveying to the archer the goal that he is seeking. This must be true of the church organization. We must have clearly defined responsibilities so that the workers will know exactly what course they are set upon. Each worker should have oral and/or written statements of the functions that he is expected to perform. He should also have a target, a goal which gives direction to his work. He should see with clarity the results that he should obtain. Whether he sets his own goal or it is set by others with his collaboration, it should be sufficiently clear that he is able to know without ambiguity whether he is high, low, or off-target.

Finally, we have feedback. The archer can see how well he is doing. He knows the direction and degree of his error. So it must be in the church. A means must be available by which the worker knows how well he is performing. He needs an adequate amount of accurate information that is relevant to his responsibilities. The church budget for Sunday school provides the Sunday school superintendent's target for expenditures. If he is to perform well in fulfilling this responsibility, he must know the budget amounts and the amount of previous expenditures for the year.

The youth director has a responsibility for aiding youth in their spiritual maturity, yet he never can perceive how accurately he has hit the mark with the same clarity as he can with the budget. Too often, through laziness or lack of thought, we push for a visible goal such as to have a certain number of youth attending the training hour. We reach the goal, but have we fulfilled the responsibility? Who knows? The goal must be relevant. Suppose we set a goal to have a certain number engaged in daily devotions and Bible study. Perhaps we are closer, yet we are not certain that spiritual maturity will result. Should our goal not be to see an increase in the fruit of the Spirit — those attributes of love, joy, peace, patience, kindness, goodness, faithfulness, humility, and self-control? Now the goal is relevant, but how do we measure it? The best measure could probably be made by the youth director himself through periodical evaluation of the youth in terms of these qualities to discern, if he is able, whether they are progressing. In effect, he would be evaluating his own performance in the area of his basic responsibilities.

Our churches need to examine closely the adequacy of their system for self-appraisal. Do your people know what their responsibilities are? Do they have relevant performance goals? Do they have adequate feedback?

It would be unfortunate to assume that the system will occur by accident. A deliberate effort is required. The leaders of the church should first define their own responsibilities and goals and set up a feedback method. They should then help others in their departments to do likewise. A form similar to that of Appendix C (page 241) may be helpful. These forms help the superintendent and teachers of Sunday school examine their past performance in areas of their responsibilities.

Three steps are outlined as to how goals and evaluation may be accomplished for yourself:

Step 1: Set three to five goals. You are encouraged to set specific goals for a quarter to be aimed at the improvement of the performance of your responsibilities. Your goals should clearly define the direction that you wish to move.

Step 2: Identify progress points that signal movement. Where possible, you should have ways of determining how well you are doing before the final results are in. This will allow you to make course corrections and get back on target.

Step 3: Plan ways to get information about your degree of success. At the outset, plans should be made for the kind and source of information required for self-evaluation. At the end of the quarter for which the goals are set, you should evaluate yourself and set goals for the next quarter.

GROUP GOALS AND EVALUATION

Another approach that is effective in business involves goal setting by a small group and subsequent evaluation by that group. It is essentially the same in its basic approach as the self-appraisal system; however, the complete process involves group activity. Let us look at the process in the church setting.

The official board is in session at the end of the first quarter in an Iowa City church. The first item of business for this special goal setting and evaluation session is to discuss performance of the first quarter. The board members have before them a copy of the goals that were set the first week of January. These goals are categorized by function; each board member carries a functional responsibility. As we begin listening in on the conversation, we see that no one person is under the floodlight of interrogation for any area. It seems as though almost everyone feels free to comment or make proposals concerning any area. Of course, the board member responsible for a given area has more information and insight, but all seem to be equally concerned.

The board finishes the evaluation and turns to the goals for the next quarter. Once again it becomes quite evident that these are group goals — not individual goals set by a group. They discuss the items that were not completed for the last quarter and set goals to finish those that are still viable. Before going to the next functional area, they discuss the new goals for the area. This procedure is repeated until all areas have been covered. The meeting is over, but it is clear as the members leave that their thoughts are still churning on goals and on solutions to road-blocks. There can be no doubt that they will keep tabs on how the efforts toward reaching these goals are progressing during the quarter, sharing ideas and encouraging one another.

The group goals and evaluation process take in a package all of the forces of the individual motivation and group dynamics to yield a powerful, positive effect upon performance. The process should find its way into every level and corner of the functioning church.

WORK PLANNING AND REVIEW

From the results of its outstanding research, General Electric insti-tuted the "Work Planning and Review" system that operates well for both industry and church. The essential ingredient is a periodic meeting of an individual worker and the leader. During their discussion they plan the daily work, review progress toward previous goals, and solve problems that are pending. Again you see that the procedure is quite similar to that of self-appraisal. However, in this approach the leader is involved with the person being appraised in an informal and flexible discussion. These discussions may be held as frequently as desired; the process begins with the identification of duties and plans. In combina-tion, these lead to a definition of the individual projects that are needed for the immediate future. At this point the two men defined the agreed-on indicators of a job well done. Plans are made for measuring quality or amount of achievement. The review of performance considers the quality and the results of performance. As a result of a change in the project, a revised or new project is agreed on and the cycle is started again. At each stage the person who will perform the project, not the leader, takes the initiative.

In accord with the purposes and pitfalls of performance evaluation, it is apparent that contemporary appraisal methods are based on funda-mental principles. The approaches are geared to the future through the process of goal setting, encouraging frequent informal assessments of how well a person is performing, and deciding on the measurements to be used in advance of the actual performance. They avoid the giving of criticism and the exercise of strong influence by the leader, placing heavy responsibility for goals and evaluations on the person rather than the leader. They assume that the individual is responsible and does not require the push-and-pull approaches of the more autocratic era of leadership.

19

Long-range Planning

"Planning is the organized application of systematic reasoning to the solution of specific practical problems. An alternative to planning is the trial and error method."[1] This quotation was taken from the *Harvard Business Review,* but its point is one which demands the attention of every individual involved in the greatest business on earth, the spreading of the Gospel of Jesus Christ. Churches have been anything but "faithful stewards" when it comes to proper management of time, money, and facilities used in the Lord's work. It is time that we make some optical corrections to overcome the malady of "administrative myopia." This correction can be made through a proper understanding of long-range planning.

What Is Long-range Planning?

Long-range planning is as important to a church as the thermostat is to a home; a thermostat controls the environment, whereas a thermometer simply records it. Seemingly, most churches simply live by a thermometer, recording the environmental changes around them and being controlled by them. What our churches desperately need today is the

---

[1]Peter Drucker, "Managing for Business Effectiveness," *Harvard Business Review.* May-June, 1963.

thermostat — the instrument that will determine the temperature and the environment. Long-range planning can be that thermostat, for through its effective application a church can act rather than react. As the ability of a congregation to *make* things happen rather than *let* things happen increases, the thermostat of long-range planning will help the leaders anticipate problems and work out solutions before the problems ever occur. Because such planning stresses using circumstances rather than fretting about misfortunes, it becomes a great deterrent to adminstrative forest fires and can promote the lush growth of vegetation which requires many years of controlled cultivation.

Long-range planning does not consist merely of the annual detailed plan which involves goals, timetables, and budgets; but it includes the challenge of determinative action that extends up to five, ten, or fifteen years, with a built-in creative flexibility to change. Long-range planning is the outworking of the wisdom of Solomon who said, "Where there is no vision, the people perish" (Prov. 29:18).

Four Basic Questions

To a large extent, long-range planning implants and encourages growth that would otherwise not occur. Obviously, the exact future of a church can seldom be predicted or determined because of external factors that interfere with the actual operation of even a well-laid plan. However, events without planning are simply left to chance. Churches can no longer exist defensively, but, assuming the offensive like a mighty army marching to war, they must mold the future rather than be molded by the present.

In order to determine the environment rather than just record it, a church employing the use of long-range planning must ask itself four basic questions: 1) Where are we now? 2) Where do we want to go? 3) How do we get there? and 4) When will we get there? When these four questions are honestly and objectively answered, the foundation on which to build a superstructure of long-range planning will be laid.

In asking the question "Where are we now?" it is imperative that the church take stock of the realistic position of its *status quo*. This involves more than just the obvious considerations of active membership, size of Sunday school, property and facility, staff and budget, but it also requires the investigation of even more strategic and informative facts. In answering the question, "Where are we now?" we must also ask, "Where have we come from?" Where were we a year ago, five years ago, and ten years ago? We must ask what we are doing and what we have been doing, as well as what our purpose is and how we are accomplishing it. To provide a proper base for long-range planning, the church must take an active inventory of its physical and spiritual assets.

The second ingredient necessary in the formulation of a long-range plan is an answer to the question, "Where do we want to go?" This is far more difficult than just evaluating where we are now. It was Winston Churchill who said, "It is wise to look ahead, but difficult to look farther than you can see." The difficulty for any church is looking farther than we can see, but it is not an impossibility if by faith we will submit ourselves to the resources of the Spirit of God. The church's direction will in part be determined by the rapidity of change in the local church. It may effect the degree or quantity of change but should not effect the quality. Where we are going will be determined by the faith, the vision, and the maturity of the leadership of the local church.

After the congregation has determined its present position and its direction for the next five, ten, or fifteen years, the third question they will ask is "How will we get there?" This will require the application of administrative guidelines set forth in other sections of this book. The fourth question, "When do we get there?" is probably the most important. It is relatively easy to plan an objective and to determine a course of action to be carried out; however, the most difficult thing is to set a realistic "target date," a time for putting the course of action into operation and testing the grain of mustard seed in the hearts of the constituency. A timetable is an invariable must.

WHAT TO INCLUDE

The process of long-range planning is a reverse cycle. Although the number and the importance of steps may vary, the process should proceed from ends to means rather than from means to ends. The following steps should be considered in establishing a program of long-range planning.

1. *Involvement of the congregation.* Though it is obvious that the entire congregation cannot be involved in the spade work of long-range planning, it is imperative that they have a meaningful involvement throughout the process, though much of the work will be done by a small group of the church leaders. The congregation as a whole must be involved in launching a long-range planning project, and should be continually informed through the lines of communication lest the plans become the property of the long-range planning committee rather than the church.

2. *Selection of a committee.* A standing committee, the size of which will be determined by the size of the church, should be authorized by the congregation. The means of selection may vary from church to church; however, the committee should be selected on the basis of competence and contribution rather than popularity.

3. *The duties of the committee* are as follows: 1) establish a realistic inventory of the spiritual and physical assets of the church, 2) seek to establish long-range priority needs of the church and the community, 3) recommend long-range goals to the congregation based on a five-, ten-, and fifteen-year projection, 4) recommend a long-range strategy

to carry out the projected goals, and 5) evaluate the long-range effectiveness of the church's programs.

Let us look at these responsibilities more closely. In determining the inventory, the long-range planning committee must ask some pertinent questions. Why do we exist? What is our mission? What is our basis of authority? These questions, answered in the light of the church's present inventory, will determine the objectives which the long-range planning committee will seek to obtain.

Along with the inventory, there is the need of analyzing the church and the community needs. To do this a number of things must be considered: 1) the past growth rate of the church — the average percentage of growth for the past five years and ten years, 2) characteristics of the church constituency, items such as economic, social, and educational background should be considered, 3) the effectiveness of present programs for the children, youth, and adults, 4) the adequacy of present church organization, staff, and facilities, 5) community growth factors, 6) community characteristics, and 7) effectiveness of church programs in meeting community needs. The items will become a springboard from which to launch long-range goals. With the raw materials of church and community needs, the committee is now ready to proceed in establishing long-range goals whose purpose is to tell what a church wants to accomplish and when. While optimistic and challenging, they should at the same time be realistic and obtainable, specific to the extent that if a church projects a 10% growth per year for the next ten years, it should determine the number of people at any given time and the required amount of space needed to accommodate them. The goals should not only deal with facilities and budget, but should also take into consideration the added staff necessary to carry out the goals.

Up to this point, the long-range planning process has considered only the ends and not the means. Determination of the ends alone will be meaningless if the church does not decide how to accomplish them through long-range strategies. Flexibility will be the key word in the development of strategies, for people and resources will change over a period of years. One must ask these questions: "In the course of action, what alternatives can be taken to achieve each goal? Which alternative is most feasible?"

The development of strategy should be the final step in long-range planning. It is here that annual programming enters into the picture, for at this point the detailed actions must be prepared to implement each process of carrying out the projected goal.

How Long-range Planning Works

As an illustration of long-range planning in action, we will describe the planning process for our own local church in the hope that this may provide a clearer framework for understanding and using the approach. In 1964, we began with our first official long-range planning committee, a committee composed of a group of men from the congregation who represented a cross section of the church. After determining the reason for their own existence from a theological basis as well as their goals of operation, the committee launched out into a three-fold area with a long-range plan as their goal. This three-pronged attack can best be described in the words of review, reaction, and results.

Review

The first order of business answered the question "Where are we?" This involved a realistic look at the active church membership, the average Sunday school attendance for the past six months, the actual giving, the number of staff to care for the membership, and a detailed accounting of the size and quality of facilities for each age group. Also included in this investigation was an objective look at the community in which the church ministered and the anticipated future of community conditions. After careful analysis of all these items, with each member of the committee researching a particular item, the long-range planning committee met again for the purpose of reviewing past performance from the present standpoint in the area of attendance, Sunday school, budget, facilities, and community. In the review a number of things became apparent: 1) There had been a 22% increase each year for the past three years in Sunday school attendance and membership. 2) There had been a 20% increase in budget giving and a 15% increase in community growth. 3) It was also noted that the projected rate of growth of the community was to double from 50,000 to 100,000 in ten years. In surveying our community, we also noted that we were in the section of the community that had the largest anticipated rate of growth.

When a composite list of our findings was formed, it provided us with a basis for immediate reaction and long-range planning.

Reaction

Being realistic and conservative, the committee decided to base its long-range plans on a 10% per-year growth rate. The 250 figure that it began with soon multipled to 644 in ten years, thereby necessitating the formulation of plans for the projected growth. The next step was to project the space needs per age group for the next ten years. This was done by determining the percentage of people in each department, comparing it with the average percentage in other Sunday schools in this nation, and then projecting that forward over a period of ten years. We found that the percentage in each department in our Sunday school was comparable to the national percentage; so we worked on that basis. The following figures denote percentages as well as the department and class size. The square-footage per person was determined by taking the figures given by Dr. Howard Hendricks, professor of Christian Education at Dallas Theological Seminary.

Department	Dept. Percent	Square Footage per Person	Max Dept. Size	Max. Class Size
Cradle Roll and Nursery (Ages 0-3)	8.0%	30	15	—
Beginner (Ages 4, 5)	8.0%	18 to 25	25	—
Primary (Grades 1-3)	10.5%	15 to 18	45	6-8
Junior (Grades 4-6)	14.5%	15 to 18	45	6-8
Jr. High (Grades 7-9)	12.0%	10 to 14	60	6-8
Sr. High (Grades 10-12)		10	60	10-12
College and Career	7.0%	10	—	20-25
Adult	40.0%	10	—	20-25

FIGURE 13 — Departmentalization Chart

After closely examining the number of facilities on hand and the number of facilities that would be available in ten years, the committee was prepared to make plans for arriving at the necessary goals.

Not only were these projections made in the area of facility, but also in the area of budget, of related programming for children, youth, and adults, and in the area of ministerial staff.

Results

After the review and the reaction were objectified, a plan of operation was proposed. This included a three-phase building program to meet the educational facility need, a projected program in eight years to care for the worship facilities, and a detailed plan for an adequate program to accommodate the growth of the congregation. Along with plans for the plant and program, a schedule for securing staff was also proposed. This was based on having one full-time staff member for each two hundred active church members or fraction thereof.

When the long-range plan was completed, it was presented to the members of the congregation, not only for their approval, but more importantly for their personal involvement. It has been gratifying to see how the proposals have been accomplished as target dates have been set, and the congregation has moved together to meet them.

Long-range planning is as important to a local church as a training program is to an athlete. An athlete may be able to play a game without training, but he will play a much better game if he has trained religiously. God can use a church that lives only from hand to mouth, day by day, but a church can certainly be far more effective, if with the Holy Spirit's guidance, it seeks to lay out its plans far in advance.

20

Annual Planning of Church Goals

$\mathbf{H}$ave you ever watched children at play? It's not unusual to see them set short-term goals through such statements as, "I want to be a fireman," "I want to be a cowboy," or "I want to be a soldier." One fact is certain — for the next five minutes their actions will reflect their intentions. Fires will be put out, cows will be roped, and the soldier will crouch down behind the tree with his rifle. And that's life. A person does what he does because he is what he is. The kind of person he is provides a major clue to the kinds of things he does.

Churches are like people. A church does what it does because it is what it is. And the kind of church it is provides a major clue to the kinds of things that it does. What does God want your church to be? The answers to this question will make up the church's goals. A church goal may be in terms of an intangible stage beyond which further progress is impossible, or in terms of a tangible result which is easily reached through guided direction aimed at target date!

The goals mirror the values of the church. Almost every organized church has a basic church covenant, that is, an expressed goal or purpose for its existence. An example is taken from the constitution of a local church which reads, "Having received the Lord Jesus Christ as our Saviour, we band ourselves together as a body of believers in the Lord Jesus Christ to provide the opportunity for worship, fellowship, instruction and service, and to proclaim the Gospel of Jesus Christ at home and abroad." All the goals of the church, both long-range and short-term, must find justification in the basic value system of the church. The goals give both guidance and direction to your efforts in planning, as a lighthouse to a boat captain, guiding his ship into port. Goals are like the North Star, enabling you to keep your bearing and to move with assurance in the direction you feel God wants you to move.

Honest evaluation may reveal that your church is characterized by one of four kinds of motion. Some churches are static, completely satisfied with the *status quo,* having no sense of direction. Goals can become guiding stars in directing the efforts of the church that does not appear to be moving at all. Other churches are moving in all directions and do not seem to be making progress in any single direction. There's much movement, but little accomplishment. This kind of church resembles the maze of disorganization in a game of pick-up sticks: there is movement, overlap, wasted effort, and little accomplishment. Other churches are moving backward and losing ground. For those who stop and wonder why, there is hope; if out of their wondering, they search and find the direction, their reverse movement can be stopped and justification for their existence salvaged. The fourth kind of church is the one that is in the race, keeping its eyes fixed on the goal determined by its value system. In this kind of goal-oriented congregation, the resources and the efforts become highly productive.

Annual goals become the means for carrying out the long-range plans. These become the ends which determine what activities or means a church will use during the following year. Thus the goals justify the activities.

Who Establishes Goals?

Many times when goals are established, they are set into operation from the top down. That is, the goals are made by one person and superimposed on a congregation whose natural response is one of resistance. One needs to realize that there is a direct relationship between the worthiness of a cause and the willingness of people to participate in the cause. Objectives are statements of cause and worthy objectives call for increased participation in order to carry them out.

If the goals are to be the objectives of the church family, they must be made by the church family and not set by the pastor. There are three ingredients necessary to make an individual willing to participate in moving toward church objectives: 1) sharing in determining what the goals will be, 2) understanding and agreeing with the goals, and 3) identifying with the goals. People and churches react with little interest when they are called on to work out someone else's goals. They are most interested when called on to work toward goals which they consider to be worthy, which they helped to determine, and with which they can personally identify.

The big question is "How can we involve our church family in establishing annual goals?" We have found that this involvement works best through small groups. Since it is impossible for any single group to determine all of the goals for the church, we ask the group to be limited to a specific area of responsibility, to be determined by the standing committee which is represented on the official board and chaired by an elder (see chapter 15 for specific details). Since every function can be found under one of these standing committees, goals for the total church program can be accomplished in this manner.

For example, let us take the missionary committee. This committee is chaired by an elder who reports to the official board and has been delegated the responsibility of overseeing the entire missionary program of the church by controlling determination of support as well as the means and expense of communication and the general oversight of the missionary program. This committee, consisting of fifteen members at large from the congregation, has its fingertips on the pulse of the missionary outreach. It is in a position to evaluate the past performance and, consequently, establish realistic goals for the coming year which will be used in giving direction to the missionary outreach. As these fifteen people of various families and interests within the church family have an opportunity of establishing the goals, they immediately have a vital interest in, and personal identification with, these and other projected goals.

After the missionary committee has set the goals, the goals are taken to the official board which in turn evaluates them and if it approves them, it adopts them as its own goals. Finally they are submitted to the entire congregation in an attractive format at which time the congregation is given an opportunity to interact with them, to ask questions about them, and finally to approve or reject them by vote. This three-step function is followed to get everyone involved by fostering a feeling of participation and a desire to implement the goals because they have come from the people and have not been forced on them.

When to Set Goals

The official legwork for goal setting should begin at least two months prior to the time the goals are to be presented to the congregation and implemented by the church. The goal setting should not be forced, but should be the result of continual evaluation during the year and research through reading and exposure to other new ideas. A working goal of each committee should be to have its list of objectives finalized at least one month before the target date of congregational approval.

WHERE GOALS ARE SET

After the preliminary goals have been drafted by the respective committees, each chairman submits these goals to the official board chairman who in turn sees that they are reproduced and collated into a single package. These are then distributed to each member of the official board in preparation for the annual leadership retreat which is held two months before the annual congregational meeting. Since our congregational meeting is in January, we have found that the weekend before Thanksgiving works best for our leaders. The leadership retreat consists of a work session for all the elders and deacons and members of staff beginning on a Friday night and continuing all day Saturday. We have held our leadership retreat at a local conference center and most recently, at a lake cabin belonging to one of the members of the congregation. The program for our retreat consists of a Friday night evaluation of the previous year's goals, a realistic look at past levels of performance, and an overall evaluation of the total church program. An in-depth opportunity for prayer climaxes the first session. The remainder of the first evening is unstructured and many men find it helpful to interact with one another concerning the possibilities for the coming year. Others take a few moments for more relaxed activity such as playing dominoes, warming their feet before a blazing fire, or snacking a bit before they go to bed. On Saturday morning we begin at 7:30 with breakfast and a time around the Word and in prayer with the Lord. Then each committee chairman presents his previously prepared goals to the board and gives an opportunity for the rest of the official board to ask questions and receive answers. Following the presentation of each committee's objectives for the coming year, members of the board are asked to adopt them officially as their own. By the end of the day each board member and each staff member has a total picture of what direction the church will be taking for the coming year and feels an identity with it. We have found this leadership retreat to be one of the most helpful and most unifying factors in the program of the church.

HOW TO WRITE GOALS

There are two kinds of goals: tangible and intangible. The following are examples of tangible goals, that might arise in the property committee: to paint all the exterior trim on the church, to purchase a new buffer to be used for polishing the floors, to replace the carpeting in the pastor's study. These are goals which can be accomplished by establishing target dates and funding money. An intangible goal might be striving to be a church that ministers unselfishly to persons in the community in Jesus' name, or to be a fellowship of maturing Christians whose learning together results in responsible living. Though these goals are worthy in themselves, their broad scope and intangible nature make the degree of their attainment uncertain and unknown.

The intangible goal of being a witness for Christ both in the community and throughout the world can be translated into a tangible goal by stating that the church family will witness for Christ, trusting the Lord for one person per week to receive Christ as personal Savior. This then makes the goal reachable and accountable.

It is best when setting goals to put them in writing and to place them in the hands of the congregation. In this way the people can be reminded of the goals and determine how they can fit into them. Putting the goals in writing also helps the church to review the goals periodically during the year to see what has been accomplished and what still needs to be done.

Now that you have established what God wants your church to be, one question yet remains. What should you do about it? Statements of goals alone are worthless: they can lie dead on a shelf. If goals are going to reflect values, direct efforts; serve as a standard for selecting means, motivate church members, or measure results, they must become guiding stars for the church's program. Goals should be the basis for planning, conducting, and evaluating your church's ministry in a long-range planning project and should be continually displayed through the lines of communication lest the plans become the property of the long-range planning committee, rather than of the church.

21

Budgeting and Accounting Procedure

Financial resources are significant as a tool in the fulfillment of the purposes and objectives of the church. Most church leaders recognize the importance of allocating funds through budgeting and expenditure under the leadership of the Holy Spirit. If there is imbalance or waste in the financial area of church operation, this will strongly tend to effect an imbalance or loss in the use of time, talent, and other resources. The importance of the use of a proper procedure in budgeting and spending is often overlooked. Since financial resources are essential for many church activities and programs, those who control the purse strings have considerable power. Ultimately, the responsibility for the distribution of funds by way of the budget is the responsibility of the deacons. Their method of exercising this responsibility and authority enjoys a measure of freedom, since it is not dictated by the revelation of Scripture. In early chapters on organization and authority, we have advocated that the exercise of our freedom within the context of today's society and church environment can best be accomplished by sharing the power as well as the responsibility among the total body of church workers. For this to be done with responsibility in such areas as evangelism, education, fellowship, and property, it must be done with the financial resources as well. Some

197

traditionalists may argue that the finances are the deacons' responsibility and must not be delegated; however, this is as erroneous as to say that the responsibility of the elders to feed the flock is limited only to them. It is obvious that while they oversee the ministry of teaching, others may and should share in this privilege, and so the deacons can and should allow others to have authority and responsibility for budgeting and expenditures under their overall direction.

In order that workers, in the body, may improve their effectiveness in the area of financial responsibility, a budget based on the needs of the congregation should be established. Well in advance of the budget's final approval, each worker should review the needs in his area for the coming year and establish a budget request to cover them. He should review these with the department leader above him, either individually or in a meeting called for that purpose. At this time, the various worker budgets are reduced, increased, or otherwise modified and are consolidated to become a departmental budget. This process moves upward until each member of the official board has a consolidated budget for his area of responsibility. After a finance committee has met to resolve any overlaps in the proposed departmental budgets, the total budget is then presented to the official board. It is at this point that most churches make a big mistake and as a result, are deprived of a great blessing. If we believe that Philippians 4:19 means that God will supply all of our needs collectively as well as individually, then after careful, prayerful consideration, our needs should dictate the budget figure. What often happens is that a total budget figure for the coming year is established on the basis of past performance. For instance, last year the budget may have been $100,000. For the coming year the deacons see only a 10% increase and thus they set a ceiling of $110,000 for the coming year. However, the needs for the coming year may be $125,000. Becoming frightened by a 25% increase instead of a 10% increase, they begin paring away at the budget until it is down to the figure of $110,000, which they think can be met. This type of process, we believe, is in direct violation to God's promises.

Whereas establishing a budget is usually looked forward to as much as having a bad case of the Asian flu, it has been our experience that when we realistically investigate our needs and are willing to trust God to meet them, it is an exciting adventure to establish something with Him which He in turn has promised to do. Having operated on this principle for the past ten years, our church has been encouraged to see the track record which reveals the fact that whether the budget was increased 10% or as much as 28%, God always provided within a few dollars of what was needed, or He gave exceedingly abundantly above all that we could expect or think.

Once the budget has been approved by the official board, it is ready to go to the congregation for their consideration and approval.

When a final budget is established, each person in an official capacity should make every effort to stay within the prescribed budget. This will do two things: (1) it will keep the confidence of the congregation in the leadership, and (2) it will be a personal testimony as to the faithfulness of the Lord in doing what He says.

A CHURCH ACCOUNTING AND REPORTING SYSTEM

Establishing a budget is only half of a good financial procedure. The other half is an adequate accounting and reporting system which is absolutely necessary if we are to do all things "properly and in an orderly manner" (1 Cor. 14:40).

As a trustee of God's financial transactions, the church must adopt a system that accurately accounts for financial matters. This may be accomplished by taking a business approach to church affairs.

Accounting for church transactions should be accomplished in a simple but adequate system designed to be operated by nonprofessional personnel without unnecessary steps that might complicate the procedures. Accordingly, only basic records are recommended for church operations of small to medium size. The objective of reporting to the church is to keep church members informed on financial matters and to encourage active participation in church affairs. Simplicity in reporting accomplishes much more than an elaborate masterpiece.

BASIC RECORDS

An adequate accounting system requires certain basic records. The basic records necessary to implement the system are a summary of receipts, a checkbook, and an account with a local bank.

As contributions are received, a receipt summary including the following data should be prepared (see page 201). A receipt summary, together with a bank deposit, should be prepared for each service for which an offering was received. This provides a record of receipts by service, which is available for retrieval when desired without maintaining lengthy subsystems which may cost more in time than they can contribute in efficiency.

A checkbook that provides for the computation of a cumulative bank balance on the stub of each check should be maintained. There should be a consecutive numbering system on the check and on the check stub and adequate space on the check stub on which to write an account number and description. As each check is written, a determination of the nature of the expenditure should be made. After reviewing the "chart of accounts" (see pages 202, 203), the appropriate account name and number should be inserted on the check stub.

A bank account provides adequate controls over funds received from contributions. On receipt of each bank statement, the bank's balance of cash on deposit should be reconciled in the cash balance in the checkbook (see page 204). Any error should be located and the correction made.

The chart of accounts should provide for adequate descriptions of church business transactions and classifications of "capital" expenditures as well as "operating" expenditures. The church budget should be prepared with a chart of existing accounts in mind and accounts should be added and deleted as desired. This provides continuity in church reporting and a basis for comparison of accounting periods.

REPORTING TO THE CHURCH

A monthly report is needed for the official church board, with an annual report required for the total church body. These reports should be structured in accord with the responsibility areas. Each member of the official board should be able to make an easy comparison between his budget items and his expenditures. Where appropriate, the report should also be categorized according to the responsibility areas of each person under his direction. For example, suppose the elder in charge of evangelism has a visitation director, an evangelism training director, and an evangelism team coordinator working under his direction. Following the procedure mentioned above, he would have a budget for each of these three areas. The period financial report should list total expenditures for each of these three areas separately. The board member should then give to his workers the financial report data of the area for which he is responsible, acquaint them with their standing, and discuss the expenditures with them.

The most important reporting requirement to the church body is an accurate account of current period receipts and expenditures with appropriate reconciliation of cash balances in comparison with the amounts budgeted (see page 205). Additionally, reports should be maintained on balances in special funds (e.g., memorial funds, scholarship funds, bequest funds). These reports should be revised only when there has been activity in the fund during the current reporting period (see page 206).

Receipts and expenditures are summarized from the two basic records: the receipts summary and the checkbook. A list of receipt summaries written during the current period should be prepared with columns to the right of the list indicating the fund for which the money was collected (see page 207).

A list of checks written during the current period should be prepared with columns indicating the purpose for which the money was spent (see page 207). When these two lists are complete, the columns are totaled and the receipts and expenditures report is prepared. The cash balance in the checkbook should agree with the cash balance on the report. The beginning cash balance should agree with the ending balance on the previous report. Many formats for reporting receipts and expenditures are acceptable. A simple example is presented on page 205. When expenditures are made for capital items, a report summarizing plant assets and current additions or deletions of plant assets should be prepared (see page 208).

A sample of a complete treasurer's monthly report showing the cumulative accounting of all records is demonstrated on pages 209ff. This can also be used as a basis for establishing a budget for the coming year.

Doing God's business in God's way will never lack God's supply.

RECEIPTS SUMMARY

_____ 19_____

Service

Sunday School   _____

Morning Worship   _____

Evening Worship   _____

Wednesday Service   _____

Other_____ _____   _____

Cash Receipts

   Coins

   Currency

   Checks   _____

   Bank Deposit   ═══════════════

Receipts Classifications

   General Fund

   Missionary Fund

   Special Fund #1

   Special Fund #2

   Special Fund #3

   Special Fund #4   _____

    Total Receipts   ═══════════════

CHART OF ACCOUNTS

Account Description	Account Number
Assets	
Cash in Bank	110
Petty Cash Fund	120
Receivables	140
Inventories:	150
Investments:	160
Bonds	161
Stocks	162
Land	163
Buildings	164
Other	165
Due From Other Funds	170
Fixed Assets:	180
Land	181
Buildings	182
Furniture & Fixtures	183
Others	184
Construction in Progress	185
Liabilities	
Notes Payable	210
Accounts Payable	220
Income Taxes Withheld	221
Social Security Withheld	222
Other Miscellaneous Accounts	229
Mortgage Payable	230
Due to Other Funds	270
Net Worth	
Investment in Plant Assets	280
Fund Balance	290

Account Description	Account Number
Revenues	
General Fund Collections	310
Missionary Fund	311
Special Fund Collections	350
Special Fund #1	351
Special Fund #2	352
Special Fund #3	353
Special Fund #4	354
Rentals	360
Interest Earned	361
Disbursements	
Salaries	500
Debt Retirement	550
Property	600
Christian Education	650
Missions	700
Worship	750
Evangelism	800
Publicity	850
Planning	910
Benevolence	920
Miscellaneous	930
Special Funds	950

ORGANIZATION AND LEADERSHIP IN THE LOCAL CHURCH

BANK RECONCILIATION

State Bank and Trust Co.

Balance on the Bank Statement $ 900.00

	Date	Amount	
Add: Deposits Outstanding	11-25	$150.00	
	11-26	300.00	
	11-30	200.00	650.00
			1,550.00

	Check No.	Amount	
Deduct Checks Outstanding	2014	25.00	
	2016	18.00	
	2029	206.00	
	2030	119.00	
	2031	201.50	
	2040	30.50	600.00

Balance per Checkbook (after subtracting service charge) $ 950.00

Balance per Last Receipts and
  Expenditures Reports — Ending Balance $ 840.00

Receipts for Current Period (per
  receipts and expenditures report)   6,890.00
  7,730.00

Disbursements for Current Period (per
  receipts and expenditures report)   6,780.00

Balance of Cash (per current receipts
  and expenditures report) $ 950.00

CASH RECEIPTS AND DISBURSEMENTS

Month of _____19____

| | Current Month | | Year to Date | |
	Actual	Budget	Actual	Budget
Receipts				
General Fund				
Interest				
Rentals				
Special Funds:				
#1				
#2				
#3				
#4				
Total Receipts				
Disbursements				
Salaries				
Debt Retirement				
Property				
Christian Education				
Missions				
Worship				
Evangelism				
Publicity				
Planning				
Benevolence				
Miscellaneous				
Special Funds				
Total Disbursements				
Current Month Surplus (Deficit)				
Cash Balance, Beginning				
Cash Balance, Ending				

CHANGES IN FUND BALANCES

Month of _____ 19___

	Missionary Fund	Special Fund #1	Special Fund #4
Balance (date of last report)	4,600.00	250.00	190.00
Add:			
Contributions	600.00	50.00	10.00
	5,200.00	300.00	200.00
Deduct:			
Salaries	900.00		
Travel Expenses	150.00		
Purchases		94.00	
Lodging		86.00	
Supplies	40.00	20.00	15.00
Rent	160.00		
Benevolence	20.00		
Printing			100.00
Total Disbursements	1,270.00	200.00	115.00
Balance (date of current report)	3,930.00	100.00	85.00

MONTH ENDED _____, 19___

Date		110 Bank Deposit	310 General Fund	311 Missionary Fund	351 Special #1	352 Special #2	353 Special #3	354 Special #4	360 Rentals	361 Interest
1-3-71	Early Church	100.00	90.00		10.00					
1-3-71	Sunday School	1000.00	1500.00	250.00	100.00	50.00	50.00			
1-3-71	11 O'clock Worship	400.00	380.00	20.00						
1-3-71	Evening Worship	200.00	160.00	40.00						
1-6-71	Prayer Worship	115.00	100.00	15.00						
1-8-71	Other								75.00	

ANALYSIS OF DISBURSEMENTS

MONTH of _____, 19___

Date	Payee	Check Number	Check Amount	230 Mortgage Payable	500 Salaries	221 Feb. Inc. Tax W/H	222 FICA W/H	600 Property	650 Chr. Ed.	700 Missions	750 Program
1-1-71		6046	200.00		260.00	(40.00)	(20.00)				
1-1-71		6047	619.50						619.50		
1-3-71		6048	8.90								

PLANT FUND CHANGES

Month of _____19____

Acct. No.		Amount
185	Construction in Progress	$ 4,500.00
182	Buildings and Improvements	35,000.00
183	Furnishings	15,000.00
181	Land	8,000.00
184	Equipment	2,500.00
	Total Plant Assets (date of last report of Plant Fund Changes)	65,000.00

	Purchase of Capital Items:		
184	Equipment (tables)	850.00	
182	Paving parking lot	300.00	
			1,150.00

	Disposition of Capital Items:		
184	Sale of Equipment (at original cost of)	200.00	
181	Donation of Land (at original cost of)	2,000.00	2,200.00

185	Construction in Progress	4,500.00
182	Buildings and Improvements	35,300.00
183	Furnishings	15,000.00
181	Land	6,000.00
184	Equipment	3,150.00
	Total Plant Assets to Date	63,950.00

PANTEGO BIBLE CHURCH
TREASURER'S REPORT
OCTOBER 25, 1972

	Four Weeks		Forty-three Weeks	
Monthly Statistics	Budget	Actual	Budget	Actual
General Fund:				
Total Receipts	$ 7,308	$ 8,461	$78,561	$73,219
*Average per week	1,827	2,115	1,827	1,703
Missionary Fund:				
Total Receipts	2,516	2,454	27,047	25,795
*Average per week	629	614	629	600

Financial Transactions Notes

Cost of Building Program:	Total	New Admin. Bldg.	Brown House	White House	Longhorn Lodge
Balance 9-25-72	$35,719	$25,993	$ 7,670	$ 1,620	$ 436
October 1972	1,535	—	49	1,460	26
Balance 10-25-72	$37,254	$25,993	$ 7,719	$ 3,080	$ 462

General Fund:	
Arlington Bank and Trust Company	$ 6,318
Arlington Savings and Loan Association	—
Petty Cash	100
Total General Fund Balance	$ 6,418
Building Fund:	
Certificate of Deposit	$10,000
Arlington Savings and Loan Association	4,275
Total Building Fund Balance	$14,275
Pantego Bible Church Memorial Fund Balance	$ 304
Property Fund:	
First National Bank	$ 44
Oak Cliff Savings and Loan Association	333
Total Property Fund Balance	$ 377

*Averages are computed on the basis of 53 Sundays in the calendar year 1972.

PANTEGO BIBLE CHURCH
GENERAL FUND
CASH RECEIPTS AND DISBURSEMENTS
MONTH OF OCTOBER 1972

Code	Account	Current Month		Year-to-Date	
		Budget	Actual	Budget	Actual
	Receipts				
401	General Fund	$ 7,308	$ 8,461	$78,561	$73,219
410	Mission Fund	2,516	2,454	27,047	25,795
450	Special Funds	—	1,287	—	45,837
	Total Receipts	9,824	12,202	105,608	144,851
	Disbursements				
500	Salaries	3,236	3,855	34,787	31,022
550	Debt Retirement	1,236	1,260	13,287	12,285
600	Property	1,712	1,350	18,404	17,556
650	Christian Education	496	723	5,332	5,209
700	Missions	2,516	2,856	27,047	25,826
750	Program	216	235	2,322	2,436
800	Evangelism	32	—	344	179
850	Publicity	60	30	645	122
910	Planning	260	—	2,795	—
920	Benevolence	24	—	258	—
930	Miscellaneous	36	—	387	1
950	Special Funds	—	2,765	—	50,622
	Total Disbursements	9,824	13,074	105,608	145,258
	Current Month Cash Flow		($ 872)		($ 407)
	General Fund Transfer		—		($ 5,258)
	Fund Balance—Beginning		7,290		12,083
	Fund Balance—Ending		$ 6,418		$ 6,418

PANTEGO BIBLE CHURCH
GENERAL FUND — SUBSIDIARY
CASH RECEIPTS AND DISBURSEMENTS
MONTH OF OCTOBER 1972

Code	Account	Current Month Budget	Actual	Year-to-Date Budget	Actual
450	Special Funds:				
451	Building Fund	$	$ 50	$	$25,087
453	Kindergarten Maint.				900
455	Banquets		1,100		1,701
460	Vending Machines		37		493
465	Encampments				2,896
470	Love Offerings				1,352
490	Transfer of Funds		100		13,408
		—	1,287	—	45,837
500	Salaries:				
501	Ministers	2,464	2,470	26,488	23,703
505	Pulpit Supply	24	—	258	160
510	Secretarial & Maint.	748	1,385	8,041	7,159
		3,236	3,855	34,787	31,022
600	Property:				
610	Insurance	76	—	817	632
612	Utilities	452	592	4,859	4,446
613	Building Maintenance	100	85	1,075	445
614	Janitorial Supplies	36	37	387	280
615	Bus Maintenance	76	32	817	318
625	New Admin. Bldg. Furn.	152	—	1,634	1,603
626	New Parking Lot	264	—	2,838	3,594
630	Trans. to Prop. Account	452	550	4,859	5,200
635	Misc. New Equipment	104	54	1,118	1,038
		1,712	1,350	18,404	17,556
650	Christian Education:				
651	Sunday School Supplies	260	848	2,795	2,713
652	V.B.S.	44	—	473	901
653	Training Hours	24	—	258	139
654	Pioneer Girls	32	73	344	286
655	Boys Brigade	36	—	387	301
626	Children's Church	32	19	344	163
657	Camps	16	(10)	172	96
658	Nursery	16	—	172	4
659	C. E. Supplies	36	(207)	387	606
		496	723	5,332	5,209

PANTEGO BIBLE CHURCH
GENERAL FUND — SUBSIDIARY
CASH RECEIPTS AND DISBURSEMENTS
MONTH OF OCTOBER 1972

Code	Account	Current Month		Year-to-Date	
		Budget	Actual	Budget	Actual
750	Program:				
751	Office Supplies	$ 152	$ 235	$ 1,634	$ 2,217
752	Music Department	36	—	387	214
753	Recreation	24	—	258	5
754	Ushering and Floral	4	—	43	—
		216	235	2,322	2,436
800	Evangelism:				
810	January Conference	16	—	172	92
811	Personal Evangel. Conf.	8	—	86	—
812	Tracts and Visitation	8	—	86	87
		32	—	344	179
850	Publicity:				
851	Church Newspaper	36	—	387	48
852	Photo Supplies	8	—	86	22
853	Advertising	8	30	86	30
854	Misc. Supplies	8	—	86	22
		60	30	645	122
950	Special Funds:				
951	Building Fund		1,535		18,876
953	Kindergarten Maint.		75		1,600
955	Banquets, Retreats, etc.		1,119		1,720
960	Vending Machines		14		547
965	Encampments		22		6,157
970	Love Offerings		—		1,672
990	Transfer of Funds		—		20,050
		—	2,765	—	50,622

22
Decision and Indecision

Decisions are the threads that weave their way through every facet of church life and bind its many activities to a common purpose. Decisions are the nutrients of life for the church body, filling the time and efforts of every church worker.

From the outset, the early church was faced with many critical decisions. There were decisions as to basic mission and purpose as Peter was led by the Spirit to include the Gentiles as recipients of the Gospel (Acts 10). Early Christians were also faced with major personnel decisions as they replaced Judas with Matthias in the apostleship (Acts 1) and as they chose the seven deacons to serve the physical needs of the believers (Acts 6). Decisions about scope, approach, and direction were made in sending Barnabas and Paul on the first missionary journey (Acts 13), and in Paul's choice to enter Macedonia rather than Asia (Acts 16). Decisions were required for the handling of interpersonal conflicts and differences of opinion as seen in the disagreement between Paul and Barnabas regarding whether or not to take John Mark on the missionary journey (Acts 15) and between Peter and Paul regarding the requirement of circumcision among the Gentile believers (Acts 15). Indeed, *The Acts of the Apostles* might as appropriately be called "the Decisions of the Apostles." At every movement, change, and activity, the apostles were clearly absorbed in the process of decision making. Many decisions in this critical early stage were earth-shakingly important whereas many others were minor and insignificant.

The decisions made in the church activities today also range from critically important to insignificant, varying from major issues of direction and purpose to minor inconsequential decisions of the dimensions of a bulletin board to be hung in the hallway. The decisions involve personnel choices, interpersonal conflicts, questions of scope and direction, finance, property, and all other church functions. The effectiveness of the church in arriving at proper decisions will go far toward determining its success.

WHERE DO WE GET DECISIONS?

A church leader is faced with decisions of three kinds: cyclical, confrontation, and innovation. Cyclical decisions are those which recur repeatedly, the repetition often allowing us to establish formal patterns for our decisions. Sunday school material is ordered each quarter, using standardized forms and procedures; worship services follow a consistent format; and the annual budget is formulated with about the same approach each year.

Confrontation decisions may be forced on us by circumstances or events. We must select a new youth worker for the Wednesday night program. We must deal with a conflict within the staff, expand our parking lot, or buy additional chairs for a Sunday school classroom. Crises are always popping up that demand a solution and require a major portion of our time.

Innovation decisions occur only when we seek them out. They do not come up naturally and therefore are not forced on us. *We must find them.* We decide to offer a kindergarten or day nursery to our community; we decide to develop a leadership training conference for our church leaders; we decide to sponsor a winter camp for adult couples; we establish a Bible chair at a local college; we decide to sponsor a community evangelical campaign. These are decisions that were not thrust on us. They are the types of decisions that require innovation.

Most church leaders become so thoroughly immersed in cyclical or confrontation decisions that they very rarely get around to innovation. We misplace the bulk of our time, effort, attention, and money on problems rather than opportunities. In the *Harvard Business Review,* Peter Drucker points out to the businessman that "a very small number of events — 10% to 20% at most — account for 90% of all results, whereas the great majority of events account for 10% or less of the results."[1] The same statement seems to be readily applicable to church decision making. We spend at least 90% of our time making the routine decisions that account for not more than 10% of the results. How can we build innovation decisions into the activities of the church organization?

---

[1]Peter Drucker, "Managing for Business Effectiveness," *Harvard Business Review,* May-June, 1963, pp. 53-60.

Perhaps the simplest procedure is by way of goal setting. Some firms have received a tremendous boost when the chief executive simply said to his men, "Look, I've just set four goals for myself for this quarter. I would like to get each of you to do the same. In a couple of weeks, I plan to call a meeting in which I'll discuss my goals with you and I hope you'll be able to share yours with me. At the end of the quarter we'll see how we do." Can you, as a church leader, think of three to five goals that you might accomplish in the next three months that are beyond your usual routine of work? If not, you have probably been in the same job too long. If you can, let us suggest that you do so and have the people working with you do the same. At the end of three months, you can see how things come out and set two or three more. As long as these do not become clubs with which to beat others, they can be real stimulants to progress.

A second approach involves setting up an innovation committee (yes, yet another committee). This group is assigned the specific role of coming up with new ideas and methods; nothing is "off limits" except the routine. They have no problems to solve, no plans to make, no quantity of items to grind out. Their function is to come up with ideas for meeting the basic purposes of the church in a way that is not now being used.

The third approach is to listen to the maverick. In most groups there is a person that always disagrees. He is always producing the hare-brained idea that leaves everyone else mumbling or staring at the floor. Try loving him; thank God for him. (I won't ask that you encourage him; he probably doesn't need it anyway.) Nothing is duller than a church board that is wallowing in agreement and thoughtless unanimity. If Paul can disagree with Peter and set him back on his ear over the circumcision issue, surely our churches can survive the test of difference of opinion. Our problem is that we have built such a mask of perfection around ourselves that we are often afraid to be open and honest in our leadership meeting. We fear disagreement as though every issue is supported on one side by God and on the other by Satan. If we get rid of this notion, then perhaps we can state our opinions honestly and listen to alternatives, deciding from among the choices available. Innovation rarely emerges from a group that simply falls into line as a solid front behind a single person or a single-minded idea.

The fourth approach — planning — we have discussed in the preceding chapters. Long-range or annual plans provide a framework for looking into the future to solve tomorrow's problems by allowing us to prepare for new methods or activities to serve our purposes. Once the need for a decision has been found or forced on us, we turn to the search for alternative approaches to a solution.

SEARCHING FOR SOLUTIONS

Suppose in establishing long-range plans your board became concerned about the under-utilization of the educational facilities. Your board felt that it was not using its facilities as fully as it should during the week days. With the problem clearly before the board, the members begin to search for alternative approaches to the use of its educational facilities.

In order to arrive at a good decision, the board must have an adequate set of alternatives — adequate in the sense that the *best* solution is among the choices under consideration and that sufficient information for an understanding and analysis of the alternatives is available. Perhaps, too, the most effective approach for beginning the search is brainstorming — a process designed to get the widest possible range of alternatives out before the group for consideration. Each board member is asked to state every possibility that comes to mind, no matter how ridiculous it may sound. Each idea is duly recorded without evaluation or comment. The breadth of the issue set out for brainstorming can vary. We might ask the board to forget that they are dealing with a church and say to them, "You have 15,000 square feet of floor space you wish to put to use. What uses might you consider for that floor space?" With more limited scope in mind, one might start the brainstorming session by saying, "We have 15,000 square feet of floor space in the church to use in any way possible. It is divided into rooms of various sizes, and some of it is carpeted. What are the possible ways to use it?" The first approach will provide a greater range of ideas, but of course, there will be a greater number that are out of the realm of possibility. The first approach takes more time, but affords more creativity in the ideas. Suppose we choose the latter and the ideas begin to pour forth. Remember, any idea is acceptable at this point. These alternatives might be presented: a medical clinic for the poor, counseling and guidance services, a private school, a private college, a kindergarten, a grammar school, a day nursery, a full 12-year school, a cleaning service, rental of office space, a bookstore, a professional building, a janitorial service, a seminary, Bible classes, a Bible institute, leadership training conferences, and so on.

Having completed a substantial list, our next step would be to have the board evaluate the list. To do this, it must develop a set of evaluation standards which will establish parameters for the alternatives. The primary and secondary purposes (see chapter 12) of the church become an initial parameter, for the church must not get outside its reason for being. Scriptural principles form another obviously related set of parameters. Other parameters may come from the local situation. The board may decide that the alternative selected must not incur expenses beyond a certain level, must not require more than a certain number of church members to direct the effort, and so on. Each idea generated in brainstorming is now put to the test of these standards. A few emerge for further study. Let us say these include a kindergarten, a psychological counseling and guidance service with fees based on ability to pay, a Bible institute, a day nursery, and a Christian bookstore.

The next step for the board is to collect data. The board must determine what monies, people, and materials will be required to pursue each alternative. To find this data, they call upon their own experiences and education, seek the aid of experts in each field, survey, investigate, and observe operations of other churches which are attempting to pursue each alternative, and read pertinent publications about the alternatives. From these many sources, they begin to project the cost and resources to be required and the return that can be expected in terms of meeting the purposes of the church. Finally, they have what approximates an analysis of cost/effectiveness (obtaining the greatest gain at the lowest cost) for each alternative, including both qualitative and quantitative information. Now they are ready to arrive at a decision.

The procedure for searching for solutions outlined for this board decision is typical of the procedure followed for almost any decision. In summary, step #1 is the brainstorming phase in which we spin out a random array of ideas; in step #2, we evaluate the ideas on the basis of the broadest parameters of purpose, Scripture, and our operational constraints; in step #3, we collect data for the purpose of analyzing the plausible alternatives; and in step #4, we summarize the data into a cost/effectiveness breakdown that allows us to compare the alternatives. Although this procedure can be used for any decision, the amount of time and effort going into each step depends upon the importance of the decision. A good decision maker must know how much effort a decision is worth and when he should stop searching and decide. Insecurity about one's ability to decide, fear of criticism from others, and/or fear of failure often cause a person to delay until the value of the decision is lost. A decision may well cost more to make than its consequences are worth on any balance sheet.

ARRIVING AT A DECISION

A decision will be made on the basis of intuition, experience, deductive logic, tryout, and considered judgment. If we have followed a thorough search process, it is unlikely that we will then turn to intuition for the decision. Yet all of us have no doubt encountered a person who behaves in the unfathomable manner that Henry Higgins attributes to Lisa Dolittle when he says,

> She will beg you for advice;
> Your reply will be concise.
> She will listen very nicely,
> Then go out and do precisely
> *What she wants!*[2]

Hard facts have little to do with such decision making.

Intuition is used when we arrive at a decision on grounds that even

---

[2]Alan Jay Lerner, *My Fair Lady,* Columbia Masterworks, 1956.

we ourselves cannot explain; we just have a feel about the problem. It is not surprising that the *best* intuitive decisions are arrived at by people of high intelligence who have a great deal of knowledge and experience on the subject. However, intuition is rarely an acceptable substitute for sound reasoning.

Experience is one of the most popular approaches to decision making. Solutions are arrived at on the basis of exposure that the decision maker has had with similar problems in the past. In using experience, we are assuming that the current problems and the previous ones have enough in common to transfer the experience. This assumption should be scrutinized carefully, for present and past conditions may be vastly different even for a similar problem.

Deductive logic is often used in some measure, usually rather haphazardly. The problem solver establishes premises related to the decision which are then used as building blocks to support a solution. If the logical process is followed with precision, the solution will achieve logical certainty. However, its actual value is largely based on the adequacy of the premises underlying the solution.

In the try-out method, the decision maker selects a tentative solution, employs the solution, and then on the basis of the results, modifies the solution through further trials. This approach is most fully applicable for decisions which involve a change in an existing program. In this context it may be viewed as a process of fine tuning in an operation, analogous to the control of a spaceship whose course is corrected in flight to make minor adjustments. In a problem like that of the board finding an effective use for its educational facilities during week-days, the try-out method would not be efficient. Changing courses would be too costly in the lives of the people involved. We cannot for example, afford to establish a day nursery, solicit the children for the operation, and then after a couple of months decide to discontinue the service. Too many people would be hurt by such a procedure.

Perhaps the most widely applicable approach is that of considered judgment. In this approach, we carefully consider all of the pertinent information that has been collected; each of the facts are carefully weighed and compared. From this data the decision maker visualizes the results of each solution and makes a judgment, choosing the one that seems most effective. A word of caution should be made at this point. We often claim to have used considered judgment, whereas, in fact, we are using intuition or experience. Considered judgment is being used only if we have carefully collected data and have mentally projected the results of the various solutions by a vicarious visualization.

WHY AREN'T DECISIONS CARRIED OUT?

A decision is of no value unless it is implemented. In the traditional concept of a church board as strictly a policy- or decision-making body, the problem of implementation is magnified. The separation of the board from functional operations is the basis of this handicap. Its decisions are made apart from day-to-day problems; consequently, it frequently fails to deal with the problems realistically. Even if the members of the board are leaders of operational departments, there is no guarantee of effective implementation of decisions. Let us consider some of the contributing elements to effective implementation:

Where possible, the people who are to carry out a decision should be the ones to make the decision.

This is perhaps most obviously demonstrated in the case of the President of the United States. Each new president tends to shuck the brainchild of the one preceding him because he wishes to make his own contribution to society and his own place in history. A similar phenomenon occurs in the case of department managers in business and other organizations. A new manager either subtly or blatantly changes the thrust of his unit to suit his personal emphasis or interest. The same principle holds for the church — a new leader will tend to plot a new course. By nature, people prefer to rear their own "brainchildren." The reasons are both psychological and practical. When we make a decision for our work unit, we consciously or subconsciously weigh the outcome in terms of our own needs. We do not have an opportunity to do this for a decision that someone else has made and that hits us cold. As a result, we take such a decision more cautiously. From the practical standpoint, when a person makes a decision, the implementation that he visualizes is one of the factors in his evaluation. By the time the decision is made, he has a clear idea as to how it will work out and is therefore primed for action. Thus, the principle of maximum delegation of decision-making authority is reinforced.

Internal communications and organization must be strong.

For an important decision to be implemented, many people will become involved. The efforts of many people must be coordinated and organized toward a single effort. Recently, Pantego Bible Church decided to build a new administration building. To reduce cost, avoid loan and interest considerations, and increase fellowship among the membership, the church decided that the members would provide most of the labor and build the wing on a "pay-as-you-go" basis. The project was led by a member who is in the construction business. He established work teams who were assigned various projects and who were led by a person who is employed in the given trade area. For the implementation of this project the communication and organization had to be strong. Group meetings, memos, posters, church bulletin announcements, announcements in worship service, and most important, the telephone, were channels that received a great deal of use in the process of carrying out the

219

project. Without proper communication and organization the project would have been a colossal failure. Most of our decisions are not as complex and do not involve as many people, yet for any decision in which two or three people are involved, the communication problems are great.

The decision must be accepted by the people involved rather than sold to them.

Often we speak of "selling" a decision to those who will carry it out. This involves persuading the majority and silencing the minority. This type of "selling" is a waste of time. If a person is to carry out a decision, he must take it as his own — either one that he makes or one that he would have made if given the choice.

> To speak of "selling" also implies that what is the right decision be subordinated to what the "customer" wants, but this is poisonous and dishonest doctrine. What is right is decided by the nature of the problem; the wishes, desires and receptivity of the "customers" are quite irrelevant. If it is the right decision they must be led to accept it whether at first they like it or not. If time has to be spent on selling a decision, it has not been made properly and is unlikely to become effective. . . . Precisely because the decision affects the work of other people, it must help these people achieve their objectives, assist them in their work, contribute to their performing better, more effectively and with a greater sense of achievement.[3]

Our problem is not one of selling decisions but rather one of tapping the internal motivation of those who will carry them out. This is augmented by their participation, but if they cannot be allowed to participate in the decision, then at least those making the decision should do so with the intent of aiding and challenging the action takers.

THE PROBLEMS OF INDECISION

In the area of indecision we are really dealing with two problems — the first is a failure to come to a decision, and the second is a decision not to decide. The failure to decide when a decision is called for is one of the most insidious cripplers of church effectiveness. Stimulated by fear and insecurity, we attempt to withdraw into other activities in the hope that the problem will pass. But it never does. It usually grows worse. Indecisiveness is the result of an inability to deal with conflict and its resultant anxiety. We choose to experience the anxieties accompanying delay because, although more prolonged, they are less acute. We often excuse our indecision with the comment "I want to pray about it some more," as though God is having a problem making up His mind. No, the problem of "indecision" lies with us. We must gain the confidence

---

[3]Peter Drucker, *The Practice of Management,* (New York: McGraw-Hill, 1954), p. 364.

to go ahead even when the solution may not be the best one. If we have a great deal of difficulty in arriving at a decision, it is probably because the alternatives available are rather close to equal in their results. If this is the case, there is little lost by making the "wrong" choice.

The decision not to decide is quite another matter. It is often among the plausible alternatives that are available to us. The famed management theorist, Chester Barnard gives four conditions in which one should decide not to decide. He says,

> The fine art of executive decision consists in not deciding questions that are not now pertinent, in not deciding prematurely, in not making decisions that cannot be made effective, and in not making decisions that others should make. Not to decide questions that are not pertinent at the time is uncommon good sense, though to raise them may be uncommon perspicacity. Not to decide questions prematurely is to refuse commitment of attitude or the development of prejudice. Not to make decisions that cannot be made effective is to refrain from destroying authority. Not to make decisions that others should make is to preserve morale, to develop competence, to fix responsibility, and to preserve authority.[4]

Our problem becomes one of knowing when these conditions exist or when we should move ahead to make a decision. In collecting the data regarding various alternative solutions, we should be alert to evidences regarding the question of timeliness. We should consider the question of the time for the decision with the same serious thought as any of the alternatives. As a clue to the judgement of when the delay is based on pertinent considerations as opposed to a desire to avoid the issue, one may study his own emotions and those of others making the decisions. If the idea of the decision brings on depression, anxiety, or hostility, then your delay is a problem of indecision. If calmness and logic prevail, then your decision to delay is wise.

---

[4]Chester Barnard, *The Functions of the Executive,* (Cambridge, Mass.: Harvard University Press, 1968), p. 194.

23

The Church Facilities

$\mathbf{T}$he Biblical imperative "not forsaking our own assembling together" (Heb. 10:25) demands a meeting of believers sometime somewhere. The meeting necessitates a place to meet. It may be large, it may be small, it may be simple, it may be elaborate. It may be a home or it may be an edifice in the business district of a large city. Whatever the structure, if believers are meeting together under New Testament principles, it is called a church, not because of the building, but because of what takes place within the building. The ecclesiastical world has been programmed to think that a building is a church and that "a church should look like a church" — in essence an untenable demand. There is no New Testament instruction as to what a building where the church meets should look like. Our concept of what a church building should look like is the result of ingrained traditionalism, the result of the medieval papacy. If we see a beautiful Gothic structure with stained-glass windows, its steeple piercing the sky, a long hallwaylike interior with rows of pews facing an elevated chancel from which the minister speaks down to the people, and if we sit back and say that that looks like a church, then we are simply admitting that our thinking has been conditioned by medieval traditionalism and not biblical direction.

Though a residential house is a very suitable place for a small con-

222

gregation to use as a meeting place, most congregations in our present structure of society find it necessary to utilize a facility which provides more space than the average-size house. This has led congregations to purchase property and to build buildings suitable for their activities. Unless the structure of our society changes so that congregations will no longer be allowed public worship and of necessity will be forced back into a house church, it seems that facilities planned for worship and service experiences and owned by local congregations are here to stay.

It should be obvious that no attempt will be made to design or describe the ideal building for church use. There is no such building. Every congregation should of necessity have its own unique kind of building because every congregation has a personality of its own. Its personality and its purpose for meeting should be reflected in the facility used as a meeting place.

Our purpose in this discussion is to set down some guidelines and principles which are applicable to virtually all building situations, though the specific details of them will depend on the context of the immediate congregation. These guidelines are contingent upon the congregation's own understanding of its purposes and needs.

The first guideline may be stated this way. The design of the church should be determined by the program and purpose of the church. In a word, it must be *functional*. At first glance, this may seem so obvious that it hardly needs mentioning, but one needs only to look around and see the atrocities that have been built because they have been designed without regard for utility. It is appalling that more care is often taken in determining what the outside of the building should look like than what the inside of the building should be used for. Remember, facilities are built to be used, not to be admired.

Function is determined by program. Program is the result of purpose and goals. Therefore, it is imperative that a congregation begin with purpose and goals when determining what kind. of a meeting place they should have.

One congregation spent months in simply defining their program and what they sought to accomplish. They concluded that the primary purpose was the followship of believers centered in the teaching of the Word of God. This purpose dictated a number of things. In order to provide an atmosphere of involving and sharing rather than of just observing and listening, they designed a circular seating arrangement, thus giving the believers an opportunity to see each other's faces rather than only the backs of the heads of those sitting in front of them. The choir was programmed into this kind of arrangement, and rather than being seated behind the pulpit, they completed the circle by being seated to the right and left of the teaching center with space reserved so that they could come together as a unit during their ministry in the worship service. Since one of the goals was to make the preaching of the Word central, the result was to situate the teaching area in the center of the congregation in such a way that the teacher was at eye level with the person seated farthest from him. Because teaching is not just verbalizing, facilities for audio-visual aids were built into the structure in order to add to its function. Comfortable seating, adequate lighting, a well-planned sound system, and provision to care for other functions of the church family such as baptism, the observance of the Lord's table, weddings, funerals and other programs of extra curricular nature were all taken into consideration in designing the facility.

"Functional," then, is the first guideline. We build for the distinct uses of each congregation rather than according to an abstract concept of an ideal church building.

The second guideline is this: concentrate on what is essential and eliminate anything superfluous. In a word, make it *simple.* The saying "Less is more" is certainly apropos in determining a facility. Over-emphasis on symbolism as a form of communication defeats the purpose of the building. Many churches give only an ambiguous statement of their purpose in symbolism, and are so cluttered with nonessentials that it is difficult to tell what is primary. Church family worship does not demand an elaborate setting. In fact, the more elaborate the trappings, the less emphasis there seems to be put on the primary purpose of a congregation worshiping and communicating with God through His Word. The simplicity of design and appointments will place the attention where it should be: on the communication of the Word and not on the admiration of the icons.

The exterior design of the building will be dictated by its interior function, but it should also be governed by the guideline of simplicity. In a day when there is much emphasis on ecology, it is wise to let this emphasis influence the planning of the structure that is to be used to house the church.

The third principle is this: Strive to make it *aesthetically beautiful.* Simplicity does not preclude beauty. It seems that churches are often at one extreme or the other; either they are overdone and gaudy or they are uninteresting and shamefully unattractive because little care has been given to simple aesthetics. The facility where believers gather to worship should be a reflection of the beauty expressed in the ancient Crusaders' hymn:

> Beautiful Savior, Lord of the nations,
> Son of God and Son of man,
> Glory and honor, praise, adoration
> Now and forever more be thine.

The essence of beauty is seen in God's creation: the firmament, the woodlands, the meadows, and the beautiful garb of spring. These things should exert their influence on the construction of the building. As much as possible, natural materials and exposure to God's creation and firmament should be incorporated into the building.

The fourth guideline is this: a building where the church meets should be adaptable for many different services and occasions. We can call this being *flexible*. There is no justification for building a facility where much of its space is used only one hour per week or designed for only one specific function or use. Our educational structures should be built with flexibility not only to accommodate a Sunday school, but also to provide for the use of the facilities throughout the week, for programs such as a Christian day school, youth activities, service projects, etc. This may mean that the same building will be used for activities for various age groups, from children through adult, for small groups as well as large, by providing flexibility in furniture design and division of space.

The same flexibility is necessary in the nave or sanctuary area. Most churches are built as if every worship service is identical and as if the attendance at all services are the same. However, this is not the case. A wedding is not the same as observance of the Lord's supper. Nor is the communion service like a service of expository teaching. With the advent of change descending upon our forms of worship, flexibility must be built into the structure to provide not only the customary spectator experience, but also a service of more involvement through discussion, small group study, a variety of teaching methods through visual-aids, role playing, dialogue, panel discussions, and informal interaction.

Most church buildings are arranged for the maximum number of worshipers. However, we do not always have a maximum number of people present, and a church that is half-full is also, and depressingly, half-empty. Flexibility is necessary to overcome this handicap.

The area which needs much creative thinking is that which deals with congregational space. In most of our churches the space is taken up with rigid pews that are fastened to the floor, giving only one possible configuration. Apart from the fact that most pews or benches are the most uncomfortable kind of seating accommodation, they also restrict versatility, visibility, and a feeling of intimacy. Total flexibility in this regard demands movable chairs designed for comfort and instructional use.

The same flexibility should be provided for the music ministry. The choir "loft" is no longer a suitable arrangement. If those participating in the music program are to identify with the congregation, by all means, choir space should not be restricted by furniture maintained in a fixed position. Provision should be made to accomodate suitably a small choral group as well as a large combined choir of adults, young people, and children.

Above all, we need to make our facilities adaptable. Every fixed wall or piece of stationary furniture eliminates just one more possibility of flexibility.

The fifth guideline is this: A building should help create a sense of oneness and community. The experience of worship cannot be second-hand. There must be involvement. Therefore our building must help us to be *intimate* in our worship. The church is an organism, not an organization. As an organism, it is described in Ephesians 5 as the body of Christ. The Peninsula Bible Church of Palo Alto, California, has done much to draw attention to the concept of "body life" as a worship experience. This body-life meeting provides believers an opportunity to share their burdens and their blessings and to bear one another's burdens through prayer, encouragement, and empathy. This concept of Christian worship will greatly influence the efforts put into overcoming the feeling of being remote from one another and from where the action really is. It will influence the appointments, the height of the ceiling, the size of the room, the angle of the wall, the location of the lectern, as well as the covering on the floor. All of these things can create a greater sense of intimacy in developing the spirit of the body life.

The sixth and last guideline is this: Buildings in which the church meets should be an example of good financial stewardship. That is, they should be soundly *economical*. The purpose of the church is to leave lasting memorials in lives rather than in buildings. It is not un-common for a church building to become a monument to the architect who designed it, rather than a reflection of the lives of people who use it. A structure can be built so that it is practical and durable, besides incorporating the other guidelines which have previously been men-tioned, and still be very economical.

The economics of the structure can be adjusted in many ways. Wise and meticulous planning will be one of the biggest factors. Impulsive planning and washroom decisions are some of the most costly factors in construction. A facility that has to be remodeled shortly after its completion because it does not meet the needs of the program can become a very costly structure, though initially built at an economical cost. Selection of an architect whose record in church buildings is of a blue-ribbon variety can in the long run save many, many dollars. This means that he is not only technically competent, but also willing to work intimately with the planning committee, being sensitive to their needs, not just determined to carry out his own ideas.

There is a final way that the economics can be affected. This method of construction is getting as rare as a Model-T Ford, but like the Model-T, it is a good arrangement if you can get it running properly. It is simply a matter of allowing the members of the congregation to become personally involved manually in some phase of the construction. There is nothing that will give an individual more pride in a facility than to know that he has had a personal part in bringing it into reality. Admittedly, in most cases, it is easier for people to give money to con-struct the building than it is to give themselves, but there is much to be said for the spirit of community that results from a common project of a visible nature. Of course, this type of building program demands some experienced craftsmen who are willing to show others what to do and who are able to involve them in the project. With the emphasis in our society on more leisure time, especially on the four-day work week and the resulting long weekends, we may do well to capitalize on this and to provide opportunities for the members to use this ample leisure time and thereby fulfill the principle of good stewardship.

These six principles — directing us to construct buildings that are functional, simple, aesthetically beautiful, flexible, intimate, and economical — are applicable to all church building projects in our time. How they will be spelled out, though, will vary as much as individual congregations differ among themselves.

Conclusion

The demands of leadership in the local church exact a broader range of capabilities than any other leadership situation. The church leader performs a scope of functions which extend from deeply personal considerations to coolly objective decisions. He is required to be a theological, biblical, and doctrinal analyst; a moral and spiritual leader; a counselor and teacher; a team leader and guide; a peacemaker; a communicator; an organizer; an administrator; a planner; and a decision maker.

In this book we have attempted to provide concepts, principles, and guidelines that will be of assistance to the church leader in wearing each of these hats. We have attempted to deal with the functions of leadership systematically and coherently, necessitating the treatment of the functions as separate units and as distinct concepts. While treating the functions of leadership in separate chapters, we have attempted to provide as much integration of the concepts as possible.

We wish to emphasize that the leadership role cannot be practiced as a set of unrelated, static activities. Indeed, it requires a continual balancing and integration of the various responsibilities. We communicate with people in small groups to organize, plan, budget, or even counsel. In so doing we confront a broad array of leadership concepts and practices.

Most students of eschatology agree that the time of Christ's return is rapidly approaching. We must use the time effectively to fulfill our mission as individuals and as local churches. It is in this context that we have presented our concepts of church organization and leadership.

We have not called for a radical upheaval of existing church structure which would bring about divisions and at least for a time curtail the work of the local congregation. Rather, we have presented concepts and principles which build directly upon bibical forms and restore new life to the body.

Many of the principles can be applied at the discretion of a single church leader, others will require the cooperative effort of the church board, and still others necessitate action by the total congregation. Each chapter attempts to stimulate thought and evoke action that will be of value to the local church in confronting the demands of the church in our generation. We urge the reader not to treat the material as merely an intellectual stimulant, but as a means of reviewing his own service and that of his congregation, and then of giving the concepts life through application, continually realizing that

> *He put all things in subjection under His feet, and gave Him as head over all things to the church, which is His body, the fulness of Him who fills all in all.*

Ephesians 1:22, 23

Appendix A

ACTIVITIES, INTEREST, AND PROFICIENCY QUESTIONNAIRE

Instructions

This questionnaire is to be used to assist your church leadership in evaluating the work of the ministry. The personal information of the first eleven items will allow a comparison of the views of persons in various age, sex, marital status, and other groups. Please do not identify yourself by name; we prefer anonymity.

Place a check mark for the response of each item which best describes you, your activities, interests, or opinions.

Thank you for your help.

ACTIVITIES, INTEREST, AND PROFICIENCY QUESTIONNAIRE

1. I am ____a.____male b.____female.

2. My age is
   - ____a. under 12. ____c. 19-25. ____e. 36-45. ____g. 56-65.
   - ____b. 13-18. ____d. 26-35. ____f. 46-55. ____h. 66 & over.

3. I am
   - ____a. single. ____c. widowed. ____e. separated.
   - ____b. married. ____d. divorced.

4. If you have children, how many?
   - ____a. one ____c. three ____e. five or more
   - ____b. two ____d. four

5. You are
   - ____a. a student. ____c. a housewife. ____e. none of these.
   - ____b. working full-time. ____d. retired.

6. How long have you been a member of this church?
   - ____a. less than a year ____c. 4-7 years ____e. more than 15 years
   - ____b. 1-3 years ____d. 8-15 years

7. How long have you attended *any* Sunday school on a regular basis?
   - ____a. less than a year ____c. 4-7 years ____e. more than 15 years
   - ____b. 1-3 years ____d. 8-15 years

8. How long have you been a Christian?
   - ____a. less than a year ____c. 4-7 years ____e. more than 15 years
   - ____b. 1-3 years ____d. 8-15 years

9. How far do you live from church?

———a. less than a mile ———c. 3-5 miles ———e. more than 10 miles

———b. 1-2 miles ———d. 6-10 miles

10. What is the total number of wage earners in your household?

———a. one ———c. three ———e. five or more

———b. two ———d. four

11. What is your TOTAL family income each year?

———a. $5,000 or less ———d. $16,000-20,000

———b. $6,000-10,000 ———e. more than $20,000

———c. $11,000-15,000

12. How often do you attend Sunday morning worship?

———a. regularly ———c. sometimes ———e. never

———b. usually ———d. seldom

13. How often do you attend Sunday evening worship?

———a. regularly ———c. sometimes ———e. never

———b. usually ———d. seldom

14. How often do you attend Wednesday evening prayer meeting?

———a. regularly ———c. somtimes ———e. never

———b. usually ———d. seldom

15. How often do you attend any fellowship group (such as Bible study, Sunday school socials, etc.)?

———a. regularly ———c. sometimes ———e. never

———b. usually ———d. seldom

16. How often do you attend a training hour meeting such as teacher training, youth fellowship, etc.

———a. regularly ———c. sometimes ———e. never

———b. usually ———d. seldom

17. How many elected or appointed offices in the church do you now hold?

———a. none ———c. two ———e. four or more

———b. one ———d. three

18. How many times in the past year has someone visited our church as the result of your invitation?

———a. none ———c. two ———e. four or more

———b. one ———d. three

19. How many people have you introduced to Jesus Christ during the past year?

———a. none ———c. two ———e. four or more

———b. one ———d. three

20. How many people have become members of this church during the past year as a result of your invitation or counsel?

———a. none ———c. two ———e. four or more

———b. one ———d. three

21. Do you read the Bible in private? How often?
    _____a. daily   _____c. once a week   _____e. very rarely
    _____b. frequently   _____d. occasionally

22. Do you have family prayer and/or Bible reading? How often?
    _____a. daily   _____c. once a week   _____e. very rarely
    _____b. frequently   _____d. occasionally

23. What percentage of your GROSS income (before taxes) does your FAMILY give to this church?
    _____a. less than 1%   _____c. 4-5%   _____e. more than 10%
    _____b. 1-3%   _____d. 7-10%

24. What percentage of your GROSS income does your family give to charitable organizations outside of the church?
    _____a. less than 1%   _____c. 4-5%   _____e. more than 10%
    _____b. 1-3%   _____d. 7-10%

25. How many hours a week do you spend in the activities of this church, *other* than worship services?
    _____a. one or less   _____c. 4-6   _____e. 11 or more
    _____b. 2-3   _____d. 7-10

26. Your involvement in Christian work since you joined our church has
    _____a. increased.   _____c. remained about the same as before.
    _____b. decreased.

27. You would become more involved in the program at the church if
    _____a. you had more time.
    _____b. you felt it wasn't going to be a lifetime job.
    _____c. you felt someone was going to share the load.
    _____d. you were given more instruction on how to do the task.
    _____e. someone asked you directly.

28. My impression of the Sunday school is that it is
    _____a. well-organized, efficiently run, and progressing in growth.
    _____b. losing its effectiveness.
    _____c. generally good.
    _____d. getting too big.
    _____e. poor.
    Comment: _____

29. More people would attend our Sunday school if
    _____a. we had better teachers.
    _____b. the classes were smaller.
    _____c. we had a better program of visitation.
    _____d. we had more advertising about it.
    _____e. more people would invite their friends.
    Comment: _____

30. I would get more out of Sunday school if
——a. the classes were smaller so we could have more discussion.
——b. we had elective classes where I could choose the study according to my need.
——c. we used quarterlies in our classes.
——d. there weren't so many distractions in our class due to noise.
——e. we had better teachers.
Comment: _____

31. The Wednesday night service is
——a. important and meaningful to me.
——b. unnecessary and a waste of time.
——c. too long.
——d. only for people who have been Christians a long time.
Comment: _____

32. Most people in a Wednesday night prayer service are there because
——a. it is the thing to do.
——b. they enjoy praying with those who come.
——c. they really go away uplifted and blessed.
——d. they have a spiritual need.
Comment: _____

33. I would like the Wednesday night service to
——a. be a large combined meeting with a Bible study and brief time for prayer.
——b. consist of small-group Bible studies with opportunity for questions and discussion.
——c. have more time for prayer and less for study.
——d. have small enough groups so that more people have an opportunity to pray.
——e. include more missionary speakers.
Comment: _____

34. The youth program of our church is
——a. the best in the city.
——b. meeting the needs of our Jr. hi., Sr. hi. and college young people.
——c. a vital part of our church.
——d. not attractive to young people today.
——e. not effective
Comment: _____

35. Our Youth program needs more
——a. interested people of our church to work in it.
——b. recreation.
——c. opportunity for young people to serve the Lord.
——d. spiritual depth.
——e. recognition.
Comment: _____

36. The relatively new position of a full-time youth pastor is
_____a. being filled acceptably and fulfilling all expectations.
_____b. satisfactory, but needs improvement.
_____c. not accomplishing what I expected.
_____d. unnecessary.
Comment: _____

37. It is my observation and opinion that our church
_____a. is growing steadily and consistently.
_____b. has had some increase during the last five years.
_____c. has had significant increase in the last five years.
_____d. is stagnant.
_____e. is dead.
Comment: _____

38. Looking into the future, I see that our church should
_____a. make plans for an enlarged auditorium in the next two years.
_____b. have two morning services.
_____c. remain its present size and not try to expand.
_____d. plan on starting another church in this area.
_____e. do none of these.
Comment: _____

39. The pulpit ministry of our pastor is
_____a. meaningful and meets my need.
_____b. hard to understand and comprehend.
_____c. not evangelistic enough.
_____d. too long-winded.
_____e. unrelated to the problems we face in the world today.
Comment: _____

40. I believe our pastor is fulfilling his pastoral responsibilities according to the following scale:
_____a. excellent
_____b. good
_____c. fair
_____d. poor
Comment: _____

41. In my observation I believe that our pastor needs improvement in
_____a. preaching.
_____b. personal relationships.
_____c. organization and administration.
_____d. visitation.
_____e. none of these.
Comment: _____

42. To my knowledge our visitation program is
    _____a. effective.
    _____b. haphazard.
    _____c. defunct.
    _____d. needed.

43. The music program at our church is
    _____a. generally tasteful and beautiful.
    _____b. acceptable.
    _____c. sometimes not up to par.
    _____d. generally not too good.
    _____e. poor.
    Comment: _____

44. The music program of our church needs
    _____a. a better selection of hymns.
    _____b. more varied involvement by the congregation.
    _____c. a youth choir.
    _____d. a junior choir.
    _____e. none of these.
    Comment: _____

45. The "faith-promise plan" for missionary giving
    _____a. is working effectively.
    _____b. is falling below expectations.
    _____c. is causing a hardship in the general fund.
    _____d. has been a real blessing.
    Comment: _____

46. Our missionary program should
    _____a. be increased to include more missionaries.
    _____b. remain about the same.
    _____c. concentrate on home missions instead of foreign.
    _____d. be reduced.
    Comment: _____

47. Our missionary budget for 19___ is
    _____a. $5,000.
    _____b. $8,700.
    _____c. $12,000.
    _____d. $19,500.
    _____e. $25,000.
    Comment: _____

48. To the best of my knowledge, I feel the spiritual condition of our church is
 _____a. excellent.
 _____b. increasing.
 _____c. declining.
 _____d. good.
 _____e. poor.
 Comment: _____

49. The social atmosphere of our church is
 _____a. warm and friendly.
 _____b. cold and unfriendly.
 _____c. cliquish.
 _____d. hard to break into, but good once you do.
 _____e. so-so.
 Comment: _____

50. The thing I like best about this church and what keeps me involved is:
 _____a. the consistent preaching and teaching of the Bible.
 _____b. the youth program.
 _____c. the people.
 _____d. the social opportunities.
 _____e. the nondenominational nature of the church.
 _____f. none of these.
 Comment: _____

51. I would like to see a week of "special meetings" in the area of
 _____a. evangelistic emphasis.
 _____b. Bible exposition.
 _____c. prophecy.
 _____d. Christian education.
 _____e. none of these.
 Comment: _____

52. The camping ministry of the church is
 _____a. over-emphasized.
 _____b. unnecessary.
 _____c. adequate.
 _____d. excellent.
 _____e. poor.
 Comment: _____

Indicate your opinion about the church programs and/or their needs by completing the following sentences.

1. If I were in a position to effect one change in the Sunday school program, I would

2. Our youth program should

3. To improve our music program, we should

4. Our worship service needs

5. For an effective visitation program, we must

6. Our evangelism outreach

7. The Wednesday night service

Appendix B

JOB TITLE: *Superintendent of Sunday School*

Communication Lines and Interactions

The superintendent of Sunday school is responsible to the official board and reports to it monthly. He works with the director of Christian education in the development of Sunday school policies and programs. He works directly with departmental superintendents in the supervision and coordination of their activities.

Responsibilities

The superintendent of Sunday school holds responsibility for the overall Sunday school program.

A. Organization
1. He integrates the activities of his department with those of other church units.
2. He assists departmental superintendents in recruiting and selecting capable teachers and workers within the department.
3. He plans and organizes the structure of a departmentalized Sunday school.

B. Administration
1. He is responsible for planning with departmental superintendents and teachers a comprehensive and well-balanced program.
2. He supervises the assistant superintendent in the ordering of Sunday school supplies and materials and in maintaining records for the Sunday school.
3. He performs a monthly and annual evaluation of the Sunday school program.

C. Leadership
1. He conducts monthly planning and evaluation meeting of the Sunday school workers.
2. He develops and executes programs for the encouragement and motivation of Sunday school workers.
3. He clarifies the responsibilities and duties of workers.
4. He keeps spiritual and academic objectives before the teachers and departmental workers.
5. He counsels personally and collectively with teachers and workers.

Self-improvement

The superintendent of Sunday school attends training seminars and conferences which are conducted locally and nationally for Sunday school superintendents. He reads periodicals and books relevant to his position.

JOB TITLE: *Director of Music*

Communication lines and Interaction

The director of music is related in his work to the music committee, the organist, and the pastor. He serves under the supervision of the official board member who is in charge of the music committee.

Responsibilities

The director of music has general responsibility for the supervision, coordination, and development of the total music program. He holds responsibilities in the following areas:

A. Music Responsibilities

1. He is responsible for planning and development of the several church choirs.
2. He works in consultation with the Pastor to select Music for worship services.
3. He arranges for special music for worship services.
4. He selects music for and directs cantatas.

B. Personnel Responsibilities

1. He works with the music committee to recruit and develop choir members and performers of special music.
2. He makes recommendations for instrumentalists and choir directors to the music committee.
3. He obtains substitute personnel as necessary.

C. Responsibilities for Instruments

1. He makes recommendations to the music committee regarding the types of musical instruments required for the music program.
2. He works in coordination with the property committee for the purchase and maintenance of musical instruments.

Appendix C

PERSONAL GROWTH INVENTORY FOR TEACHERS

This inventory is designed to aid you in examining your performance as a teacher. Please place a "P" (present) to represent what is true for you *now* and an "F" (future) to represent the level you wish to attain within the next three months.

EXAMPLE: Ability to listen

					P		F					
none   always

---

1. I understand the wants and interests of the group with which I work.

not at all   completely

2. I have developed methods that are especially suited to the age group I teach.

not at all   completely

3. I prayerfully prepare for lessons by study.

never   always

4. I use a written lesson plan for each Sunday school lesson.

never   always

5. ' attend worship services.

never   always

6. I have used opportunities to improve my ability to teach.

never   always

7. I arrive early to greet each person as he or she arrives for class.

never   always

8. I have a deep spiritual and prayerful concern for the members of my class.

no   complete

9. I visit members of the class in their homes.

no   twice
each week

10. I encourage and attend social activities of the class.

no   much

11. I attempt to improve my relationship to the pupils by keeping personal information about them and their families and taking an interest in them.

never   always

12. I attend workers' meetings and departmental meetings.

never   always

13. I attend laymen's training programs and conferences.

never   always

14. I read magazines and books concerning teaching.

never   often

15. I have regular personal devotional periods.

never   always

16. I use a variety of teaching methods for a lesson (story, lecture, discussion, question-and-answer, projects, and teaching aids).

never   always

17. My pupils are genuinely interested throughout the lesson time.

never   always

Steps in Achieving Your Personal Growth Goals

Step 1   Examine yourself, secure feedback from others, and set your goals. Set only from one to three goals. Work on these intensively.

Step 2   Analyze the factors that will support or block your personal growth plans.

Step 3   Plan ways to lessen the effects of the hindering forces in your life and to encourage the supporting forces. Set realistic targets. Discuss these with others.

Goals for improvement during the next three (3) months

_____

_____

_____

_____

_____

Factors that will help to reach the growth goals

_____

_____

_____

_____

Factors that tend to hinder you in your personal growth goals

_____

_____

_____

_____

_____

PERSONAL GROWTH INVENTORY FOR SUPERINTENDENTS

This inventory is designed to aid you in examining your performance as a super-intendent. Place a "P" (present) to represent what is true for you *now* and an "F" (future) to represent the level you wish to attain within the next three months.

EXAMPLE: Ability to listen

| | | | | P | F | | | | | |

none   always able

1. I prayerfully prepare for Sunday morning.

never   always

2. I attend worship services.

never   always

3. I arrive early to greet each person as he or she arrives for Sunday school.

never   always

4. I have a deep spiritual and prayerful concern for the members of my department.

no   complete

5. I encourage, plan, and attend social activities of the department.

never   always

6. I attend workers' meetings.

never   always

7. I hold departmental meetings with teachers.

never   every two months

8. I attend laymen's training programs and conferences.

never   always

9. I read magazines and books concerning superintending Sunday school.

```
|___|___|___|___|___|___|___|___|___|___|
never                                    often
```

10. I have regular personal devotional periods.

```
|___|___|___|___|___|___|___|___|___|___|
never                                    always
```

11. I hold a yearly meeting with the departmental teachers to plan for curriculum, parties, training sessions, projects, etc.

```
|___|___|___|___|___|___|___|___|___|___|
never                                    annually
```

12. I have concrete written goals for my department.

```
|___|___|___|___|___|___|___|___|___|___|
no                                       complete
```

13. I sit in with each teacher some time during a class period (with advance notice).

```
|___|___|___|___|___|___|___|___|___|___|
never                                    2 or 3 times
                                         during the year
```

14. I visit teachers in their homes.

```
|___|___|___|___|___|___|___|___|___|___|
never                                    2 or 3 times a year
```

15. I work with teachers to prepare a system of visitation, assure that adequate facilities are available, and discuss duties of teachers.

```
|___|___|___|___|___|___|___|___|___|___|
never                                    often
```

16. I work with the Sunday school superintendent to acquaint him with needs of personnel, facilities, literature, etc.

```
|___|___|___|___|___|___|___|___|___|___|
never                                    often
```

245

ORGANIZATION AND LEADERSHIP IN THE LOCAL CHURCH

Steps in Achieving Your Personal Growth Goals

Step 1   Examine yourself, secure feedback from others, and set your goals. Set only from one to three goals. Work on these intensively.

Step 2   Analyze the factors that will support or block your personal growth plans.

Step 3   Plan ways to lessen the effects of the hindering forces in your life and to encourage the supporting forces. Set realistic targets. Discuss these with others.

Goals for improvement during the next three (3) months

_____

_____

_____

_____

_____

Factors that will help to reach the growth goals

_____

_____

_____

_____

_____

Factors that tend to hinder you in your personal growth goals

_____

_____

_____

_____

_____

Bibliography

Introduction

Richards, Lawrence. *A New Face for the Church*. Grand Rapids: Zondervan Publishing House, 1970.

Schaeffer, Francis. *The Church at the End of the 20th Century*. Downers Grove, Ill.: Inter-Varsity Press, 1970.

Chapter 1

Bischof, Ledford J. *Interpreting Personality Theories*. New York: Harper & Row, 1964.

Rogers, Carl R. *Client-Centered Therapy*. New York: Houghton Mifflin, 1965.

Chapter 2

Coleman, Lyman. *Growth by Groups: Prologue*. Huntingdon Valley, Penn.: Christian Outreach, 1967.

Epp, Theodore. *Principles of Spiritual Growth*. Lincoln, Neb.: Back-to-the-Bible Publishers, 1967.

Osborne, Cecil. *The Art of Understanding Yourself*. Grand Rapids: Zondervan Publishing House, 1967.

Pentecost, J. Dwight. *Pattern for Maturity*. Chicago: Moody Press, 1966.

Richards, Lawrence. *A New Face for the Church*. Grand Rapids: Zondervan Publishing House, 1970.

Chapter 3

Hodges, Zane C. "The Purpose of Tongues," *Bibliotheca Sacra,* vol. 120, no. 479. Dallas: Hicks Printing Company, 1963.

Stedman, Ray. *Body Life*. Glendale, Calif.: Regal Books, 1972.

Taylor, Howard and Mary G. *Hudson Taylor's Spiritual Secret*. Chicago: Moody Press.

Walvoord, John F. *The Holy Spirit*. Wheaton, Ill.: Van Kampen Press, 1954.

Chapter 5

Kobayashi, Shigeru. *Creative Management*. New York: American Management Association, 1971.
Personnel Psychology, 20(4), 1967.

Wofford, Jerry C. "Behavior Styles and Performance Effectiveness,"
——— "Factor Analysis of Managerial Behavior Variables," *Journal of Applied Psychology,* vol. 54(2), 1970.
——— "Managerial Behavior, Situational Factors, and Productivity and Morale," *Administrative Science Quarterly,* vol. 16(1), 1971.

Chapter 6

Coleman, James C. *Abnormal Psychology and Modern Life,* 3rd ed. New York: Scott, Foresman and Company, 1964.

Herzberg, Fredrick. *Work and the Nature of Man.* Cleveland: The World Publishing Company, 1966.

McGregor, Douglas. *The Human Side of Enterprise.* New York: McGraw-Hill, 1960.

Vroom, V. H. *Motivation for Work.* New York: John Wiley and Sons, 1964.

Chapter 7

Bales, Robert. *Small Groups.* New York: Knopf, 1955.

Cartwright, Dorwin, and Zunder, Alvin. *Groups Dynamics,* 3rd ed. New York: Harper & Row, 1968.

Kemp, C. Gratton. *Perspectives on the Group Process.* Boston: Houghton Mifflin Company, 1970.

Seashore, Stanley. *Applying Modern Management Principles.* Ann Arbor, Mich.: Foundation for Research on Human Behavior, 1963.

Zaleznik, Abraham, and Moment, David. *The Dynamics of Interpersonal Behavior.* New York: John Wiley and Sons, 1964.

Chapter 8

Beckhard, Richard. *Organization Development: Strategies and Models.* Reading, Mass.: Addison-Wesley Publishing Company, 1969.

Boulding, Kenneth. *Conflict Management in Organizations.* Ann Arbor, Mich.: Foundation for Research on Human Behavior, 1961.

Horney, Karen, *Our Inner Conflicts: A Constructive Theory of Neurosis.* New York: W. W. Norton, 1945.

Lawrence, Paul R. and Lorsch, Jay W. *Developing Organizations: Diagnosis and Action.* Reading, Mass.: Addison-Wesley Publishing Company, 1969.

Moore, Franklin. *Management Organization and Practice.* New York: Harper & Row, 1964.

Chapter 9

Drucker, Peter. *The Practice of Management.* New York: Harper & Row, 1954.

Sisk, Henry L. *Principles of Management.* Dallas: Southwestern Publishing Company, 1969.

Chapter 10

Bennis, Warren G. *Changing Organizations.* New York: McGraw-Hill, 1966.

Blake, Robert R., and Mouton, Jane Srygley. *Building a Dynamic Corporation Through Grid Organization Development.* Reading, Mass.: Addison-Wesley Publishing Company, 1969.

Coch, Lester, and French, J. R. P., Jr. "Overcoming Resistance to Change." *Human Relations,* vol. 1(4), 1948.

Dalton, G. E. et al. *Organization Change and Development.* Homewood, Ill.: Irwin-Dorsey, 1970.

Likert, Rensis. *Human Organization.* New York: McGraw-Hill, 1967.

Richards, Lawrence. *A New Face for the Church.* Grand Rapids: Zondervan Publishing House, 1970.

Chapter 11

Schaeffer, Francis. *The Church at the End of the 20th Century.* Downers Grove, Ill.: Inter-Varisty, 1970.

Chapter 12

Leonard, George. *Education and Ecstasy.* New York: Delacort Press, 1968.

McGregor, Douglas. *The Human Side of Enterprise.* New York: McGraw-Hill, 1960.

Odiorne, George S. *Management by Objectives.* New York: Pitman, 1965.

Chapter 13

Leavitt, Harold. *Managerial Psychology,* 2nd ed. Chicago: University of Chicago Press, 1968.

Likert, Rensis. *New Patterns of Management.* New York: McGraw-Hill, 1961.

Chapter 14

Bennis, Warren G. *Changing Organizations.* New York: McGraw-Hill Book Co., 1966.

French, J. R. P. and Raven, Bertram. "The Bases of Social Power," ed., D. Cartwright and A. Zander, *Group Dynamics: Research and Theory.* New York: Harper and Row, 1968, pp. 259-270.

Chapter 15

Kobayashi, Shigeru. *Creative Management.* New York: American Management Association, 1971.

Likert, Rensis. *Human Organization.* New York: McGraw-Hill, 1969.

Chapter 16

Cargo, Rocco, Jr., and Yanouzas, John N. *Formal Organization: A Systems Approach.* Homewood, Ill.: Richard D. Irwin and The Dorsey Press, 1967.

Litterer, Joseph A. *The Analysis of Organizations.* New York: John Wiley and Sons, 1965.

Chapter 18

Foundation for Research on Human Behavior. *Performance Appraisal.* Ann Arbor, Mich., 1968.

Kay, E.; French, J. R. P.; and Meyers, H. *A Study of the Performance Appraisal Interview.* New York: Behavioral Research Service, General Electric Company, 1962.

McGregor, Douglas. *The Human Side of Enterprise.* New York: McGraw-Hill, 1960.

Chapter 19

Vernon, Vance O. "Tools for Long-Range Planning," *Church Administration,* January, 1968.

Drucker, Peter. "Managing for Business Effectiveness," *Harvard Business Review.* May-June, 1963.

Chapter 22

Bernard, Chester. *The Functions of the Executive.* Cambridge, Mass.: Harvard University Press, 1968.

Drucker, Peter. "Managing for Business Effectiveness," *Harvard Business Review.* May-June, 1963.

————. *The Practice of Management.* New York: McGraw-Hill, 1954.

Ford, George L. *Manual on Management for Christian Workers.* Grand Rapids: Zondervan Publishing House, 1964.

Hendricks, Howard G. and Sell, Charles M. *Church Management Manual.* Dallas: Dallas Theological Seminary, 1961.

Index

Abilities, 43, 54, 59, 62, 160, 182, 187
Accounting, 199-212
Achievement, 23, 26, 27, 29
    Dynamic-achievement, 69, 73, 74, 75
Administration, 173, 186
Anxiety, 26, 86, 180
Authority, 90, 153-154, 157-159, 162, 166, 168, 172, 177, 189, 197, 219
    see also Delegation, Power

Bales, Robert, 90
Bennis, Warren G., 124, 153
Board, church (official), 143, 144, 150, 160, 161, 163, 167, 168, 169, 170, 183, 194, 197, 198, 200, 216-217
Body of Christ, building up, 14, 48
Body life, 12, 13, 40, 47
    see also Growth, Spiritual maturity
Boulding, Kenneth, 107
Budget, 197-199
Buildings, 222-227

Candidating, 175-176
Change, 121-130, 158, 161, 188
Children's church, 62, 145, 149, 150, 160
Coch, Lester, 127
Coleman, Lyman, 42
Committees,
    Benevolence, 147, 149
    Building, 32
    Finance and budget, 32, 147, 149
    Innovation, 215
    Long-range planning, 188, 189, 196
    Missions, 145, 149, 194
    Music, 147, 149, 161
    Personnel, 56, 62, 63, 147, 149, 161, 176
    Property, 32, 147, 149
    Publicity, 147, 149

Communication, 95, 110-120, 135, 150, 151, 157, 160, 161, 166, 167, 169, 177, 178, 188, 196
    Networks, 90
    Styles, 116
Community, 125, 133, 134-136, 171, 188, 189, 190
Conflict, 98, 104, 105, 180
Confrontation, 99, 105, 106, 107, 180, 214
Conscience, 24, 25, 27, 30, 31
Cromwell, 62

Decision making, 161, 162, 168, 213-221
Defensiveness, 112
Delegation, 156, 165, 168, 198, 219
Director of Christian education, 169, 173, 175, 177
Disbursements, 210-212
Discipleship, 64, 65
Drucker, Peter 186
Dynamic-achievement, 69, 73, 74, 75
Dynamics, group, 184

Epp, Theodore, 34
Equipping the saints, 13, 48
    see also Body of Christ
Esteem, 23, 26, 27, 29
Evaluation, 179-185, 216
Evangelism, 145, 149, 197, 200
Expenses,
    Moving, 176
    Traveling, 176

Facilities, church, 222-227
Faith, 26, 35-36, 173
Feedback, 44, 107, 183
Fellowship, 38-40, 42, 147, 149, 162, 164, 178, 197
    see also Groups
Financial
    Stewardship, 226
    Transactions, 209
Form, 12, 13, 183, 229

Freedoms, 12, 13, 153, 197
French, J. R. P., Jr., 127
Fruit of the Spirit, 25, 34, 182

Goals, 83, 91, 109, 176, 177, 179-185, 189, 192-196, 215
Group achievement and order, 69, 73, 74, 75
Groups,
Cohesiveness, 95, 161
Dynamics, 184
Effectiveness, 96
Fellowship, 40
Growth, 42
In team-centered organization, 160
Instruction, 44
Norms, 92
Small, 84, 88-97, 143, 183, 188
Structure, 89
Yokefellow, 41-42
Growth, spiritual, 33-45, 191

Herzberg, Fredrick, 82
Hodges, Zane C., 49
Holy Spirit, 25-26, 27, 31, 32, 49, 84, 102, 106, 178, 188, 191, 197
Influence of, 25-26
Horney, Karen, 98

Indecision, 213-221
"Inner law," 14, 23, 24, 27, 28, 31, 102
Innovation, 127, 128, 214, 215
Integrity therapy, 42
Interpersonal conflict, 13, 98, 109, 166
Personality conflict, 178
Interpersonal hostility, 112

Job description, 157, 168-169, 175
Job enrichment, 83
Job title, 169-170

Kay, E., 180

Laity, 172
Lawrence, Paul, 129

Leadership, 64, 69-78, 152-158, 176, 177, 178, 188, 195, 228
Leonard, George, 139
Likert, Rensis, 124, 143

Membership profile, 57
Moore, Franklin, 104
Motivation, 31, 79-87, 155, 163, 178, 182, 184
Motivational dimension, 22, 23
Motivational forces, 25, 26, 28-29, 31
Music, 173, 175, 177, 225

Need, 23, 80, 81, 175, 188, 189, 198
Educational, 191
Neurotic reaction, 86

Objectives, 137-141, 151, 166, 167, 189
Organism (Church), 133, 134, 136, 172
Organization,
Characteristics, 143
Church, 142-155, 172, 176, 182, 197, 214, 228
Dynamic, 151
Structure of, 161, 171
Structuring, 142, 165-170
Osborne, Cecil, 41

Personal enhancement, 70, 73, 74, 75
Personal interaction, 69, 73, 74, 75, 78
Personnel, 173
Enlisting people, 56, 62, 63, 170, 191
Selection, 55-63, 173, 175, 182, 188
Planning, 14, 186-191, 215
Power, 23, 29, 77
Coercive, 153, 155, 156
Expert, 153, 156
Referent, 153, 154
Reward, 155
see also Authority
Problems, 171, 187, 220
Problem solving, 161, 165, 184, 187, 215-217
Psychotic disorder, 87

Receipts, 210-212
Recognition, 23, 29, 53, 84, 155
Recruitment, 56, 62
  see also Personnel
Reformation, the, 172
Reporting, 200
Resistance to change, 121, 129-130,
  157, 160-161
Resolution of conflict, 104, 105
Resources, 188
Responsibility, 177, 182, 183, 197
Richards, Lawrence O., 41, 44, 112,
  124
Role, 228
  Conflict, 100

Satisfaction, 85
Schaeffer, Francis, 12, 13
Seashore, Stanley, 96
Secure and easygoing, 70, 73, 74,
  75, 78
Self, 24
Shaw, Malcolm E., 116
Small church, 145, 149, 171, 222
Solution to problems (see Problems)
Spiritual gifts, 14, 46-54, 172
  Administration, 51, 54
  Cheerful mercy, 52
  Evangelism, 50
  Exhortation, 51
  Faith, 52
  Giving, 52
  Helps, 51
  Pastor-teacher, 50, 54

Teaching, 49
  Use, 54
Spiritual growth, 38-39, 41, 43
  see also Growth
Spiritual maturation, 37-38
Spiritual maturity, 13, 33-34, 182,
  188
Staff, 151, 171-178, 187, 189, 190,
  191
Stedman, Ray, 40
Sunday school, 32, 44, 145, 149,
  150, 160, 162-164, 169, 179,
  182, 187, 190, 214

T-Group, 108, 109
Taylor, Howard, 52
Taylor, Hudson, 52
Taylor, Mary G., 52
Teaching, 65
Team-centered organization, 158,
  159-164
Three-dimensional man, 22, 32
Training, 55, 56, 63, 64, 165, 182

Walvoord, John F., 49
Wofford, Jerry C., 72
Word, the, 35, 36, 38, 40, 43, 45
Worship, 147, 149, 191, 214, 224
Work of service, 14, 48

Youth, 32, 147, 149, 173, 175, 177,
  182
  Director, 182, 183